NOW READ ON

Now Read On brings together literatures in English from around the world, combining an excellent choice of texts with sound methodological guidance. It contains approximately eighty texts and extracts from countries and continents including:

Africa	Australia	Great Britain	India
Southeast Asia	New Zealand	the Caribbean	the USA

Designed as a course for native and non-native English-speakers in *how* to read literature, this anthology begins with short starter texts and questions, and develops in complexity as the reader progresses through the book. *Now Read On* provides the user with

- hands-on experience of working with a plurality of texts and voices from around the world
- questions, exercises, pointers, and commentary, accompanying the passages of literature, and providing the student with the tools and confidence to evaluate any text critically
- an understanding of the major genres – poetry, short stories, drama, and novels.

John McRae is Special Professor of Language in Literature Studies at the University of Nottingham. His publications include *The Language of Poetry* (Routledge), *The Routledge History of Literature in English* (with Ronald Carter), and *The Penguin Guide to English Literature* (with Ronald Carter).

Malachi Edwin Vethamani is Lecturer and teacher trainer in the Department of Education at the Faculty of Educational Studies, Universiti Putra Malaysia. His Ph.D. thesis at the University of Nottingham was on language and point of view in Southeast Asian fiction. He has written widely on the teaching of literature and language, and on new literatures in English, and is himself a short-story writer.

NOW READ ON

A course in
multicultural reading

John McRae
and
Malachi Edwin Vethamani

LONDON AND NEW YORK

First published 1999 by Routledge
11 New Fetter Lane, London EC4P 4EE

Simultaneously published in the USA and Canada
by Routledge
29 West 35th Street, New York, NY 10001

© 1999 John McRae and Malachi Edwin Vethamani

Typeset in Galliard and Avante Garde by
Keystroke, Jacaranda Lodge, Wolverhampton
Printed and bound in Great Britain by
Clays Ltd, St Ives PLC

British Library Cataloguing in Publication Data
A catalogue record for this book is available from the British Library

Library of Congress Cataloging in Publication Data
Now read on : a course in multicultural reading
  John McRae & Malachi Edwin Vethamani.
      p.   cm.
    Includes bibliographical references and index.
    1. Commonwealth literature (English) 2. Pluralism (Social
sciences)—Commonwealth countries—Literary collections.
    3. Commonwealth countries—Cultural relations—Literary collections.
    4. Ethnic groups—Commonwealth countries—Literary collections.
    5. Pluralism (Social sciences)—Great Britain—Literary collections.
    6. Great Britain—Cultural relations—Literary collections.
    7. Ethnic groups—Great Britain—Literary collections. 8. English
language—Textbooks for foreign speakers. I. McRae, John.
II. Vethamani, Malachi Edwin, 1955- .
    PR9085.N69 1999
    820.8—dc21   98–38478
                                                               CIP

ISBN 0–415–18216–6 (hbk)
     0–415–18217–4 (pbk)

CONTENTS

PART I

PART II

ACKNOWLEDGEMENTS

Achebe, Chinua *Things Fall Apart*, 1958

Agard, John 'Rainbow' from *Mangoes and Bullets*, 1985, reprinted by permission of Serpent's Tail Ltd

Bond, Edward 'Bingo' from *Penguin Modern Poets*, 1996, reprinted by permission of Random House

Brock, Edwin *Song of the Battery Hen*, reprinted by permission of Secker and Warburg

Desai, Anita *A Village by the Sea* copyright Anita Desai, 1982, reprinted by permission of the author c/o Rogers, White and Coleridge

Fernanco, Lloyd *Scorpion Orchid*, 1953, reprinted by permission of HarperCollins Publishers

Frame, Janet *You are Now Entering the Human Heart*, 1984, from *Penguin Book of Short Stories*, reprinted by permission of the author and Curtis Brown (Aust) Pty Ltd, Sydney

Hemingway, Ernest *A Farewell to Arms*, 1929, reprinted by permission of the estate of Ernest Hemingway and Jonathan Cape

Ramli Ibrahim *In the Name of Love*, reprinted by permission of Skoob Books Ltd

Jhabvala, Ruth Prawer, *Like Birds, Like Fishes*, reprinted by permission of the author and John Murray Publishers Ltd

Lawrence, D.H. *Sons and Lovers*, 1948, reprinted by permission of Laurence Pollinger Ltd and the Estate of Frieda Lawrence Ravagli, and Viking Penguin, a division of Penguin Puttnam Inc.

Lee, Harper *To Kill a Mockingbird*, 1960, by permission of Heinemann

x

Lim, Catherine *The Journey*, reprinted by permission of Heinemann Southeast Asia

Mahesh, Dattani *Dance Like a Man* from *Final Solutions and Other Plays*, reprinted by permission of East West Books (Madras) PVT. Ltd

Maniam, K.S. *The Return*, reprinted by permission of Skoob Books

Marshall, James Vance *Walkabout*, 1954, reprinted by permission of John Johnson Ltd

Maugham, W. Somerset *The Force of Circumstance* from *Collected Short Stories*, 1984, reprinted by permission of Heinemann

Orwell, George *Keep the Aspidistra Flying*, 1936, copyright Mark Hamilton as the Literary Executor of the Estate of the Late Sonia Brownell Orwell, reprinted by permission of Mark Secker and Warburg Ltd and A&M Heath and Co. Ltd, and Laurence Pollinger Ltd

Paley, Grace *Mother* from *Later the Same Day*, reprinted by permission of Little Brown

Pinter, Harold *A Night Out* from *A Slight Ache and Other Plays*, 1968, reprinted by permission of Faber and Faber Ltd

Roy, Arundhati *The God of Small Things*, 1997, reprinted by permission of HarperCollins Publishers and David Godwin Associates

Sen, Sudeep *New York Times* from *New York Times* (London: The Many Press, 1993) and *Postmarked India: New and Selected Poems* (New Delhi: HarperCollins, 1997)

Steinbeck, John *Of Mice and Men*, 1938, reprinted by permission of Heinemann

Sudham, Pira *Rains*, reprinted by permission of the author

Williams, William Carlos 'This is Just to Say' from *Collected Poems 1909–1959*, 1987, eds., Wilton, E., and Macgowan, C., reprinted by permission of Laurence Pollinger Ltd, Carcanet Press, and New Directions Publishing Corporation

Every effort has been made to trace and contact copyright holders before publication. If any copyright holders have queries they are invited to contact the publishers.

In this book we are going to look at a lot of *texts*. They will be from all sorts of places, and all sorts of periods – and they will be about all sorts of subjects and ideas.

There is no special secret to literature – it is about every one of us, and everyone should be able to enjoy it.

This book is intended to give you some ways of reading and ways of thinking about the texts you read.

The first step is to find *how* a text works, how it does what it does. There is no point in knowing *about* a text or its author or period if we do not know *how* the text achieves its effects.

What we are concerned with first and foremost, therefore, is text as process – the processes of how texts work. That is what is often missing in the reading and study of literature. The background, context, history, and criticism come later.

The ways of reading that you learn in this book can be applied to *any* text, to anything on your literature programme – and to anything outside it: newspapers, songs, advertisements, any kind of text that you come across. We are talking about literature with a small 'l' and leading on to the study of literature as a specialist subject.

Reading opens up questions, makes us think – and very often there are no correct answers. The questions are not designed to test you on right or wrong. Rather, they focus on things you might want to think about and to explore further. So, you will be encouraged to offer *your own* ideas and opinions, not just to memorise other people's views.

Very often, the best answers will be phrased as 'it could be . . . ' or 'it might mean . . . ' – and a lot of discussion will take place as the issues and interpretations are shared around the class. There is an old saying 'there are more questions than answers' but, in this area of study, there are often a lot of possible answers to any single question. Of course, there are things we can get wrong – simply because of misreading, misunderstanding, or not knowing something crucial about what we are reading.

Interpretation is the key to reading literature. And as long as you can justify your answer from the text, basing your judgement on objective criteria as well as on some of your own subjective views, you will be able to answer any kind of questions that examiners might ask.

Whenever you read, you should trust what you know rather than worry about what you don't know. You will find that you know a lot more than you thought you did. For what *you* bring to the text is every bit as important as what the author brings to the text: the author depends on the reader to *make* the text come to life.

There is nothing to be afraid of – and there is a lot to look forward to.

Terms you will find useful

lexis	the words
syntax	the way the words are put together
cohesion	the system of links through a text
graphology	the look of the text, punctuation, layout
phonology	the sounds of the text
semantics	the study of meaning and how meaning is achieved
dialect	language as it is spoken, reflecting local and social conditions
register	the tone of the text
period	modern or older; and the intertextual influences on the text
function	what the text does, the effect it has on the reader
style	the combination of all these elements in any single text

You will be looking at these aspects throughout the book. You will be finding what you think are the *key words*, what the most important *ideas* are, and what *effect* the texts have on you.

The *response* of the reader can be influenced by many things – even the look of the text. In fact, that is the first thing. You must learn to trust your ability to *read, react, and respond* to any text you read.

Remember that any text is only as difficult as what you are asked to do with it. Don't be put off by what critics have said: their opinions are often useful, but often they can get in the way between you and the text.

Don't look for the meaning: usually there is a lot of *meaning potential* and room for you to interpret, discuss, and reach your own conclusions.

Finding texts you enjoy is part of the learning process. As you proceed with the texts in this book, you will find that you are learning to read all sorts of texts and all sorts of language – you are learning to read the world, and learning ways to respond to what you read.

You will find that you remember many different things: that is a very important step. Remember the memorable, instead of memorising the forgettable – this can be your slogan.

Teachers are increasingly aware that the teaching of literature is undergoing a change: the focus is more on *processes* than on *facts*, on students' interaction with texts, on opinions and interpretation rather than received opinion.

Ways of reading

Linguistic	*Traditional*
words, links, contexts	plot, character, setting
movement between beginning and end	intention
contrast, conflicts, binaries	meaning
interpretation, interaction, opinion	criticism

The linguistic approach gives the reader more tools to handle the more 'traditional' questions. It does not ignore them; rather, it reaches them through more careful, aware reading, and helps the reader to answer *any* questions about the text in a fuller way.

The concentration is on *how* a text expresses what it says, to reach a fuller understanding of *what* it says, and *why*.

The following questions may be useful for a poetic text:

Vocabulary
- Is it simple or complex?
- Is it concrete or abstract?
- Is it referential or emotive?
- Are the adjectives used in normal collocations with nouns, or in unusual ones?
- What associations do they evoke?

Content
- Whose voice(s) can you hear in the poem?

- If someone is being addressed, who is it?
- What kind of time and place is the poem set in?
- What is the message of the poem?
- What is the tone: serious, reflective, ironic, satirical?
- Is the poem narrative, descriptive, lyrical, pastoral, epic, or what?
- Can it be read at different levels?

Form

- What is the metre, stress, pattern, if any?
- Is there a rhyme scheme? If so, what?
- What elements can you identify on the phonological level (alliteration, assonance, enjambement)?
- Does the poem follow any set form of layout (ballad, sonnet, etc.)?
- What other visual elements are there?

Figures of speech

- Can you find examples of parallelism and antithesis?
- Are there any metaphors or similes?
- Is the imagery connected with any particular sense or semantic field?
- In what way is the language different from ordinary language?
- What is the overall effect of the poem after the first reading?

This book aims to be an exercise in *enabling*: it shows students how to approach reading, explores all four genres, and offers a range of new non-canonical writings from Southeast Asia, India, Australia, and Africa, to stand beside texts from literature of Britain, Ireland and America.

There are over eighty texts, including thirteen complete short stories, points of entry for eight novels, and stepping stones to help readers through another six novels. The focus is on language-based approaches, giving students *procedural* rather than *declarative* knowledge – they learn *how* to read any text rather than learning *about* the literature they read.

The authors would not wish to prescribe an itinerary through the book. It can be used over two academic years, or used as preparation for examinations: a section on examination strategies is vitally important to the book, illustrating how students must be confident of their ability to answer *any* exam question once they have worked through the texts in the book.

The authors would consider the following texts the 'musts' in order for students to gain a working familiarity with language/ literature interface: Part I, Section 1, 'Poetry', pages 1–11; Part I, Section 2, 'Short Stories', pages 12–17; Part II, Section 6, 'Short Stories', pages 80–89. In general, it is recommended that readers start with shorter texts and gradually move on to longer texts. Otherwise, both teachers and students should feel free to use the book flexibly.

Clearly, students and teachers will want some historical background: *The Routledge History of Literature in English* by Ronald Carter and John McRae (1997) is the best recent overview. Teachers may also want the methodological support of *Literature with a Small 'l'* by John McRae (Macmillan/Prentice Hall 1991/97), *The Extensive Reading Handbook* by Gail Ellis and John McRae (Penguin 1991), and *Language, Literature and the Learner*, edited by Ronald Carter and John MacRae (Longman 1996).

We will conclude with some wise words, written over twenty years ago by Jonathan Culler: 'our examinations are not designed merely to check whether [the student] has read and remembered certain books but to test his or her progress as a reader of literature'.

That should be our watchword – we want more and more students to take up the literature option, to enjoy reading and studying literature, and to achieve good results in their examinations. Along the way, they will develop their language awareness, text awareness, and cultural awareness, and will become better readers of the world they live in.

John McRae/Malachi Edwin Vethamani
Nottingham/Kuala Lumpur, December 1997

PART I

The first thing we have to ask is – what is a poem anyway?
Think about it, and make some notes about what makes a poem.

....

....

So, which of these texts is *more* a poem for you?

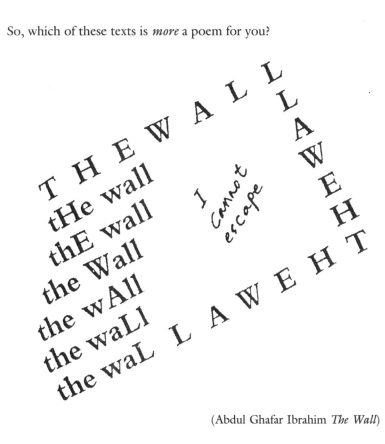

(Abdul Ghafar Ibrahim *The Wall*)

You ask me if I have ever been to prison.
Been to prison!
Your world of murderers and thieves
of hatred and jealousy
and . . . you ask me if I have ever been to prison!

I answer
Yes
I am still there
trying to escape . . .

(Mutabaruka [Allan Hope] You Ask Me)

This is just to say I have eaten the plums that were in the icebox and which you were probably saving for breakfast. Forgive me, they were delicious, so sweet and so cold.

(William Carlos Williams This Is Just to Say)

What might make them seem *not* to be like the usual kind of poems?

Now let's look at them one at a time.
In the first one, make a list of the separate words you can find.

....

....

Look at the words in the middle, 'I cannot escape'. Would it be very different if these words were not there? What would the effect be? What difference would there be if we put the words 'no escape' in the middle instead of an empty space or the words 'I cannot escape'?

Is the text positive or negative, in your opinion? Is it about a wall keeping someone in, or keeping someone out? Is it a real wall? What could the wall be, in your interpretation? Who could 'I' be?

Does the second text have anything in common with the first one? What similarities can you find between the two? And what differences?

Who might 'you' be? And 'me'?

Look at the graphology, particularly the use of dots. . . . Would it be different if the dots were not there? What kind of difference might it make?

Is this text more positive or more negative than the first one? Compare your reactions with others in the class. Does everyone have the same opinion?

When, and where, do you think this text might have been written? Is it modern or old, particular or universal? – discuss your opinions and reactions.

The third text perhaps looks *least* like a poem. What does it look like? Where might it be found? In terms of language functions, what is the text trying to do? In your home, would you (or anyone else) leave a message like this? Can you give the basic message, in five or six words?

Playing with the words

If we take away the final five words, what difference does it make to the whole text? And the first five words? Would it be different if it was 'very sweet and very cold'? How sweet and cold were the plums?

How many of the following things does the text do: gives information, tells a story, communicates enjoyment, apologises, makes suppositions, identifies the speakers (addresser/addressee)? Check with the question about functions earlier – how many did you identify? Who do you think might be speaking, and to whom? What kind of relationship do you imagine between the addresser (who writes the message) and the addressee (who receives it)?

Is there anything you would not have written – 'icebox', for instance? What does that word tell us? Do you think this is a modern text or an older one?

It does not look like a poem, in any of the usual ways. Try writing it as a poem, and see how you would want it to look, as well as how you want it to express its subject matter.

Compare versions around the class. Did anyone change the words, alter the emphasis (perhaps beginning 'Forgive me . . . ')? Is it possible to choose the 'best' version? Or do most of them have some good qualities?

The original version of the text written as a poem is on page 209. Check it out – do you prefer this version or one of the class ones? Why?

Now we will look at a text which certainly looks like a real poem, with verses, and a rather more usual poetic subject. As you read for the first time, don't worry about the missing words – watch how the last line of each verse is different from the first three.

I came to you at ____
With silvery dew on sleeping lotus
Sparkling in my gay hands;
You put my flowers in the sun.

I danced to you at ____
With bright raintree blooms
Flaming in my ardent arms;
You dropped my blossoms in the pond.

I crept to you at ____
With pale lilac orchids
Trembling on my uncertain lips;
You shredded my petals in the sand.

I strode to you at ____
With gravel hard and cold
Clenched in my bitter fists;
You offered me your hybrid orchids,
And ____

(Hilary Tham)

What can you say about the last lines, verse by verse? How many different kinds of flowers or plants can you find?

Is the poem as a whole positive or negative, in your opinion?

Read it again, suggesting words to fill in the gaps. Now compare your suggestions, and decide which of them work best, both in terms of grammar and in terms of poetry.

Is the last line a happy ending or not, for most of the class?

Which of the two ('I' or 'you') do you think is male, and which female?

Compare the verbs in the first line of each verse. And compare the adjectives in the second lines. Is there a progression? What does the semicolon at the end of each third line indicate, in your opinion?

Suggest a title for the poem. (Check the missing words and title on page 209.)

Now we have two texts which look fairly similar. In two groups, read one each, in order to tell the other group what it's about and how it works.

```
hello      who's    there      this is    me
this is    me       who is     that,      hello
hello      who is   that       this is    me


who is     that     this is    me         here
this is    me       who is     that       hello
who is     that     this is    me


I'm        there    here       here       I am
who is     that     hello      hello      who's there
I'm        there    here


I'm        here     here       I am       there
who        hello    hello      who is     there
I'm        here


here       here     I am       there      who
hello      hello    who is     there      I am
there
```

(Abdul Ghafar Ibrahim *Hello*)


```
Her face       Her tongue     Her wit
so fair        so sweet       so sharp
first bent     then drew      then hit
mine eye       mine ear       my heart


Mine eye       Mine ear       My heart
to like        to learn       to love
her face       her tongue     her wit
doth lead      doth teach     doth move


Her face       Her tongue     Her wit
with beams     with sound     with art
doth blind     doth charm     doth knit
mine eye       mine ear       my heart


Mine eye       Mine ear       My heart
with life      with hope      with skill
her face       her tongue     her wit
doth feed      doth feast     doth fill
```

O face	O tongue	O wit
with frowns	with checks	with smart
wrong not	vex not	wound not
mine eye	mine ear	my heart

This eye	This ear	This heart
shall joy	shall yield	shall swear
her face	her tongue	her wit
to serve	to trust	to fear.

(Sir Arthur Gorges *Her Face*)

Is it easy to say what the text you read says and does? What do the two texts have in common? And how are they different? Can your text be read in different directions (up or down, along, diagonally)? Does it make a difference how it is read?

Which is simpler? What makes it simpler?

Is one of the texts older? How can you tell?

Which has more of a story? Is it a happy or a sad story? Where does it become clear how happy or sad it is?

Check any words or concepts which are unfamiliar. Are they unfamiliar just because they are archaic, older forms? Or are there other reasons?

Would it be easy to *perform* your text (in groups, or lines, one voice per phrase, for instance)? You might want to try various ways of performing the two texts.

Now look at these two texts. What do you find in common in them?

These natives are unintelligent –
We can't understand their language.

(Chinweizu *Colonizer's Logic*)

Goodbye, Europeans
And without a grudge
I, myself, am not offended
Goodbye, every one to his own home
Without any fuss
Goodbye provided you disturb us no more
Let him follow you
He who believes you indispensable.

(J.R.D.A. Dubreka *Goodbye, Europeans*)

Who do you imagine is speaking in each? What attitudes are revealed? Do the texts seem to be related in any way?

The next poem contains a different kind of 'goodbye'. As you read, see if you can find what reasons are given for the ending.

> So, we'll go no more a-roving
> So late into the night,
> Though the heart be still as loving,
> And the moon be still as bright.
>
> 5   For the sword outwears its sheath,
> And the soul wears out the breast,
> And the heart must pause to breathe,
> And love itself have rest.
>
> Though the night was made for loving,
> 10   And the day returns too soon,
> Yet we'll go no more a-roving
> By the light of the moon.
>
> (Lord Byron *So We'll Go No More A-Roving*)

What do you think 'a-roving' means?

Look at the first words of each verse. What does each of them do, in terms of cohesion? Does the word 'Yet' in line 11 continue, or contrast with, what has gone before?

Has the love ended, or not, in your opinion? How important is the idea of time passing?

What do you think the poem is really about? Who is the speaker addressing?

In the following poem, there are three blanks. The same word has been deleted each time. Read the poem, and choose a word which you think is appropriate.

> We two are like partners in the _____ ,
> Approaching nearer, nearer and nearer;
> But just when one would think we'd meet at last,
> We turn away, reverse our steps, withdraw.

And like the _____ too, my life seems now,
With steps mechanical, repeated, meaningless;
Arms swinging back and forth, expressing nothing,
Feet pacing up and down the floor, going nowhere.

I am tired of going through these _____ motions,
Long to break this impasse of reserve;
If only at one point our hands could clasp,
What rich variety of movement and gesture could be ours.

(Fadzillah Amin)

Compare your choices around the class.

Describe the movement of the partners in the poem. Does the movement of the partners tell you anything about their relationship?

Read the second stanza again. Are the last words in the second, third, and fourth lines positive or negative? What do they indicate?

Read the last two lines of the poem. What does the speaker wish the partners had done? Would you consider these lines as positive or negative? What effect does the word 'could' have in these lines? How is the verb different from the verb in the first line of the poem?

Ask your teacher (or see page 210) for the missing word.

Do you know what it is? It is a dance. What do you think the movements in the dance symbolise? Can you think of other dances which have similar movements?

What you have learned

Looking back at the texts in this section, is it easy to say that any of them is more poetic than others? Is the language of the texts similar or different? Compare them under these headings:

form (graphology)	subject/theme	language	effect
....	....	....	....
....	....	....	....
....	....	....	....

Which of the texts did you like best? Can you say why? Is your liking (or disliking) subjective, or can you suggest objective reasons (maybe relating to the list you have just made)?

Research

There is poetry everywhere around us: in advertisements, songs, greetings cards, etc. Find some samples of poetry (in any language) and bring them into class to compare them with the texts in the book.

Look at them under the headings you had earlier, and see if you can begin to see how each text works as a poem, and to suggest objectively why some are not as good as others.

A story has a beginning, a middle, and an end – but (as they say) not necessarily in that order! But what is a story? Almost anything can be a story: think of a joke you could tell the whole class. It will have a structure just like a story.

> There's a woman standing at a bus stop with a dog on a lead. Along comes a man and stands beside her.
>
> 'Good morning,' he says.
>
> 'Good morning,' she replies.
>
> 'Nice dog,' he says.
>
> 'Thank you,' she says.
>
> 'Does your dog bite?' he asks.
>
> 'No,' she says.
>
> So the man leans down and begins to stroke the dog. The dog turns round and bites his hand.
>
> 'You said your dog didn't bite!' the man complains.
>
> 'It's not my dog,' the woman replies.

The simplest form of story has:

- a premise
- development
- complication
- dénouement (conclusion; often the twist in the tale).

Check these in the jokes you have told, and in the joke above. How far does this structure hold?

When we read, we have *expectations* – often we think we know what to expect but then the author, or the person telling the joke, surprises us. This is the use of the *expectation gap*. It is what makes us laugh; it is often what gives a short story its punch, its effect.

As we read the next story, check your expectations sentence by sentence. Cover up the lines below, so that each line can come as a surprise.

Two Dogs, who had been fighting for a bone,

What kind of story is it? Do you have positive or negative expectations of this kind of story? What do you normally have at the end of this kind of story? What do you think the Dogs will do now?

without advantage to either,

What does this phrase mean? Can you express it more simply?

referred their dispute to a Sheep.

That is quite a complex sentence. Tell the story again in the present tense, making it into three simple sentences. What difference does that make to the tone of the story so far?

Is this the end of the story? How can you tell?

The Sheep patiently heard their arguments, then

Suggest what the Sheep did. Will it be positive or negative? Is this going to give the moral to the story? How far are we from the end of the story, do you think?

flung the bone into a pond.

Is *this* the end of the story? How can you tell? Did the Sheep do what you expected? How do you think the Dogs will react? Invent different continuations for the story.

Trace the structure through, in terms of premise, development, etc. Where are we now, in that progress?

'Why did you do that?' asked the Dogs.

(Ambrose Bierce *The Disinterested Arbiter*)

How far are we from the end now? What kind of ending do you expect? What would you feel if you could not find the ending? (The complete story is on page 210.)

Write a short paragraph about how this story plays with your expectations of the fable, and the effect it had on you.

Now an opportunity to put a story together, seeing how our structural elements might work. Try arranging the following sentences to make a complete story – but don't leave anything out. Discuss some of the possibilities as you work on the story.

1   All the shutters of the hospital were nailed shut.
2   When they fired the first volley he was sitting down in the water with his head on his knees.
3   There were pools of water in the courtyard.
4   They tried to hold him up against the wall but he sat down in a puddle of water.
5   One of the ministers was sick with typhoid.
6   Two soldiers carried him downstairs and out into the rain.
7   There were wet dead leaves on the paving of the courtyard.
8   Finally the officer told the soldiers it was no good trying to make him stand up.
9   They shot the six cabinet ministers at half past six in the morning against the wall of a hospital.
10   It rained hard.
11   The other five stood very quietly against the wall.

(Ernest Hemingway *In Our Times*)

Where did you want to put the descriptive sentences? If you were making a video of the episode, how would you use the descriptions?

Is there anything you *cannot* use as the opening of the story? Compare the various openings you have suggested.

Are there any sentences which automatically go together? What difficulties did you encounter in putting versions of the story together? Look at: cohesion, description as opposed to narration, and the structure of the story.

The original story is on page 210. Check how different it is from your own versions. What effect does this version create, compared to your own version? How visual is the original version? Was your own version more visual? How?

The next text is also a fable – but a little different. Read the whole fable; then make notes about it under the following headings:

Expectations	Is it predictable, or are there unexpected elements?
Traditional	What is traditional, what is not?
Tone	Is it serious or not? (How can you tell?) (And where can you tell?)
Moral	Is it a genuine moral, or is there a hidden moral too?
Characters	Are they generalised or individual?
Language	Is it simple, complex, abstract, realistic? How does it fit the tone of the fable?
Symbols	Is it highly symbolic? Is it too obvious? Is it easy to understand what the fable is getting at, or not?
Function	Is the author using the fable form to tell a different kind of story? What is it really about, in your opinion?

Once upon a time an artist who had painted a small and very beautiful picture placed it so that he could see it in the mirror. He said, 'This doubles the distance and softens it, and it is twice as lovely as it was before.'

The animals out in the woods heard of this through the housecat, who was greatly admired by them because he was so learned, and so refined and civilized, and so polite and high-bred, and could tell them so much which they didn't know before, and were not certain about afterward. They were much excited about this new piece of gossip, and they asked questions, so as to get a full understanding of it. They asked what a picture was, and the cat explained.

'It is a flat thing,' he said; 'wonderfully flat, enchantingly flat and elegant. And, oh, so beautiful!'

That excited them almost to a frenzy, and they said they would give the world to see it. Then the bear asked:

'What is it that makes it so beautiful?'

'It's the looks of it,' said the cat.

This filled them with admiration and uncertainty, and they were more excited than ever. Then the cow asked:

'What is a mirror?'

'It is a hole in the wall,' said the cat. 'You look in it, and there you see the picture, and it is so dainty and charming and ethereal and inspiring in its unimaginable beauty that your head turns round and round, and you almost swoon with ecstasy.'

The ass had not said anything as yet; he now began to throw doubts. He said there had never been anything as beautiful as this before, and probably wasn't now. He said that when it took a whole basketful of sesquipedalian adjectives to whoop up a thing of beauty, it was time for suspicion.

It was easy to see that these doubts were having an effect upon the animals, so the cat went off offended. The subject was dropped for a couple of days, but in the meantime curiosity was taking a fresh start, and there was a revival of interest perceptible. Then the animals assailed the ass for spoiling what could possibly have been a pleasure to them, on a mere suspicion that the picture was not beautiful, without any evidence that such was the case. The ass was not troubled; he was calm, and said there was one way to find out who was in the right, himself or the cat: he would go and look in that hole, and come back and tell what he found there. The animals felt relieved and grateful, and asked him to go at once – which he did.

But he did not know where he ought to stand; and, so, through error, he stood between the picture and the mirror. The result was that the picture had no chance, and didn't show up. He returned home and said:

'The cat lied. There was nothing in that hole but an ass. There wasn't a sign of a flat thing visible. It was a handsome ass, and friendly, but just an ass, and nothing more.'

The elephant asked:

'Did you see it good and clear? Were you close to it?'

'I saw it good and clear, O Hathi, King of Beasts. I was so close that I touched noses with it.'

'This is very strange,' said the elephant; 'the cat was always truthful before – as far as we could make out. Let another witness try. Go, Baloo, look in the hole, and come and report.'

So the bear went. When he came back, he said:

'Both the cat and the ass have lied; there was nothing in the hole but a bear.'

Great was the surprise and puzzlement of the animals. Each was now anxious to make the test himself and get at the straight truth. The elephant sent them one at a time.

First, the cow. She found nothing in the hole but a cow.

The tiger found nothing in it but a tiger.

The lion found nothing in it but a lion.

The leopard found nothing in it but a leopard.

The camel found a camel, and nothing more.

The Hathi was wroth, and said he would have the truth, if he had to go and fetch it himself. When he returned, he abused his whole subjectry for liars, and was in an unappeasable fury with the moral and mental blindness of the cat. He said anybody but a near-sighted fool could see that there was nothing in the hole but an elephant.

MORAL, BY THE CAT

You can find in a text whatever you bring, if you will stand between it and the mirror of your imagination. You may not see your ears, but they will be there.

(Samuel Clemens *A Fable*)

Compare your results with the rest of the class, and discuss how well this fable works. Is it like the fable of the two Dogs, or not? What comments are there in the fable which you think might reflect the author's own views, or his sense of humour?

Is the moral a good one?

The next story is a little bit longer. As you start reading, what expectations are created? What are the words and phrases which create your expectations?

> The room was quiet in the dimness of early evening. Dr James Graham, key scientist of a very important project, sat in his favourite chair, thinking. It was so still that he could hear the turning of pages in the next room as his son leafed through a picture book.
>
> Often Graham did his best work, his most creative thinking, under these circumstances, sitting alone in an unlighted room in his own apartment after the day's regular work. But tonight his mind would not work constructively. Mostly he thought about his mentally arrested son – his only son – in the next room. The thoughts were loving thoughts, not the bitter anguish he had felt years ago when he had first learned of the boy's condition. The boy was happy, wasn't that the main thing? And to how many men is given a child who will always be a child, who will not grow up to leave him? Certainly that was a rationalization, but what is wrong with rationalization when it – The doorbell rang.

Part 1

What kind of atmosphere do you think the author wants to create? What is the story going to be about? What kind of story might it be?

What are the most important things you have noticed so far?

> Graham rose and turned on lights in the almost-dark room before he went through the hallway to the door. He was not annoyed; tonight, at this moment, almost any interruption to his thoughts was welcome.
>
> He opened the door. A stranger stood there: he said, 'Dr Graham? My name is Niemand; I'd like to talk to you. May I come in a moment?'
>
> Graham looked at him. He was a small man, nondescript, obviously harmless – possibly a reporter or an insurance agent.
>
> But it didn't matter what he was. Graham found himself saying, 'Of course. Come in, Mr Niemand.' A few minutes of conversation, he justified himself by thinking, might divert his thoughts and clear his mind.

'Sit down,' he said, in the living room. 'Care for a drink?'

Niemand said, 'No, thank you.' He sat in the chair; Graham sat on the sofa.

The small man interlocked his fingers; he leaned forward. He said, 'Dr Graham, you are the man whose scientific work is more likely than that of any other man to end the human race's chance for survival.'

Part 2

Have your expectations changed at all? Do you still think the same as you did at the end of Part 1? What do you think Mr Niemand will do? Is his name significant, do you think (it means 'no man' in German)?

Now read on. As the story begins to get exciting, why not give a musical underlining to moments you think are significant – as in a movie!

A crackpot, Graham thought. Too late now he realized that he should have asked the man's business before admitting him. It would be an embarrassing interview – he disliked being rude, yet only rudeness was effective.

'Dr Graham, the weapon on which you are working – '

The visitor stopped and turned his head as the door that led to a bedroom opened and a boy of fifteen came in. The boy didn't notice Niemand; he ran to Graham.

'Daddy, will you read to me now?' The boy of fifteen laughed the sweet laugh of a child of four.

Graham put an arm around the boy. He looked at his visitor, wondering whether he had known about the boy. From the lack of surprise on Niemand's face, Graham felt sure he had known.

'Harry' – Graham's voice was warm with affection – 'Daddy's busy. Just for a little while. Go back to your room; I'll come and read to you soon.'

'*Chicken Little*? You'll read me *Chicken Little*?'

'If you wish. Now run along. Wait. Harry, this is Mr Niemand;'

The boy smiled bashfully at the visitor. Niemand said, 'Hi, Harry,' and smiled back at him, holding out his hand. Graham, watching, was sure now that Niemand had known; the smile and the gesture were for the boy's mental age, not his physical one.

The boy took Niemand's hand. For a moment it seemed that he was going to climb into Niemand's lap, and Graham pulled him back gently. He said, 'Go to your room now, Harry.'

Part 3

Where did you want musical effects? What words begin to increase the tension of the story?

Do you know the story *Chicken Little*? Is it necessary to know about it?

Why does Graham stop Harry going to Mr Niemand, do you think? Why has Mr Niemand come to the house?

Now read on. Why does Graham want Mr Niemand to leave?

The boy skipped back to the bedroom, not closing the door.

Niemand's eyes met Graham's and he said, 'I like him,' with obvious sincerity. He added, 'I hope that what you're going to read to him will always be true.'

Graham didn't understand. Niemand said, '*Chicken Little*, I mean. It's a fine story – but may Chicken Little always be wrong about the sky falling down.'

Graham suddenly had liked Niemand when Niemand had shown liking for the boy. Now he remembered that he must close the interview quickly. He rose, in dismissal.

He said, 'I fear you're wasting your time and mine, Mr Niemand. I know all the arguments, everything you can say I've heard a thousand times. Possibly there is truth in what you believe, but it does not concern me. I'm a scientist, and only a scientist. Yes, it is public knowledge that I am working on a weapon, a rather ultimate one. But, for me personally, that is only a by-product of the fact that I am advancing science. I have thought it through, and I have found that that is my only concern.'

'But, Dr Graham, is humanity *ready* for an ultimate weapon?'

Graham frowned, 'I have told you my point of view, Mr Niemand.'

Part 4

What is Graham's point of view about his work, in your own words?

Chicken Little thought the sky had fallen down – a pot had fallen on his head, and he couldn't see! Does this link with anything in this story?

What do you think will happen now? Now read on.

Niemand rose slowly from the chair. He said, 'Very well, if you do not choose to discuss it, I'll say no more.' He passed a hand across his forehead. 'I'll leave, Dr Graham. I wonder, though . . . may I change my mind about the drink you offered me?'

Graham's irritation faded. He said, 'Certainly. Will whisky and water do?'
'Admirably.'

Graham excused himself and went into the kitchen. He got the decanter of whisky, another of water, ice cubes, glasses.

When he returned to the living room, Niemand was just leaving the boy's bedroom. He heard Niemand's 'Good night, Harry,' and Harry's happy 'Night, Mr Niemand.'

Graham made drinks. A little later, Niemand declined a second one and started to leave.

Niemand said, 'I took the liberty of bringing a small gift to your son, doctor. I gave it to him while you were getting drinks for us. I hope you'll forgive me.'

'Of course. Thank you. Good night.'

Graham closed the door; he walked through the living room into Harry's room. He said, 'All right, Harry. Now, I'll read to – '

Part 5

Is there more tension now? What has caused it?
   Why does Graham not finish his last sentence?
   How is the story going to end? Now read on.

There was sudden sweat on his forehead, but he forced his face and his voice to be calm as he stepped to the side of the bed. 'May I see that, Harry?' When he had it safely, his hands shook as he examined it.

   He thought, *only a madman would give a loaded revolver to an idiot.*

(Fredric Brown *The Weapon*)

Part 6

Why is the story called *The Weapon*? What is it about? – How many answers are there to that question?

   What did you think of the last line? Is the ending hinted at earlier in the story, in any way?

   Did you enjoy the story? Did it work? Does the ending raise more issues, or close the argument? Did it follow our structure formula? Trace the form through, to see if it did.

   What kind of effect did the story have on you? Is it a story you will remember, do you think? If so, what are the elements that make it memorable?

Here is one version of the Chicken Little story. What kind of reader is it intended for, do you think? Would you prefer the version where the pot had fallen on his head?

Once upon a time there was a little chick called Chicken Licken. One day, as he was playing, an acorn fell on his head. 'Help!' thought Chicken Licken. 'The sky is falling down!' And he ran off to tell the King.

On the way, Chicken Licken met Henny Penny. 'Oh! Henny Penny!' cried Chicken Licken. 'The sky is falling down and I'm off to tell the King.' 'Then I shall come too,' said Henny Penny. So Chicken Licken and Henny Penny hurried off to find the King.

On the way, Chicken Licken and Henny Penny met Cocky Locky. 'Oh! Cocky Locky!' cried Chicken Licken. 'The sky is falling down and we're off to tell the King.' 'Then I shall come too,' said Cocky Locky. So Chicken Licken, Henny Penny and Cocky Locky hurried off to find the King.

On the way, Chicken Licken, Henny Penny and Cocky Locky met Ducky Lucky. 'Oh! Ducky Lucky!' cried Chicken Licken. 'The sky is falling down and we're off to tell the King.' 'Then I shall come too,' said Ducky Lucky. So Chicken Licken, Henny Penny, Cocky Locky and Ducky Lucky hurried off to find the King.

On the way, Chicken Licken, Henny Penny, Cocky Locky and Ducky Lucky met Drakey Lakey. 'Oh! Drakey Lakey!' cried Chicken Licken. 'The sky is falling down and we're off to tell the King.' 'Then I shall come too,' said Drakey Lakey. So Chicken Licken, Henny Penny, Cocky Locky, Ducky Lucky and Drakey Lakey hurried off to find the King.

On the way, Chicken Licken, Henny Penny, Cocky Locky, Ducky Lucky and Drakey Lakey met Goosey Loosey. 'Oh! Goosey Loosey!' cried Chicken Licken. 'The sky is falling down and we're off to tell the King.' 'Then I shall come too,' said Goosey Loosey. So Chicken Licken, Henny Penny, Cocky Locky, Ducky Lucky, Drakey Lakey and Goosey Loosey hurried off to find the King.

On the way, Chicken Licken, Henny Penny, Cocky Locky, Ducky Lucky, Drakey Lakey and Goosey Loosey met Turkey Lurkey. 'Oh! Turkey Lurkey!' cried Chicken Licken. 'The sky is falling down and we're off to tell the King.' 'Then I shall come too,' said Turkey Lurkey. So Chicken Licken, Henny Penny, Cocky Locky, Ducky Lucky, Drakey Lakey, Goosey Loosey and Turkey Lurkey hurried off to find the King.

But on the way, they met Foxy Loxy! 'Good morning,' said Foxy Loxy. 'Where are you all going in such a hurry?' 'Oh! Foxy Loxy!' cried Chicken Licken. 'The sky is falling down and we're off to tell the King.' 'Follow me,' said Foxy Loxy. 'I know just where to find the King.' So Chicken Licken,

Henny Penny, Cocky Locky, Ducky Lucky, Drakey Lakey, Goosey Loosey and Turkey Lurkey all followed Foxy Loxy.

But he didn't take them to the King. He led them straight to his den, where his wife and all the little foxes were waiting for their dinner. Then the foxes ate up Chicken Licken, Henny Penny, Cocky Locky, Ducky Lucky, Drakey Lakey, Goosey Loosey and Turkey Lurkey. And Chicken Licken never did find the King to tell him that the sky was falling down.

(*Chicken Licken*)

The next story you can read all in one go. As you read, decide when the story really begins. . . .

One day I was listening to the AM radio. I heard a song: 'Oh, I Long to See My Mother in the Doorway.' By God! I said, I understand that song. I have often longed to see my mother in the doorway. As a matter of fact, she did stand frequently in various doorways looking at me. She stood one day, just so, at the front door, the darkness of the hall behind her. She said sadly, If you come home at 4 A.M. when you're seventeen, what time will you come home when you're twenty? She asked this question without humor or meanness. She had begun her worried preparations for death. She would not be present, she thought, when I was twenty. So she wondered.

Another time she stood in the doorway of my room. I had just issued a political manifesto attacking the family's position on the Soviet Union. She said, Go to sleep for godsakes, you damn fool, you and your Communist ideas. We saw them already, Papa and me, in 1905. We guessed it all.

At the door of the kitchen she said, You never finish your lunch. You run around senselessly. What will become of you?

Then she died.

Naturally for the rest of my life I longed to see her, not only in doorways, in a great number of places – in the dining room with my aunts, at the window looking up and down the block, in the country garden among zinnias and marigolds, in the living room with my father.

They sat in comfortable leather chairs. They were listening to Mozart. They looked at one another amazed. It seemed to them that they'd just learned the first English words. It seemed to them that he had just proudly handed in a 100 percent correct exam to the American anatomy professor. It seemed as though she'd just quit the shop for the kitchen.

I wish I could see her in the doorway of the living room.

She stood there a minute. Then she sat beside him. They owned an expensive record player. They were listening to Bach. She said to him, Talk to me a little. We don't talk so much anymore.

I'm tired, he said. Can't you see? I saw maybe thirty people today. All sick, all talk talk talk talk. Listen to the music, he said. I believe you once had perfect pitch. I'm tired, he said.

Then she died.

(Grace Paley)

How many possible answers are there to the pre-reading question?

Where did the parents come from? What did the father do when they arrived in America? And the mother? Is the 'I' male or female, in your opinion?

How many shifts in time are there in the story? Trace them through.

What is the story about? How many of these *could* it be about: mothers, death, families, politics, music, doorways, lack of communication, the passing of time, emigration, anything else?

Suggest a title for the story. (Grace Paley's title is given on p. 210.)

The point of entry into the next story looks at a successful man. As you read, what can you tell about his past?

He wondered how, with such an environment, he had managed to be where he was now. How culturally deprived had been his environment, how starved of the requisites of mental and emotional growth. Thank God Annabelle and Mark would never know such deprivation. He never had a toy; he remembered that the only toy he had had was a plastic bear with a broken nose which his mother had asked from someone for him, and he had treasured this toy and kept it hidden from his sisters.

One of his sisters had died. It was tetanus. She had stepped on a rusty nail, and his mother had applied some medicine, but three days later, she was dead. He remembered how grief-stricken his mother, grandmother and aunt were. The ignorance of those days! The women were convinced that an evil spirit had entered his sister's body, and caused her death. Evil spirits, evil spirits – they were said to cause every illness and misfortune. How many deaths had been caused as a result of this belief – Richard felt grateful for the regular medical check-ups that he and his family were able to have. The nurse now appeared to summon him into the consulting room and he thought, Good. I shall be well in time for my golf. Shall pick up Mabel from the hairdresser's, and then drive on to a nice, relaxing game.

(Catherine Lim *The Journey*)

List the things you have found about his past, under these headings:

deprivation　　　　*health*　　　　*ignorance*

....　　　.......................　　　.........................

....　　　.......................　　　.........................

What does 'such', in the first line, tell you? What does it refer to – the present or the past? Are there any other contrasts between past and present? What are they? What can you tell about his family when he was young? And his present family?

   Now read the passage again, and underline the verbs which refer to *past*, *present*, and *future*. The verbs bring out one of the basic contrasts of the passage: between how 'he' lives now, and how he lived in the past. Make some statements about the differences, using some of these phrases to begin:

- There is a change from . . .
- There is a movement from . . .
- He does not like some things about the past, such as . . .
- There is a difference between . . .

How does he feel now, about the present?

   How many children does he have? How are their lives different from his own? What does he think about his own future? And his children's future?

   Is there anything in the text you feel you do not understand yet? Check with others in the class to make sure.

   Think of some adjectives of your own to describe his feelings. Then decide which of these adjectives you think are appropriate to him, and which are not, saying why: happy, unhappy, regretful, self-satisfied, complacent, secure, worried, proud, superior. Do you think he rejects his past life? What is his attitude to his past life, in your own words? And to his present life?

   Where is he? What is he waiting for? What will he do afterwards? Who do you think Mabel is? What kind of person is he?

   What do you think will happen next in the story? Will it be a happy story? Pick out some more contrasts which make binaries or opposites: positive/negative, happy/sad, life/death, past/present, present/future, etc.

The story is called *The Journey*. What kind of journey might it be?

You might be asked: What is the story about? Which of these gives the best idea? Discuss why each is not a complete answer to the question:

- a man thinking about his past
- a man satisfied with his life
- a man waiting to see a consultant
- a man going to play golf

The complete story is on pages 211–16. Now read on, and see if your ideas about the man and his story were justified. After you have read the whole story, look again at the question 'What is the story about?' How many things is it about, in your opinion? Which of these do you think are most important?

Can you pick out the premise, development, complication, and dénouement? Are there clear turning points between these moments?

Look again at the contrasts and binaries you found. Are there more you could add to that list?

Look again at the point-of-entry passage. Where is it in the overall structure of the story? How much of the whole story is contained in it, and how much is missing?

Is there anything you could take away from the story without damaging it? Is there anything you would add?

What do you think the author intends to make us think about in this story? Our past, our roots, our family, our health, other people's problems, success, the past and the present, or other things? Discuss these ideas in class, and see what opinions emerge.

What you have learned

Make a list of the new words you have found, which you want to remember. Make a note, in two or three sentences, of what struck you most about this story. Write down some of the things you did not like about the story.

What will you remember about it? How would you sell it to someone, encouraging them to read it?

In the following extract you will read about two people. As you read, try to decide what work the husband does and what work the wife does.

My wife has no respect for my work. For that matter I have no respect for hers either. She tells me I am feeding mindless pap to the masses – or rather, that I am trying unsuccessfully to feed it since, as I point out, the masses show no inclination to swallow. I am pandering to the lowest common denominator. I am sacrificing my undeniable talents, squandering my undoubted gifts, selling my soul. I tell her she is practising a sophisticated form of voodoo under the pretence of using science. She tells me that last year she earned $78,000, or was it eighty-two? She tells me that my declared income over the last twelve months amounted to $6,149. End of argument.

My wife Stephanie – she hates to be called Steve as the boys at work do – sees me as a kind of glorified houseboy and to my chagrin that is what she sometimes calls me before her guests when we have dinner parties. I am good at cleaning and tidying up. In between trying to write songs I clean the house immaculately and struggle for inspiration over the kitchen sink:

> *Don't say it's the song, and not the singer*
> *If you no longer want me, I don't want to linger,*
> *Used to count your lovers on the fingers of one finger,*
> *But now I'm reading the signs.*

It doesn't always come. My wife says that my lyrics sound like badly translated Brecht poems. I am not sure whether or not this is a compliment.

She does, however, appreciate my cleaning efforts. She calls me her Mr Moto. Have I mentioned my wife's sense of humour? Sometimes she shows her appreciation in thoughtful little ways, bringing me home flowers or a box of chocolates, or inviting me out to our favourite restaurant. I put on after-shave lotion before she comes home.

(Laurie Clancy *Reading the Signs*)

Who earns more money? Do you think the wife's comment on his lyrics is a compliment? What is 'It', immmediately after the lyric?

Now read the extract again. What do you think of the words 'undeniable talents' and 'undoubted gifts'? Do you think the husband or wife chose the adjectives? What positive things does she say about him?

Why does she not respect her husband's work? Why does he not respect the wife's work? Why does he say 'End of argument'? Who has won?

Why do you think the wife's colleagues call her by a man's name, Steve?

What does the wife like about the husband?

When do you think this story was set: around the 1970s? 1980s? 1990s? Sometime in the future? Sometime in the distant past? How can you tell?

Describe the relationship between the two people. Is there anything unusual about their relationship? What do you think of their relationship? Why?

What do you think the story is about?

List the stories you have read, and then compare some of the features, like structure, characters, actions, language. Decide which (one, or more than one) you like best, and write a review of it – the review should make other people really want to read the story.

The difference between a play and the other kinds of text we read is simple: a play text is mostly just the dialogue, and the *performance* fills in the rest.

If we cannot see a performance, it is up to us, the readers, to fill in the gaps for ourselves. We have to imagine: who the characters are, where they are (the setting), how they speak and move in relation to each other (tone, proxemics), how they do what they do – and so on.

For some readers, this makes plays more difficult to read. But actually it opens up a wonderful world of opportunity to interpret and experiment, which tells us a lot about how texts work, and shows us how much meaning potential there is in even the simplest text.

The first text is a good example. How many speakers might there be?

> What are you writing?
> Nothing.
>
>   [*They drink.*]
>
> Not writing?
> No.
> Why not?
> Nothing to say.
> Doesn't stop others. Written out?
> Yes.
>
>   [*They drink.*]
>
> Now, what are you writing?
> Nothing.
>
>   (Edward Bond *Bingo*)

Since we do not know the characters' names, or the setting, we have complete freedom to interpret the text – to build up a context, to create characters, and to make a performance. Among the questions we have to ask and answer are:

How many characters are there? (At least two; as many as . . . ?) Where are they? Are they standing, sitting, walking, running, jogging . . . ? What are they drinking? (Or are these words spoken too?)

What is their mood – angry, inquisitive, reluctant, happy, sad . . . ?

Is the scene fast or slow, loud or quiet? Is there any humour in it?

Are there any words or phrases which cause difficulty? If so, the performance should *show* the possible meaning.

In groups of five or six, discuss all these questions, make some decisions, and then rehearse a performance of the scene. The performance should be enough to *show* the answers to all the questions. Do not have someone explain the setting or characters before the performance – make it clear by *showing* rather than telling. (There will also be decisions within the group – choosing the director and performers, finding props and settings, organising the 'stage', getting the performance ready.)

Possible scenarios: students and teachers during a test (but what about the drinking?); news conference with a famous writer; tea party of romantic lady novelists; television interview (rehearsal and take); journalists during a war; writers in a café or bar; prisoners trying to get a message out, with jailer(s) watching . . . and others.

The various performances will show differences in all the aspects discussed, plus *intonation* and emphasis, pace and attitude. Discuss some of these things and how well they worked – or did not work, and why.

'Written out' may have caused some problems – it means a writer has nothing more to say or write.

Now look at the names of the speakers (page 217). Does it make the situation clearer – or do you prefer the version you performed? Would you say this version is positive or negative? How would you perform it, in terms of tone, pace, and attitude? If you saw it as negative, try it now the other way round: utterly positive, if you played it negatively; very negatively, if you played it positively. Does it still work?

What you have learned

- How a text can be *open* – and how to explore the meaning potential of an open text.
- How to *show* rather than *tell* how a text might work.
- Some terminology: *proxemics* – the attitudes of people in relation to·each other (sitting or standing, threatening or friendly, etc.); *turn-taking* – the order of speakers following each other, or interrupting, in conversation.

Now we can apply some of these ideas to more drama texts. Look closely at the following five snippets from longer texts, and make decisions about:

- how open they are
- what kinds of difficulty or problems they contain for actors and directors (language, theme, action, characters, setting, etc.)
- what the whole play might be about
- which you would *most* like to work on, and which you would *least* enjoy working on – saying why, of course.

CECILY [*thoughtfully and sadly*]: Whatever unfortunate entanglement my dear boy may have got into, I will never reproach him with it after we are married.
GWENDOLEN: Do you allude to me, Miss Cardew, as an entanglement? You are presumptuous. On an occasion like this it becomes more than a moral duty to speak one's mind. It becomes a pleasure.
CECILY: Do you suggest, Miss Fairfax, that I entrapped Ernest into an engagement? How dare you? This is no time for wearing the shallow mask of manners. When I see a spade I call it a spade.
GWENDOLEN [*satirically*]: I am glad to say that I have never seen a spade. It is obvious that our social spheres have been widely different.

(Oscar Wilde *The Importance of Being Earnest*)

AMANDA: What's happened to yours?
ELYOT: Didn't you hear her screaming? She's downstairs in the dining-room I think.
AMANDA: Mine is being grand, in the bar.
ELYOT: It really is awfully difficult.
AMANDA: Have you known her long?
ELYOT: About four months, we met in a house party in Norfolk.

AMANDA: Very flat, Norfolk.

ELYOT: How old is dear Victor?

AMANDA: Thirty-four, or five; and Sibyl?

ELYOT: I blush to tell you, only twenty-three.

(Noël Coward *Private Lives*)

BLUNTSCHLI: There are only two sorts of soldiers: old ones and young ones. I've served fourteen years: half of your fellows never smelt powder before. Why, how is it that you've just beaten us? Sheer ignorance of the art of war, nothing else. [*Indignantly.*] I never saw anything so unprofessional.

RAINA [*ironically*]: Oh! Was it unprofessional to beat you?

BLUNTSCHLI: Well, come! Is it professional to throw a regiment of cavalry on a battery of machine guns, with the dead certainty that if the guns go off not a horse or man will ever get within fifty yards of the fire? I couldn't believe my eyes when I saw it.

RAINA [*eagerly turning to him, as all her enthusiasm and her dreams of glory rush back on her*]: Did you see the great cavalry charge? Oh, tell me about it. Describe it to me.

BLUNTSCHLI: You never saw a cavalry charge, did you?

RAINA: How could I?

BLUNTSCHLI: Ah, perhaps not. No: of course not! Well, it's a funny sight. It's like slinging a handful of peas against a window pane: first one comes; then two or three close behind him; and then all the rest in a lump.

RAINA [*her eyes dilating as she raises her clasped hands ecstatically*]: Yes, first One! the bravest of the brave!

(George Bernard Shaw *Arms and the Man*)

SERVANT: Madam, Mrs Candour is below, and if your ladyship's at leisure, will leave her carriage.

LADY SNEERWELL: Beg her to walk in.

[*Exit Servant.*]

LADY SNEERWELL: Now, Maria, here is a character to your taste; for though Mrs Candour is a little talkative, everybody allows her to be the best natured and best sort of woman.

MARIA: Yes, – with a very gross affectation of good nature and benevolence, she does more mischief than the direct malice of old Crabtree.

JOSEPH: I'faith 'tis true, Lady Sneerwell: whenever I hear the current running against the character of my friends, I never think them in such danger as when Candour undertakes their defence.

(Richard Brinsley Sheridan *The School for Scandal*)

RUMSEY: Can you cook now?
ELLEN: Shall I cook for you?
RUMSEY: Yes.
ELLEN: Next time I come. I will.

[*Pause.*]

RUMSEY: Do you like music?
ELLEN: Yes.
RUMSEY: I'll play you music.

[*Pause.*]

RUMSEY: Look at your reflection.
ELLEN: Where?
RUMSEY: In the window.
ELLEN: It's very dark outside.
RUMSEY: It's high up.
ELLEN: Does it get darker the higher you get?
RUMSEY: No.

[*Silence.*]
(Harold Pinter *Silence*)

Conclusions

Write notes on each text summarising the group discussions. Which texts would you like to know more about? Which would you be happy to leave aside right now?

The dates when these plays were written cover almost 200 years. Try to decide which was written when: 1969, 1930, 1894, 1895, and 1777. Do these dates tell you anything about the society or the context of the plays?

We will now look at different scenes from two of these plays. Read both scenes, and make notes about:

- any similarities between them, and
- what you would want to bring out of a performance of either scene.

CECILY: May I offer you some tea, Miss Fairfax?
GWENDOLEN [*with elaborate politeness*]: Thank you. [*Aside.*] Detestable girl! But I require tea.
CECILY [*sweetly*]: Sugar?
GWENDOLEN [*superciliously*]: No, thank you. Sugar is not fashionable any more.

[CECILY *looks angrily at her, takes up the tongs and puts four lumps of sugar into the cup.*]

CECILY [*severely*]: Cake or bread and butter?

GWENDOLEN [*in a bored manner*]: Bread and butter, please. Cake is rarely seen at the best houses nowadays.

CECILY [*cuts a very large slice of cake and puts it on the tray*]: Hand that to Miss Fairfax.

[MERRIMAN *does so, and goes out with footman.* GWENDOLEN *drinks the tea and makes a grimace. Puts down cup at once, reaches out her hand to the bread and butter, looks at it, and finds it is cake. Rises in indignation.*]

GWENDOLEN: You have filled my tea with lumps of sugar, and though I asked most distinctly for bread and butter, you have given me cake. I am known for the gentleness of my disposition, and the extraordinary sweetness of my nature, but I warn you, Miss Cardew, you may go too far.

CECILY [*rising*]: To save my poor, innocent, trusting boy from the machinations of any other girl there are no lengths to which I would not go.

GWENDOLEN: From the moment I saw you I distrusted you. I felt that you were false and deceitful. I am never deceived in such matters. My first impressions of people are invariably right.

CECILY: It seems to me, Miss Fairfax, that I am trespassing on your valuable time. No doubt you have many other calls of a similar character to make in the neighbourhood.

(Oscar Wilde *The Importance of Being Earnest*)

BATES: Will we meet to-night?

ELLEN: I don't know.

[*Pause.*]

BATES: Come with me to-night.

ELLEN: Where?

BATES: Anywhere. For a walk.

[*Pause.*]

ELLEN: I don't want to walk.

BATES: Why not?

[*Pause.*]

ELLEN: I want to go somewhere else.

[*Pause.*]

BATES: Where?

ELLEN: I don't know.

[*Pause.*]

BATES: What's wrong with a walk?

ELLEN: I don't want to walk.

[*Pause.*]

BATES: What do you want to do?
ELLEN: I don't know.

[*Pause.*]

BATES: Do you want to go anywhere else?
ELLEN: Yes.
BATES: Where?
ELLEN: I don't know.

[*Pause.*]

BATES: Do you want me to buy you a drink?
ELLEN: No.

[*Pause.*]

BATES: Come for a walk.
ELLEN: No.

[*Pause.*]

BATES: All right. I'll take you on a bus to the town. I know a place. My cousin runs it.

(Harold Pinter *Silence*)

Trace the changes in the girls' moods during the first scene. Which of these do they go through: shyness, friendliness, intimacy, confusion, distance, dislike, separation? Mark the points where any of these change – the turning points in the scene.

Whatever happens, the characters try to be polite to each other. Pick out the words and phrases which indicate this politeness. How can you tell it is sometimes false?

Make a list of any problems or difficulties which might influence the staging of the scene. How can these be overcome? What do you think the butler, Merriman, might do while he is onstage, even though he doesn't speak at all?

Pick out the lines you think will make the audience laugh.

How do you think this scene relates to the short scene you read earlier?

Now we can look at the other scene. There are a lot of pauses. How long do you think a pause might be?

Try playing the scene, based on an adjective to describe the mood (but don't tell the rest of the class what adjective you are using!). Possible adjectives: fast, slow, loud, quiet, running, angry, violent, aggressive, seductive, sexy, threatening, happy, sad, funny, all male, all female. What kind of setting do you imagine for the scene?

Now for a famous scene. Imagine witches, a storm, and lots of sound effects. As you read, what kind of voices do you imagine the witches have?

> [*Thunder and lightning. Enter three* WITCHES.]
>
> FIRST WITCH: When shall we three meet again?
>> In thunder, lightning, or in rain?
> SECOND WITCH: When the hurlyburly's done,
>> When the battle's lost and won.
> THIRD WITCH: That will be ere the set of sun.
> FIRST WITCH: Where the place?
> SECOND WITCH: Upon the heath.
> THIRD WITCH: There to meet with Macbeth.
> FIRST WITCH: I come, Graymalkin!
> SECOND WITCH: Paddock calls: – anon!
> ALL: Fair is foul, and foul is fair;
>> Hover through the fog and filthy air.

(William Shakespeare *Macbeth*)

How much is the scene about the future, and how much about the past? What is happening offstage during this scene (check line 3)?

What elements of the scene cause difficulty? Are they important for the staging and performance?

There are quite a few examples of *ambivalence* in the scene ('lost'/'won', for instance) – how many can you find?

What kind of sound effects and scenic effects would you want in staging the scene? Discuss it, cast it, and try a performance. Are the witches meant to be frightening, funny, realistic, or what?

Why do you think the witches talk about Macbeth? What are they going to do with him, do you think?

As you read the following extract, decide what Looka and Popova have in common. How does each react to this?

The action takes place in a drawing-room of Madame Popova's house in the country. POPOVA *in deep mourning, keeping her eyes fixed on a photograph, and* LOOKA.

LOOKA: It's not right, Madam. . . . You're just killing yourself. The cook and the chambermaid have gone to pick strawberries in the wood . . . every living thing's happy . . . even the cat knows how to enjoy herself – promenading in the courtyard and chasing birds. . . . And you sit indoors all day, as if you were in a nunnery, taking no pleasure in anything. Yes indeed! I believe it's nearly a year since you went out of the house!

POPOVA: And I never will go out. . . . Why should I? My life is over. He lies in his grave – I have buried myself in these four walls. . . . We are both dead.

LOOKA: There you go again! I wish I didn't have to listen to it! Nikolai Mihailovich's dead, that's as it had to be – it was God's will, and the Kingdom of Heaven be his! You've done your mourning, and now that'll do – it's time to stop. Surely you can't go on weeping and wearing mourning all your life? I lost my missus too. . . . Well, what of it? I grieved and cried for a month or so, and that was enough for her. Suppose I kept on wailing like Lazarus all my life – it would be more than the old woman was worth. [*Sighs.*] You've forgotten all your neighbors. . . . You don't visit them, and you won't receive them. We live like spiders, if you'll pardon me saying so – we don't see the light of day. The mice have eaten our liveries. . . . It's not as though there weren't any nice people about – the district is full of them. . . . There's a regiment stationed at Ryblovo, and the officers are proper lollipops – you simply can't take your eyes off them! In the camp there's never a Friday goes by without a ball, and the military band plays music every day, they say. Ah! Madam, my dear lady! You're young, pretty, blooming with health – all you need is to live and enjoy yourself to the full. . . . You know, beauty isn't given you to keep for ever! In another ten years you may be wanting to show off before the officers too – spreading your tail like a peacock – but it will be too late then!

POPOVA [*resolutely*]: I must ask you never to speak to me like this again! You know quite well that ever since Nikolai Mihailovich died, life has lost all its value to me. It may seem to you that I'm alive, but that's only what you think! I made a vow never to take off this mourning, never to look at the light of day till I go to my grave. . . . Do you hear? May his departed spirit see how I love him. . . . Yes, I know, it was no secret to you that he was often mean to me, harsh, and . . . and even unfaithful. But I will be faithful to the grave, and I will let him see how well I can love. There, from the other side of the grave, he will see me just as I was before he died. . . .

LOOKA: Instead of talking like that, you'd do better to take a walk in the garden or maybe have Toby or Giant put into harness and go and drop in on your neighbors. . . .

POPOVA: Oh! [*Weeps.*]

LOOKA: Madam! My dear lady! . . . What is the matter? God be with you!

POPOVA: He was so fond of Toby! He always used to drive him when he went to visit the Korchaghins and the Vlasovs. How wonderfully he used to drive!

How graceful he looked when he pulled at the reins with all his strength!
Do you remember? Toby, Toby! Tell them to give him an extra bag of oats
today.

LOOKA: Yes, Madam.

[*A loud ring at the door.*]

POPOVA [*starts*]: Who is that? Say that I'm not seeing anyone!

LOOKA: Yes, Madam. [*Goes out.*]

What does Looka's attitude to his wife's death tell us about him? Do
you find Looka's attitude sympathetic, cynical, or what? Does Looka
approve of Popova's mourning her husband's death? Why? What
does he want her to do?

Do you think Popova is sincere in her mourning of her husband's
death? Is there any line in the text which supports your view?

Now read the next extract. Underline the adjectives that Popova uses
to describe herself. Do you see her in the same light?

POPOVA [*alone, looking at the photograph*]: You shall see, Nicolas, how well
I can love and forgive. . . . My love will only fade away when I do, when my
poor heart stops beating. [*Laughs, half-weeping.*] Aren't you ashamed of
yourself? I'm such a good little woman, such a loyal wife, I've shut myself up
and I'll remain faithful to you all my life, while you . . . aren't you ashamed of
yourself, you fatty? How you deceived me, and made scenes, and left me on
my own for weeks on end! . . .

LOOKA [*enters, flustered*]: Madam, there's someone asking for you. He wants
to see you. . . .

POPOVA: But didn't you tell him that I'm not seeing anybody since my husband died?

LOOKA: I did, but he won't listen: he says it's a very urgent matter.

POPOVA: I won't see *anybody*!

LOOKA: I kept telling him, but . . . he's a proper devil . . . he swore and shoved
past me . . . he's in the dining-room now.

POPOVA [*irritably*]: Very well, show him in. . . . How rude these people are!

[LOOKA *goes out.*]

How difficult they are! What do they want from me? Why will they keep upsetting my peace of mind? [*Sighs.*] No, it looks as if I really shall have to enter
a convent. . . . [*Ponders.*] Yes, a convent. . . .

[*Enter* LOOKA *with* SMIRNOV.]

(Anton Chekhov *The Bear*)

Now that you have learned of Popova's motives for remaining in mourning, do you approve of her actions? Why?

How much of the contrast between the characters can you bring out in a performance?

SECTION FOUR

NOVELS

We are going to look at some *points of entry* which tell us quite a lot about the whole novel they come from. As you read the first passage, what do you think the two sides of the argument represent?

Then, quite mechanically and more distinctly, the conversation began again inside him.

'She's dead. What was it all for – her struggle?'

That was his despair wanting to go after her.

5   'You're alive.'

'She's not.'

'She is – in you.'

'You've got to keep alive for her sake,' said his will in him.

Something felt sulky, as if it would not rouse.

10   'You've got to carry forward her living, and what she had done, go on with it.'

But he did not want to. He wanted to give up.

'But you can go on with your painting,' said the will in him. 'Or else you can beget children. They both carry on her effort.'

15   'Painting is not living.'

'Then live.'

'Marry whom?' came the sulky question.

'As best you can.'

'Miriam?'

20   But he did not trust that.

He rose suddenly, went straight to bed. When he got inside his bedroom and closed the door, he stood with clenched fists.

'Mater, my dear – ' he began, with the whole force of his soul. Then he stopped. He would not say it. He would not admit that he wanted to die,

25   to have done. He would not own that life had beaten him, or that death had beaten him.

Going straight to sleep, he slept at once, abandoning himself to the sleep.

(D.H. Lawrence)

Can you say who the participants in the 'conversation' are?

Which of these polarities have you found in the text: alive/dead, inside/outside, waking/sleeping, conscious/unconscious? Mark where each of them is found, then write *who* or *what* each adjective represents.

Who do you think (a) Miriam, and (b) Mater are?

Can you think of another word for 'sulky' (lines 9 and 17)? Is it part of his conscious or his unconscious feelings?

What words tell you that the mother's life was not easy?

Why do you think he wants to die?

Compare the first sentence and the last sentence. What movement is there in the text between the beginning and the end? What has happened before this passage begins?

What might be positive in his life? How does the positive balance against the negative aspects? What do you think he will do?

The title of the novel is *Sons and Lovers.* How does the passage relate to that title?

In the next passage, there are two very different settings, and three stages to the story. Even just looking at the text, you can see the stages of the story – mark where the three main stages seem to be, before you read. As you read, what are the first signs you can find of the move from one setting to the other?

I ate the ham and eggs and drank the beer. The ham and eggs were in a round dish – the ham underneath and the eggs on top. It was very hot and at the first mouthful I had to take a drink of beer to cool my mouth. I was hungry and I asked the waiter for another order. I drank several glasses of beer. I was not thinking at all but read the paper of the man opposite me. It was about the breakthrough on the British front. When he realized I was reading the back of his paper he folded it over. I thought of asking the waiter for a paper, but I could not concentrate. It was hot in the café and the air was bad. Many of the people at the tables knew one another. There were several card games going on. The waiters were busy bringing drinks from the bar to the tables. Two men came in and could find no place to sit. They stood opposite the table where I was. I ordered another beer. I was not ready to leave yet. It was too soon to go back to the hospital. I tried not to think and to be perfectly calm. The men stood around but no one was leaving, so they went out. I drank another beer. There was quite a pile of saucers now on the table in front of me. The man opposite me had taken off his spectacles, put them away in a case, folded his paper and put it in his pocket and now sat holding his liqueur glass and looking out at the room. Suddenly I knew I had to get back. I called the waiter, paid the reckoning, got into my coat, put on my hat and started out the door. I walked through the rain up to the hospital.

Upstairs I met the nurse coming down the hall.

'I just called you at the hotel,' she said. Something dropped inside me.

'What is wrong?'

'Mrs Henry has a haemorrhage.'

'Can I go in?'

'No, not yet. The doctor is with her.'

'Is it dangerous?'

'It is very dangerous.' The nurse went into the room and shut the door. I sat outside in the hall. Everything was gone inside of me. I did not think. I could not think. I knew she was going to die and I prayed that she would not. Don't let her die. Oh God, please don't let her die. I'll do anything for you if you won't let her die. Please, please, please, dear God, don't let her die. Dear God, don't let her die. Please, please, please, don't let her die. God, please make her not die. I'll do anything you say if you don't let her die. You took the baby but don't let her die – that was all right but don't let her die. Please, please, dear God, don't let her die.

(Ernest Hemingway *A Farewell to Arms*)

Briefly, what are the main characteristics of each stage?

First   *setting*   *characters*   *action*

            ....

            ....

Second   *setting*   *characters*   *action*

            ....

            ....

Third   *setting*   *characters*   *action*

            ....

            ....

Why do you think he tells us in such detail about what he is eating and drinking? How can you tell that he does not belong to the place? What sign is there that the story takes place in wartime? What do these sentences tell us: 'I was not ready to leave yet', and 'Suddenly I knew I had to get back'?

In the dialogue section, what is strange about 'Can I go in?' What is the most striking moment for you?

Looking at the first paragraph, what is the dominant pronoun? What is the longest sentence? Why do you think the writer uses so many very short sentences?

What effect does the final paragraph have on you? Do you think Mrs Henry will die?

What can you tell about the whole novel from this extract?

The next novel looks at one man's reactions to being rejected. As you read about Gordon, what would you say are the key words in the passage?

Gordon gazed at the thing with wordless hatred. Perhaps no snub in the world is so deadly as this, because none is so unanswerable. Suddenly he loathed his own poem and was acutely ashamed of it. He felt it the weakest, silliest poem ever written. Without looking at it again he tore it
5   into small bits and flung them into the wastepaper basket. He would put that poem out of mind for ever. The rejection slip, however, he did not tear up yet. He fingered it, feeling its loathly sleekness. Such an elegant little thing, printed in admirable type. You could tell at a glance that it came from a 'good' magazine – a snooty highbrow magazine with the money of
10   a publishing house behind it. Money, money! Money and culture! It was a stupid thing that he had done. Fancy sending a poem to a paper like the *Primrose*! As though they'd accept poems from people like *him*. The mere fact that the poem wasn't typed would tell them what kind of person he was. He might as well have dropped a card on Buckingham Palace. He
15   thought of the people who wrote for the *Primrose*; a coterie of moneyed highbrows – those sleek, refined young animals who suck in money and culture with their mother's milk. The idea of trying to horn in among that pansy crowd! But he cursed them all the same. The sods! The bloody sods! 'The Editor regrets!' Why be so bloody mealy-mouthed about it?
20   Why not say outright, 'We don't want your bloody poems. We only take poems from chaps we were at Cambridge with. You proletarians keep your distance'? The bloody, hypocritical sods!

At last he crumpled up the rejection slip, threw it away, and stood up.

Better get to bed while he had the energy to undress. Bed was the
25   only place that was warm. But wait. Wind the clock, set the alarm. He
went through the familiar action with a sense of deadly staleness. His eye
fell upon the aspidistra. Two years he had inhabited this vile room; two
mortal years in which nothing had been accomplished. Seven hundred
wasted days, all ending in the lonely bed. Snubs, failures, insults, all of
30   them unavenged. Money, money, all is money! Because he had no money
the Dorings snubbed him, because he had no money the *Primrose* had
turned down his poem, because he had no money Rosemary wouldn't
sleep with him. Social failure, artistic failure, sexual failure – they are all
the same. And lack of money is at the bottom of them all.

(George Orwell)

Why is Gordon unhappy? Is his unhappiness particular, or general,
or both? How many contrasts can you find in terms of:

• people
• places
• moods
• positive/negative?

What is 'the thing' in line 1? Check through to line 6, and then say
also what the 'snub' is – is it the same thing? Who says, 'We don't
want your bloody poems'? Are the words actually spoken? Who are
'the sods'?

   The idea of 'Who chose the adjective?' can give us an insight
into the character's mind; who chose the adjectives 'elegant' (line 7)
and 'admirable' (line 8), for instance? How can you tell what
Gordon thinks about the rejection slip? Find adjectives chosen by
Gordon which reflect his state of mind or his views on the *Primrose*
people. With any of the adjectives you don't know, are they positive
or negative? Are any of them actually positive but used negatively?

   Do you sympathise with Gordon or with someone else? Why do
you think this is – because he is a good poet, because he has been
rejected, because we have only his own point of view, because he is a
nice character, because you identify with his problems?

Contrast these two sentences: 'Without looking at it again . . . '
(lines 4–5), and 'At last he crumpled up the rejection slip . . . ' (line
23). Look at them in terms of:

- verbs
- movement
- mood.

What do they show of how Gordon's frame of mind has changed between the two paragraphs?

Think of some adjectives to describe Gordon's mood in the first paragraph:

....

And in the second:

....

What effects do you notice in the second paragraph in terms of:

- verbs in the imperative
- repetition
- parallelism?

Who actually uses the imperative in sentences like 'But wait' (line 25)?

Look at the whole passage again, and see how often you can notice the author's trick of moving in and out of Gordon's mind. Adjectives, imperatives, and reported speech will show you some of the changes.

This text reaches a climax – where would you say the climax happens?

What is the effect of the final sentences? Do they represent Gordon's thoughts, or only the author's, in your opinion?

Vocabulary

There are a lot of words you probably don't know in this text. How many of them do you *need* to know? If you could only know *three* words, which would they be? Discuss them in groups, and reach a decision. Are there other words you *want* to know?

What can you tell about the society Gordon lives in? Why does he think of Buckingham Palace? Which of these themes do you think is most important: failure, rejection, loneliness, class difference, money, artistic creativity, ambition?

Do you think Gordon is a good poet? How can you tell? What do you think of the *Primrose* people? Has Gordon's opinion of them influenced yours?

What do you think the novel is going to be about? Do you think Gordon will be a success or will he continue to be a failure? Who or what are his main enemies?

The novel is called *Keep the Aspidistra Flying*. Was 'aspidistra' one of the words you needed or wanted to know? An aspidistra was the house plant which became a symbol of the working class in England in the 1930s. What, then, do you think the title indicates about the focus of the novel?

Sometimes we can find a key event in a novel as a point of entry – the heart of the story. As you read this point of entry to *No Harvest But a Thorn*, how does the story tie in with the title?

Jeha ran on, leaping over the wide gaps in the ridge.

Only three plots had been completed. Another eleven huge plots to go. Who would clear all those plots? Who?

Jeha ran on.

'What's happened?' she asked as she neared the spot where Lahuma lay.

'What's happened?' she yelled.

Sanah rushed up to her and took her hand. They went up close to Lahuma. The earth where he lay was wet with red blood. And the blood flowed into the rice field: Lahuma's blood merged with the muddy water of the rice field. And the blood still flowed from the sole of his right foot.

'*Nibong!*'[1] said a neighbour who was tying something around Lahuma's foot.

'*Nibong* thorn?'

'Yes,' said Milah who was standing near by.

'Where was that thorn?'

Nobody answered.

'Where?' she demanded.

Sanah pointed to the spot where her father had fallen. Jeha tore herself free of her eldest daughter's grasp. She leapt to the middle of the rice-plot. She bent and groped under the water at that spot. She groped with both hands as though groping for catfish in a new muddy nook.

---

1 *nibong* – a tall tufted palm, used for flooring

'Where? Where?' she kept asking as she groped.

Sanah jumped into the water and groped too.

'Ha! Here it is! Here it is!' Jeha shouted as with both hands she pulled at something embedded in the earth. Sanah helped and they pulled out an old *nibong* stem about a *depa*[2] long. The stem was covered with hard, knobbly, mud-steeped thorns. Among the thorns there was one that had been broken off.

'Ha! Here it is!' Jeha yelled again in fury. She lifted the *nibong* stem on to her shoulder. She carried it on to a ridge. The crowd stared at the *nibong* stem as though it were something strange.

'Has the end come out?' Jeha asked.

What do you think the relationship is between Jeha, Lahuma, Sanah, and Milah? What had Lahuma been doing? How much of the work had been completed? Why do you think Sanah wanted to pull the whole *nibong* stem out? Why is Jeha's last question important?

What can you tell about the society and its main concerns?

Now read on. A little later in the novel, we find Jeha thinking about her life, and Lahuma. What impression do these lines give of the life of the family?

Jeha thought of all the torments of past years. Year by year Lahuma had toiled with all his might.

Flood will come. You must fight.

I will fight, declared Jeha.

The crabs will come.

I will fight them with these hands.

The birds will come to eat up your rice.

I will fight, Jeha declared again in her mind.

Worms will nest in the leaves of your rice plants.

I will fight. Jeha is still alive. My children are still alive.

Next year?

Next year too I will fight them all.

And the year after?

I will fight. I will fight them all. I will fight together with Sanah, Milah, Jenab, Semek, Liah, Lebar, Kiah.

(Shahnon Ahmad *No Harvest But a Thorn*)

---

2 *depa* – the span of arms outstretched

General discussion

Do you prefer the English title or the original? Why? In Malay this literally translates as *Steps Along the Way*. How much do you think the scenes you have read are a good representation of a kind of life? How universal do you find it?

In the next story we meet two twins who are very good at reading – they even read backwards! As you read, what signs do you find of their attitudes to life and to other people?

The twins were precocious with their reading. They had raced through *Old Dog Tom*, *Janet and John* and their *Ronald Ridout Workbooks*. Baby Kochamma, who had been put in charge of their formal education, had read them a version of *The Tempest* abridged by Charles and Mary Lamb.

'*Where the bee sucks, there suck I*,' Estha and Rahel would go about saying. '*In a cowslip's bell I lie*.'

So when Baby Kochamma's Australian missionary friend, Miss Mitten, gave Estha and Rahel a baby book – *The Adventures of Susie Squirrel* – as a present when she visited Ayemenem, they were deeply offended. First they read it forwards. Miss Mitten, who belonged to a sect of born-again Christians, said that she was a Little Disappointed in them when they read it aloud to her, backwards.

'*ehT serutevdA fo eisuS lerriuqS. enO gnirps gninrom eisuS lerriuqS ekow pu*.'

They showed Miss Mitten how it was possible to read both *Malayalam* and *Madam I'm Adam* backwards as well as forwards. She wasn't amused and it turned out that she didn't even know what Malayalam was. They told her it was the language everyone spoke in Kerala. She said she had been under the impression that it was called Keralese. Estha, who had by then taken an active dislike to Miss Mitten, told her that as far as he was concerned it was a Highly Stupid Impression.

Miss Mitten complained to Baby Kochamma about Estha's rudeness, and about their reading backwards. She told Baby Kochamma that she had seen Satan in their eyes. *nataS in their seye*.

They were made to write *In future we will not read backwards. In future we will not read backwards*. A hundred times. Forwards.

A few months later Miss Mitten was killed by a milk van in Hobart, across the road from a cricket oval. To the twins there was hidden justice in the fact that the milk van had been *reversing*.

The story is set in Kerala. What can you tell about the place? It is in southern India – do you find many signs of Indian culture? What does that tell you about the twins' education?

Just before this scene, this is what is happening. Does it contain any more indications of their cultural background?

It was Chacko's idea to have a billboard painted and installed on the Plymouth's roof rack. On the way to Cochin now, it rattled and made fallingoff noises.

Near Vaikom they had to stop to buy some rope to secure it more firmly. That delayed them by another twenty minutes. Rahel began to worry about being late for *The Sound of Music*.

Then, as they approached the outskirts of Cochin, the red and white arm of the railway level-crossing gate went down. Rahel knew that this had happened because she had been hoping that it wouldn't.

She hadn't learned to control her Hopes yet. Estha said that that was a Bad Sign.

So now they were going to miss the beginning of the picture. When Julie Andrews starts off as a speck on the hill and gets bigger and bigger till she bursts on to the screen with her voice like cold water and her breath like peppermint.

The red sign on the red and white arm said STOP in white.

'POTS,' Rahel said.

A yellow hoarding said BE INDIAN, BUY INDIAN in red.

'NAIDNI YUB, NAIDNI EB,' Estha said.

(Arundhati Roy *The God of Small Things*)

'Be Indian, buy Indian.' Does that tie in with the twins' reading, and the movie? Why, then, do you think it is important for them to tell Miss Mitten about their local language?

Do you find Miss Mitten's death funny, or cruel, or what?

Turn to *Colonizer's Logic* on page 8 – does it tie in with anything in this story, do you think?

Read the following extract, and decide who 'I' is.

'I was born in Malacca speaking Portuguese. That's because the Portuguese colonised us so many years ago. The Dutch didn't stay long enough, or I suppose it's a toss up I would be speaking Dutch instead now. Anyway the result was no one outside understood the Portuguese I spoke. Then, because the British had ousted the Dutch, I learnt English and forgot my Portuguese. It was like taking out the parts and organs of my body and replacing them with others. Then the Japs came and we were told to forget English, learn Japanese. So once more I began taking out parts and putting in new ones – unlearning my language and learning another. Now it seems I must unlearn it once more and learn Malay.' He said passionately, 'What I want to say, Sabran, is this. I've gone through the process so many times, I can't anymore. Say I'm a colonial creature because I speak English. I'm tired, tired, I can't learn anymore. It may not have got into my bones, but it's gone deep enough for it to hurt when trying to remove it. You want to unlace all my nerves and tie them up in a different set of knots. How many more times?' His voice had risen. 'How many times? Can you tell me that? The process is simply repeating itself, why can't it stop?'

(Lloyd Fernando Scorpion Orchid)

Check your answer around the class. Pick out the languages 'I' has had to learn. Why did he learn them? What is the 'it' referred to in lines 13–14: 'It may not have got into my bones, but it's gone deep enough for it to hurt when trying to remove it'?

What is the tone in the last sentence? Is it the same as the first sentence? What does he compare the learning of each new language with? Do you think this is an appropriate comparison? Which word indicates that he wants to stop learning more languages? Why? What does the learning of each language symbolise?

What is Sabran's relationship with the speaker, in your opinion? Do you sympathise with the speaker?

In this short extract from a novel, we have a point of entry to the whole story. As you read about Hari and Lila, ask yourself some questions about where Hari has been, and why. Make notes of your answers.

'Lila, Bela, Kamal!' he called.

In an instant Lila was at the door, her old purple sari gathered about her, her face peeping out, brown and curious. When she saw him, she gasped. They stared at each other. Then she ran out crying, 'Hari! Hari, I knew you would come. It's Diwali tomorrow and I knew you'd come!'

'How did you know? I didn't write.'

'Oh, I knew, I knew you would,' Lila smiled. 'And we made sweets for you, Hari – come and eat.'

Hari wanted to ask a hundred questions, all at once, about their mother, their father, Bela and Kamal, about the village and Biju's boat and everything.

Instead, he followed Lila into the house. Old and shabby it might be, but how shady and cool it was. He felt grateful for it, just as it was, and stood breathing in its air silently. Only the invisible pigeons could be heard, letting flow their musical notes like soft, feathered bubbles trickling through the air.

Then Lila came towards him with a brass tray on the palm of her hand. It was heaped with the sweets she had made of rice powder and cream, sugar and flour and semolina, and coconut.

Hari said, 'But I must wash first: I am dusty.'

(Anita Desai *A Village by the Sea*)

What is the relationship between Hari and Lila, do you think? Who are the other people mentioned?

What lines or images do you like best in the passage? Has Hari been away for a long time? How can you tell? Suggest reasons why he might have gone away. Where do you think he has been? Is it far away? Where are they? What did Hari miss while he was away? How can you tell? How has he travelled back?

Read the passage again. How many senses are involved? Compare the first line and the last line – what movement has there been?

Did Lila know Hari would come? Why does she say she did, *three* times? What can you tell about the place they are now?

Who chose the adjectives 'old and shabby', 'shady and cool', do you think? Why do 'old and shabby' come before the subject, 'it'? What is different about the main verb in the last sentence in this paragraph? What contrasts, or binaries, can you find in the text: outside/inside, away/back . . . ?

What colours do you find in the text? What can you tell about the sweets Lila has made?

How old do you think Hari and Lila are? Has anything changed about Hari since he went away?

What do you think the main themes of the whole novel might be, judging from this point of entry?

PART II

SECTION FIVE

POETRY

We are going to move further, in this section, with our analysis of *processes* of how texts work. What can you tell about the 'I' and 'me' in these two poems?

In my country they jail you
for what they think you think.
My uncle once said to me:
they'll implant a microchip
in our minds
on to a screen at John Vorster Square.
I was scared:
by day I guard my tongue
by night my dreams.

(Pitika Ntuli *In My Country*)

Blessed are the dehumanized
For they have nothing to lose
But their patience.

False gods killed the poet in me. Now
I dig graves
With artistic precision.

(Keorapetse Kgositsile)

Can you tell where the poets are? (They are in the same country.) Pick out binaries of past and present. What is the atmosphere of these lines for you?

The second text is called *Mandela's Sermon*. What does that add to your understanding?

What attitudes do you find here? Is it culturally surprising to you?

You must pay the price
Of wanting to marry
A university graduate,
A Ph.D. at that!
She's worth every bit
Of six thousand naira;
We must uphold tradition.

Agreed, but then
Can you give a guarantee
She's not shop-soiled –
All those years on the campus,
Swotting and sweating,
Sucking up to lecturers
For all those degrees?

Shop-soiled, you ask?
What do you mean 'shop-soiled'?
Our daughter's not old clothes,
She's not old books
That get soiled in the shop;
She's old wine, matured over the years
For the discerning taste.

Shop-soiled she may not be,
Matured no doubt she is;
But then is she untouched?
Has nobody removed the cork,
All those years in the varsity?

That we cannot tell you,
That's your business to find out
On your nuptial night
In the privacy of your bedroom.

In that case, in-laws, dear,
Can I return her then
And obtain a refund
According to tradition
If I should discover
Someone has sipped the wine
Before I got there?

(Mabel Segun *Bride Price*)

How can you tell it is a dialogue? Who are the speakers? What is important to the man? And to the 'in-laws, dear'?

Compare this with the story by Siew Yue Killingley on pages 154–5.

Is this an appropriate answer from the bride?

> Father when I was a child, you promised me
> We would never be separated.
> Mother when I was a child, you promised me
> We would never be separated.
> But what of today?
> Have you not broken your word?
> Am I not leaving now?

(Bini Bride's Complaint)

Now we are going to look at the heart of a poem, and see how far the point of entry can show us what the poem is doing. Where is the poem set, do you think? What might the missing words be?

> Water, water, everywhere,
> And all the boards did shrink;
> Water, water, everywhere
> —— —— drop to drink.

Compare your choices of words to fill the gaps in the last line. What are 'the boards' part of? Why is the water undrinkable?

Now read on. How does the next verse help to make the situation clearer? What single word might fill the gaps?

> Day after day, day after day,
> We stuck, —— breath —— motion;
> As idle as a painted ship
> Upon a painted ocean.

Who could 'we' be?

The original words in the first verse were 'Nor any', and, in the second, 'nor' twice. Did anybody think of these? How different are the other possible choices? What image do you have of the ship?

We often look at the very beginning and the very end of a text to see how much movement there has been during the whole text.

Now read on, and see what movement you can find between these
two sets of lines:

  _____ _____ an ancient Mariner,
And he stoppeth one of three

   A sadder and a wiser man
He rose the morrow morn.

What do you expect the first words to be? Why? Do you think 'He'
in the final line is the mariner or the 'one of three'? What might have
made him 'sadder' and 'wiser' – anything to do with the verses you
read earlier? Is there any movement from present to future? And
what tenses were the verbs in the earlier verses? (The opening words
of the poem are 'It is'.)

Is 'A sadder and a wiser man' positive or negative, do you think?
How might these words relate to these ideas: 'man must suffer to be
wise'; 'innocence and experience'?

Now read on: there are fourteen verses at the heart of the whole
poem, which might clarify some of the questions we have been
looking at. As you read them, mark any moments which relate to
what you have already read, and to the questions you are still not
clear about. Before you read, cover up the commentary at the right-
hand side. (You can refer to it after you have read the verses.)

The Sun now rose upon the right:
Out of the mist came he,
Still hid in mist, and on the left
Went down into the sea.

And the good south wind still blew behind,
But no sweet bird did follow,
Nor any day for food or play
Came to the mariners' hollo!

And I had done an hellish thing,   *His shipmates cry out against the ancient*
And it would work 'em woe: *Mariner, for killing the bird of good luck.*
For all averred, I had killed the bird
That made the breeze to blow.
Ah wretch! said they, the bird to slay,
That made the breeze to blow!

Nor dim nor red, like God's own head,
The glorious Sun uprist:
Then all averred, I had killed the bird
That brought the fog and mist.
'Twas right, said they, such birds to slay,
That bring the fog and mist.

*But when the fog cleared off, they justify
the same, and thus make themselves
accomplices in the crime.*

The fair breeze blew, the white foam flew,
The furrow followed free:
We were the first that ever burst
Into that silent sea.

*The fair breeze continues: the ship enters
the Pacific Ocean, and sails northward,
even till it reaches the Line. The ship hath
been suddenly becalmed.*

Down dropt the breeze, the sails dropt down,
'Twas sad as sad can be;
And we did speak only to break
The silence of the sea!

All in a hot and copper sky,
The bloody Sun, at noon,
Right up above the mast did stand,
No bigger than the Moon.

Day after day, day after day,
We stuck, nor breath nor motion;
As idle as a painted ship
Upon a painted ocean.

Water, water, everywhere,
And all the boards did shrink;
Water, water, everywhere,
Nor any drop to drink.

And the Albatross begins to be avenged.

The very deep did rot: O Christ!
That ever this should be!
Yea, slimy things did crawl with legs
Upon the slimy sea.

About, about, in reel and rout
The death-fires danced at night;
The water, like a witch's oils,
Burnt green, and blue, and white.

And in some dreams assured were
Of the spirit that plagued us so:
Nine fathom deep he had followed us
From the land of mist and snow.

And every tongue, through utter drought
Was withered at the root;
We could not speak, no more than if
We had been choked with soot.

Ah! well a-day! what evil looks
Had I from old and young!
Instead of the cross, the Albatross
About my neck was hung.

*A Spirit had followed them; one of the
invisible inhabitants of this planet, neither
departed souls nor angels; concerning
whom the learned Jew Josephus, and the
Platonic Constantinopolitan, Michael
Psellus, may be consulted. They are very
numerous, and there is no climate or
element without one or more.*

*The shipmates, in their sore distress,
would fain throw the whole guilt on the
ancient Mariner: in sign whereof they hang
the dead seabird round his neck.*

(Samuel Taylor Coleridge
The Rime of the Ancient Mariner)

What has the 'I' of the poem done? Why was it a terrible deed? The Ancient Mariner tells his story to 'one of three' wedding guests he stops in the first verse. Why do you think he has to tell his story? Why should it make the wedding guest 'A sadder and a wiser man'? What will he have learned from the story?

The poem is in the form of a ballad. If we look up the word 'ballad' in the dictionary, we will find these definitions:

- a short story told in verse
- a simple song
- a popular love song.

The *Rime* is neither a song, nor a love song, nor particularly short, but simple and popular it certainly is. Simplicity is a quality which makes the ballad memorable both for the teller and the audience. Like all well-told stories, in order to keep the listener/reader interested, it alternates straightforward narration with dialogue, descriptive bits with comments either by the narrator himself or by characters involved in the story.

In groups, pick out:

- narrative elements
- descriptive elements
- comments by the narrator
- comments by others.

Then share your findings with the rest of the class.

In the same groups, find out about the sound patterns which make the poem easier to remember, in particular considering the following aspects:

- rhyme
- rhythm
- repetitions
- alliteration and assonance.

Pick out examples of 'archaic' language – you should be able to identify about eighteen!

Did the commentary, which Coleridge himself provided, make your task easier? Why do you think Coleridge gave a prose summary of the story as well?

In what way do the third and fourth verses differ from the other verses? How do verses 5 and 6 contrast in terms of rhythm? Form and content interact beautifully here, as well as in many other parts of the poem. Where?

What images convey the ideas of (a) corruption, and (b) an evil spirit, in the later verses? Who or what do you think 'the spirit' is (see verse 12)? What dimension, if any, does the commentary give to it? Which images have struck you most? Can you venture some reason for their being more memorable than others?

Vocabulary

Here are some of the words from the text which may be unfamiliar. Group them together as *adjectives, verbs, nouns, other.*

hid	wretch	'twas	dropt	idle	plagued
hellish	slay	foam	copper	shrink	root
woe	dim	furrow	mast	slimy	
averred	uprist	burst	stuck	mist	

Which words do you *need to know* of these, and which can you simply imagine the meaning of?

Find out more about Coleridge's life and works, and report your findings to the rest of the class. Find a complete edition of *The Rime of the Ancient Mariner*. Form six groups. Each group should read one of the remaining six sections of the poem and make a summary of it. Report back in order, from section 1 to section 7, so as to reconstruct the entire poem.

Conclusions

Why do you think Coleridge chose the ballad form for the poem? Discuss, then write about how appropriate you think it is.

Was the poem too long? Which parts could you cut, if any?

What is the poem mainly about, in your opinion: a horror story, guilt, innocence and experience, the old passing on wisdom to the young, time, suffering, a voyage, a combination of some of these, something else?

Is the Albatross a symbol, in some way, do you think? Or is it not necessary to think in terms of symbolism?

What would you say are the key words of the poem? And the key images?

La Belle Dame sans Merci is also a ballad – but much shorter! Have you any idea what the title might mean? Discuss some of the things that happen traditionally when someone is *suffering* because of love. What happens to his energy, complexion, dreams? As you read the poem, pick out which stanzas are negative and which are positive.

> O, what can ail thee, knight-at-arms,
> Alone and palely loitering?
> The sedge has withered from the lake,
> And no birds sing.
>
> 5   O, what can ail thee, knight-at-arms,
> So haggard and so woe-begone?
> The squirrel's granary is full,
> And the harvest's done.
>
> I see a lily on thy brow,
> 10 With anguish moist and fever dew;
> And on thy cheeks a fading rose
> Fast withereth too.

I met a lady in the meads,
Full beautiful – a faery's child

15 Her hair was long, her foot was light,
And her eyes were wild.

I made a garland for her head,
And bracelets too, and fragrant zone;
She looked at me as she did love,

20 And made sweet moan.

I set her on my pacing steed,
And nothing else saw all day long;
For sidelong would she bend, and sing
A faery's song.

25 She found me roots of relish sweet,
And honey wild, and manna dew,
And sure in language strange she said –
'I love thee true.'

She took me to her elfin grot,

30 And there she wept and sighed full sore,
And there I shut her wild wild eyes
With kisses four.

And there she lullèd me asleep
And there I dreamed – Ah! woe betide!

35 The latest dream I ever dreamed
On the cold hill side.

I saw pale kings and princes too,
Pale warriors, death-pale were they all;
They cried – 'La Belle Dame sans Merci

40 Hath thee in thrall!'

I saw their starved lips in the gloom,
With horried warning gapèd wide,
And I awoke and found me here,
On the cold hill's side.

45   And this is why I sojourn here
      Alone and palely loitering,
      Though sedge has withered from the lake,
      And no birds sing.

(John Keats *La Belle Dame sans Merci*)

Is the whole poem positive or negative? What lines tell you?

The first two lines of the first two stanzas are questions. Where are these questions answered? Is 'thee' in line 1 the same person as 'thy' in line 9? What is the third stanza about? How does it tie in with the things you discussed before reading the poem? How many voices are there in the text? Is 'I' in line 9 the same as 'I' in line 13? Does it make a difference?

How many signs are there the 'she' loved him? At what point does the love story change? What causes the change?

What season is it? Are there any lines that portray the season positively? How do they contrast with other lines about the setting? What kind of thing do you think 'sedge' is? Is it important to know precisely what it is? Why do you think 'no birds sing'? Where are the birds?

How many opposites or binaries can you find, such as 'no birds'/ 'the squirrel's granary is full'? What colours predominate?

What do you think these words might have in common: 'faery's child', 'faery's song', 'language strange', 'elfin grot'?

The knight is a medieval figure. What words and phrases *sound* as if they are medieval rather than modern? Would 'has' be better than 'hath', for example? What sounds and images strike you most in the poem? What do you think 'thrall' means? The modern word 'enthralled' has a similar meaning – is it positive or negative in its modern sense? And in the poem?

Look at the rhyme and rhythms of the poem. How do they compare with the *Ancient Mariner*? How effective are they, for you? What is the atmosphere of the poem: mysterious, frightening, magic, lovely, romantic, something else?

Has the knight passed from innocence to experience? Was the love real? What has death got to do with it? Do you think the poem is against women, in any way? Would the title in English have been just as good – 'The Beautiful Woman without Pity'? Why, or why not?

This section looks at some of the best-known poems in English. But the fact that they are well-known should not be a problem, if we look at them as if they were new, and they did not have a reputation preceding them.

The Charge of the Light Brigade was written to commemorate a famous event in the Crimean War, in the mid-1850s. As you read the first three verses, pick out lines which show something heroic about the Charge.

I

Half a league, half a league,
Half a league onward,
All in the valley of Death
Rode the six hundred.
5   'Forward, the Light Brigade,
Charge for the guns!' he said:
Into the valley of Death
Rode the six hundred.

II

'Forward, the Light Brigade,'
10   Was there a man dismay'd?
Not tho' the soldier knew
Some one had blunder'd:
Their's not to make reply.
Their's not to reason why,
15   Their's but to do and die:
Into the valley of Death
Rode the six hundred.

III

Cannon to right of them,
Cannon to left of them,
20   Cannon in front of them
Volly'd and thunder'd,
Storm'd at with shot and shell,
Boldly they rode and well,
Into the jaws of Death,
25   Into the mouth of Hell
Rode the six hundred.

Check how far a 'league' is in your dictionary. Is the distance realistic? What other elements give you the idea of distance? How many negative elements are there so far? What do they contrast with?

What words give *sounds* to the text? What lines tell you that the Charge was a mistake?

Who is 'he' (line 6)? How many of the lines does he speak? What noun do 'volly'd and thunder'd' (line 21) go with? And what pronoun goes with 'Storm'd at' (line 22)?

Now read on: the rest of the poem tells us who the enemy were, and whether all of the 'six hundred' returned. Find these points as you read.

IV

Flash'd all their sabres bare,
Flash'd as they turn'd in air
Sabring the gunners there,
30   Charging an army, while
All the world wonder'd:
Plunged in the battery-smoke
Right thro' the line they broke;
Cossack and Russian
35   Reel'd from the sabre-stroke
Shatter'd and sunder'd.
Then they rode back, but not
Not the six hundred.

V

Cannon to right of them,
40   Cannon to left of them,
Cannon behind them
Volly'd and thunder'd;
Storm'd at with shot and shell,
While horse and hero fell,
45   They that had fought so well
Came thro' the jaws of Death,
Back from the mouth of Hell,
All that was left of them,
Left of six hundred.

VI

50   When can their glory fade?
O the wild charge they made!
All the world wonder'd.
Honour the charge they made!
Honour the Light Brigade,
55   Noble six hundred!

(Alfred, Lord Tennyson *The Charge of the Light Brigade*)

Pick out lines which give you a *visual* picture of what happened, and lines which give *sounds*. There are a lot of repeated lines in the whole poem. Check through them and decide:

- how often they are repeated
- if they are 'heroic' or not
- if their meaning has changed during the poem
- why you think they are repeated so many times.

Look at line 31. How different is it from the rest of the poem? If we take away the final verse, how would the poem as a whole be different?

What can you tell about the soldiers in the Charge? And their commanders? How heroic was the Charge? Does the poem question their heroism, or only affirm it?

Do you think this poem reads differently to us from how it appeared to the Victorians? What differences in perception might there be?

As you read the next text, pick out as many positive words as you can find.

> I wandered lonely as a cloud
> That floats on high o'er vales and hills,
> When all at once I saw a crowd,
> A host of golden daffodils:
> 5   Beside the lake, beneath the trees,
> Fluttering and dancing in the breeze.
>
> Continuous as the stars that shine
> And twinkle on the Milky Way,
> They stretched in never-ending line
> 10   Along the margin of a bay:
> Ten thousand saw I at a glance.
> Tossing their heads in sprightly dance.
>
> The waves beside them danced, but they
> Out-did the sparkling waves in glee:
> 15   A poet could not but be gay,
> In such a jocund company:
> I gazed – and gazed – but little thought
> What wealth the show to me had brought.

> For oft, when on my couch I lie
> 20   In vacant or in pensive mood,
> They flash upon that inward eye
> Which is the bliss of solitude:
> And then my heart with pleasure fills,
> And dances with the daffodils.
>
> (William Wordsworth *Daffodils*)

Are there any words you don't know, which you can definitely say are positive? Look at line 22. Is the 'solitude' related to the 'lonely' in line 1? Follow through the verbs telling us what 'I' did in lines 1 to 19. List his actions:

....

....

Are there any differences between the verbs of *seeing* in the poem?

Where are the daffodils? Many people don't know what daffodils are. If you didn't know what daffodils were, which of the following would you imagine they might be: birds, butterflies, colours, something else?

What are 'they' (line 9)? How is line 11 different from what has gone before, in terms of syntax? How many daffodils did he see? What are 'them' and 'they' in line 13?

There are three things in line 15 which you might comment on. What are they? Discuss how the word 'gay' has changed its meaning; whether 'could not but' means he did or didn't; and how 'a poet' is different from 'I'. What word in line 16 means the same as 'gay' in line 15?

What did he *not* do in lines 17–18? How does the tense of the verb show a time shift in line 18?

Compare the very first line and the very last: what differences are there? Sum them up as:

there is a move from .... to ....

....

....

....

Look back at the whole poem. Where do you think the *main* turning point between past and present is?

In line 21, something happens which is different from everything else in the poem. What has changed about the subject? What, in the poem, is 'the bliss of solitude' (line 22)? Look again at the question as to whether this solitude is the same as the feeling in line 1 – have you changed your opinion, or confirmed it? Look at some little words in the last verse: 'For', 'when', and 'then'. Why are they important?

Conclusions

What do you think this poem is about: flowers, memory, nature, past and present, the poet, or something else? Many critics have said that the poet remembers the daffodils, and say the poem is about the joy of memory. Does the active verb in line 21 challenge that reading, in your opinion? Could the poet have written, 'I remember the daffodils'? Would that have been different? For many people, the poem is simply about the beauty of nature and its effect on humanity. Is that reading valid, in your opinion? Which reading(s) do you prefer?

Research

You might want to find out some more about the Romantic poets, and their attitudes to time and nature.

The next few texts are less familiar – but no less enjoyable!

What do you see when you see a rainbow? Is it a masculine- or a feminine-sounding word, 'rainbow'? The next text plays with that idea. Where do you think the voice comes from? See if you find any cultural references to help you place it.

When you see
de rainbow
you know
God know
wha he doing –
one big smile
across the sky –
I tell you
God got style
the man got style

When you see
raincloud pass
and de rainbow
make a show
I tell you
is God doing
limbo
the man doing
limbo

But sometimes
you know
when I see
de rainbow
so full of glow
and curving
like she bearing child
I does want know
if God
ain't a woman

If that is so
the woman got style
man she got style

(John Agard *Rainbow*)

What aspects of the language make this sound like spoken English?
Do you think the poet is being serious? How can you tell?

Read the next poem, and underline the lines which refer to the
woman's present state, her past life, and her future.

The dulang-washer, squinting like a witch,
Squats with rag-wrapped head and begging-bowl.
The sun mocks her with false gold.
Still she bows her head acquiescently.

How will she die? In memory of movement,
The monotonous rhythm of search
And discarding. Changeless streams and gravel
Will dim her sight, exchanging gold-dust

For rocks in the head. No glamour of departure
Enshrines her travel, the shift
From landscape to landscape a meagre drift.

(Shirley Lim *The Dulang-Washer*)

Why do you think the dulang-washer is described as 'a witch'? What
had been the woman's work? What has she become now? How had
she lived her life as a dulang-washer?

What does the speaker mean by 'exchanging gold-dust/For rocks
in the head'? What is the 'travel' the speaker refers to? What does the
dulang-washer have to look forward to? Do you think the speaker is
sympathetic towards the dulang-washer? Are you?

The next poem is called *Woman Work* – a woman speaks about the
things she does. As you read, what *positive* ideas do you find?

I've got the children to tend
The clothes to mend
The floor to mop
The food to shop
Then the chicken to fry
The baby to dry
I got company to feed
The garden to weed
I've got the shirts to press
The tots to dress
The cane to be cut
I gotta clean up this hut
Then see about the sick
And the cotton to pick.

Shine on me, sunshine
Rain on me, rain
Fall softly, dewdrops
And cool my brow again.

Storm, blow me from here
With your fiercest wind
Let me float across the sky
'Til I can rest again.

Fall gently, snowflakes
Cover me with white
Cold icy kisses and
Let me rest tonight.

Sun, rain, curving sky
Mountain, oceans, leaf and stone
Star shine, moon glow
You're all that I can call my own.

(Maya Angelou Woman Work)

There are many *daily* jobs mentioned. What are they contrasted with? List them under separate headings:

daily	*special*
....	....
....	....
....	....
....	....

Do the special things have anything in common?

Are there any words you would not have used? Think what words you might have used, then try them in the line, and see if you think yours are better. Look at the rhymes, and mark where they change their order. Do you think the changes reflect any changes in the tone of the words?

In the first part of the poem, most of the verbs follow 'I've got . . . ', and make lists; in the second part, there are a lot of imperative forms. Mark all the imperatives. Are they realistic – that is, can they really be done? How does this contrast with the first part?

What are the things she can call her own? Could the last line be written with 'I've got . . . '? Would you prefer it with 'I've got . . . ', or is it better to be different from the first part of the poem?

Issues

Is this a good reflection of women's roles? Or is it exaggerated? Could a man have written it? Does the second part reflect reality or dreams? Do you think many women feel like this? Is the speaker complaining, do you think? Should she try to change her life?

Discuss around the class any comparisons or contrasts between this text and the situation of women as you know it. (This could also be the subject of an essay or assignment. What other texts you have read touch on similar issues? You could use them to bring out contrasts or to show other situations and points of view.)

Contrast what Maya Angelou says with this. Is it positive or negative about men? You may want to write a reply, or a continuation!

Men are, men are, men are.
men are strong
men are tough
men are surly, men are rough
men have mates
men drink beer
men are brave and don't show fear
men slap backs
men sing songs
men are men and men are strong
men don't touch
men aren't drips
men shake hands with vice-like grips.

men like fighting
men like cars
men like shouting with men in bars
men like football
and now and then
men like men like men like men
no they don't
men beat up queers
men live with their mums for years and years
men have beards
and hairy chests
men walk through blizzards in string vests.

men can embrace
and bare their soul
but only if they've scored a goal
men leap tall buildings
men are tough
men don't know when they've had enough
men drive fast cars with wide wheels
men like fur-lined steering wheels
men have muscles
men have sweat

men wear trousers
men have flies
men kick sand in each other's eyes
men stand alone
men show no fears
men have hobbies and hairy ears
men have willies
men have bums
men are good at science and sums
men aren't loving
men don't dance
men don't change their underpants.

men climb mountains
in the snow
men don't cook and men don't sew
men are bosses
men are chums
men build office blocks and slums
men make bombs
men make wars
men are stupid, men are bores
men ignore
what women see
and call our story history.

(The Joeys *Men Are*)

How serious is it? What about the contrast in the final lines?

Now we look at a poem which is about nature, and one person's reaction to it. As you read, decide what the 'narrow Fellow' actually is.

> A narrow Fellow in the Grass
> Occasionally rides –
> You may have met Him – did you not
> His notice sudden is –
>
> 5   The Grass divides as with a Comb –
> A spotted shaft is seen –
> And then it closes at your feet
> And opens further on –
>
> He likes a Boggy Acre
> 10   A Floor too cool for Corn –
> Yet when a Boy, and Barefoot –
> I more than once at Noon
>
> Have passed I thought a Whiplash
> Unbraiding in the Sun
> 15   When stooping to secure it
> It wrinkled and was gone –
>
> Several of Nature's People
> I know and they know me –
> I feel for them a transport
> 20   Of cordiality –
>
> But never met this Fellow
> Attended, or alone
> Without a tighter breathing
> And Zero at the Bone –

(Emily Dickinson *A narrow Fellow in the Grass*)

Probably the first thing you noticed was the dashes. Do they affect the way you read? How does the absence of dashes in verses 4 and 6 affect the flow of the poem?

Some people say the 'narrow Fellow' is a snake; others that it might be a shadow. Which of the two do you prefer? Can you find words in the text which prove your idea right?

What ideas of movement do you find in the second verse? Are there any words which make the movement clear?

Who is the speaker? In what words is the present indicated, and the past? Why might it be significant that the speaker was 'Barefoot'? Why do you think the 'narrow Fellow' likes 'a Boggy Acre' and a cool floor? Pick out any words which tell you about the speed the narrow fellow can move at.

There are changes, little turning points, at lines 11 and 17. How are they indicated? What word would you probably not have used in line 17? How does the personal identification strike you?

Is the speaker's relationship with nature generally positive or negative? Does the final verse change this in any way? What causes 'a tighter breathing'? Have you ever felt 'Zero at the Bone'? What kind of feeling is it?

As well as her use of dashes, Emily Dickinson uses capital letters more than most people. Does this help the poem in any way, or do you find it distracting? Does it make the words with capital letters seem more important?

Compare this poem (a) with others of Emily Dickinson's, and (b) with other nature poems you may have read.

Now read the following lines, and decide to whom these lines are spoken.

> do not make this wind our hangman
> and the sea where our souls are soaked
> our hearts are buried,
> where they cannot find us.

Read the four lines again. Where do you think the speaker is at the time these lines are spoken? What does the speaker fear? Who do you think 'our' refers to? What do you think their occupation is? Who does 'they' refer to? Now read the whole poem.

> three small souls in a frail old sampan
> in the bowl of the sea
> between the teeth of the waves.
> between the sea and the home
> there was no choice
> against the big winds
> and the capricious sea.

the wind has no heart
nor the sky nor the sea,
and the heart was for words of prayer;
time, between the stretches of a red imagination
was a promise of hope,
for the heart knows its logic
and the pains of the whipping winds.

what of the wives, sons and daughters,
the tomorrow, the eye of the day,
the rice and the fish, the school fees?
on land how heavy the soul is loaded:
to survive was as difficult as to die,
to go down into the bottom of the sea-dish,
the bare dish:
to swim into time and hope.

the early morning nets, the boats,
the friends, the chattering gregariousness,
and the see-saw
on the fulcrum of the shore.

the harsh land pushed them
into the uncertain sea
deep into the eclipsing experience of death.
but yet to be responsible is to love
and to love is to live,
to be rich in life.

do not make this wind our hangman
the sea where our souls are soaked
and our hearts are buried,
where they cannot find us.

(Muhammad Haji Salleh)

Where are the fishermen as the poem opens? Pick out the contrasts involving the boat, the men, the wind, and the sea. What difficulties do the fishermen face on land and sea?

Land   *Sea*

....

....

....

Pick out words later in the poem which show how the fishermen are torn *between* the sea and the shore. There is one invented word – why is it appropriate?

What do you think the poet wants to suggest in these lines?

the wind has no heart
nor the sky nor the sea, . . .

Do you see these lines as positive or negative, hopeful or desperate?
What risks are involved in these lines?

to go down into the bottom of the sea-dish,
the bare dish:
to swim into time and hope.

What is the state of mind here?

What words bring out a sense of inevitability? Do you think they imply any of these: resignation, acceptance, destiny, fate, the will of God, the human condition? Would the poem be very different if the last two lines were taken away? And if all the last four were taken away?

The title of the poem is *Three Beserah Fishermen*. Do you think it is important that they come from Beserah, a small village in Malaysia? Could the poem be about more than just fishermen, in your opinion? Look back at the poem and see what universal elements there might be.

The sinking of the *Titanic* in 1912 was one of the most shocking disasters of the twentieth century. What do you know about it? See what you can find out about it. Can you think of major disasters in our time which have had a shocking effect on you?

The poet Thomas Hardy, shocked by the news of the loss of the *Titanic*, wrote a very famous poem about it. He imagines that, all the time the ship was being built, some spirit which he calls the Immanent Will was simultaneously building the iceberg which caused the ship to sink.

Before you read the poem, look at the shape of it. What do you find unusual about it? As you read, how much of the ship do you find is actually described?

I

In a solitude of the sea
Deep from human vanity,
And the Pride of Life that planned her, stilly couches she.

II

Steel chambers, late the pyres
5   Of her salamandrine fires,
Cold currents thrid, and turn to rhythmic tidal waves.

III

Over the mirrors meant
To glass the opulent
The sea-worm crawls – grotesque, slimed, dumb, indifferent.

IV

10   Jewels in joy designed
To ravish the sensuous mind
Lie lightless, all their sparkles bleared and black and blind.

V

Dim moon-eyed fishes near
Gaze at the gilded gear
15   And query: 'What does this vaingloriousness down here?'

VI

Well: while was fashioning
This creature of cleaving wing,
The Immanent Will that stirs and urges everything

VII

Prepared a sinister mate
20   For her – so gaily great –
A Shape of Ice, for the time far and dissociate.

VIII

And as the smart ship grew
In stature, grace, and hue,
In shadowy silent distance grew the Iceberg too.

IX

25   Alien they seemed to be:
No mortal eye could see
The intimate wedding of their later history,

X

Or sign that they were bent
By paths coincident
30   On being anon twin halves of one august event,

XI

Till the Spinner of the Years
Said 'Now!' And each one hears,
And consummation comes, and jars two hemispheres.

(Thomas Hardy *The Convergence of the Twain*)

Which verse tells you: where the ship is; the contrasts between where it should have been and where it is now; what the Immanent Will was making?

Look at the first line of verse VI. What does 'Well' tell us?

Pick out as many adjectives as you can which point out the negative aspects of the *Titanic* now. What adjectives contrast with these?

There are a lot of very unusual words in the poem. Mark them, and say what you *think* they might mean. Then decide which words you *really need* to know, and which words you don't need to know. Finally, look up one or two of the words, and try to decide if the synonyms would have been more appropriate, or less.

Can you find anything to contrast with 'Pride of Life' (line 3)? 'So gaily great' (line 20) describes the ship very positively. Then the iceberg begins to grow – where does this growth end? Which word in the last verse suggests the end of the process?

A lot of the syntax of the poem is unusual (the initial lines of verses VI and IX, for example). Look at them, and rewrite them in more usual ways. Is it the form and shape of the poem which makes Hardy write like this, do you think? What do you notice about the rhymes in the poem?

In the final verse, who does Hardy imagine bringing the two great constructions together?

What is the overall effect of the poem for you: shock, confusion, pessimism, admiration, or something else? Hardy has often been described as both pessimistic and ironic in his writings. Does this poem bear out this description, in your opinion?

Does this poem give you a deeper idea of the tragedy of the sinking of the *Titanic*? Or does it leave you cold?

SHORT STORIES

Many of the passages in this section are quite self-contained, but they can also be points of entry for the whole story. The first passage tells us something about two characters, a daughter and her mother. As you read, which of the two do you sympathise with more?

So poor Virginia was worn out. She was thin as a rail. Her nerves were frayed to bits. And she could never forget her beastly work. She would come home at tea-time speechless and done for. Her mother, tortured by the sight of her, longed to say: 'Has anything gone wrong, Virginia? Have you had anything particularly trying at the office today?' But she learned to hold her tongue, and say nothing. The question would be the last straw to Virginia's poor overwrought nerves, and there would be a little scene which, despite Mrs Bodoin's calm and forbearance, offended the elder woman to the quick. She had learned, by bitter experience, to leave her child alone, as one would leave a frail tube of vitriol alone. But, of course, she could not keep her *mind* off Virginia. That was impossible. And poor Virginia, under the strain of work and the strain of her mother's awful ceaseless mind, was at the very end of her strength and resources.

Mrs Bodoin had always disliked the fact of Virginia's doing a job. But now she hated it. She hated the whole government office with violent and virulent hate. Not only was it undignified for Virginia to be tied up there, but it was turning her, Mrs Bodoin's daughter, into a thin, nagging, fearsome old maid. Could anything be more utterly English and humiliating to a well-born Irishwoman?

Check round the class who sympathises more with Virginia, and who with her mother.

Think of some adjectives to describe the mother. Then see which of the following adjectives you think are suitable for the mother: 'understanding', 'snobbish', 'worried', 'bossy', 'nervous', 'calm', 'patient'. Do you think there are any of these adjectives that Mrs

Bodoin would use to describe herself? Any she would definitely not use?

What about Virginia? What adjectives can you think of to describe her? Physically, what do you think Virginia looks like? And Mrs Bodoin?

What contrasts are there in the passage? Begin a list:

....

....

Then contrast the very first sentence with the very last one, and see how many things you can find to say:

language   'There is a movement from . . . '
content (character and subject) 'There is a difference between . . . '

Things you might want to look for: short/long sentences, characters, names, statements/questions, adjectives . . .

What new information do we find out about the mother in the last sentence? If we take the last sentence away, how does it affect the whole text?

What would you say are the main contrasts in the passage? Are they between people, or ideas, or social attitudes? Or all three?

Who chose the adjectives? There are three possible answers: the author (who of course chose all of them!), and also each of the two characters. Look at the second paragraph again. What would you say is the key word?

> Mrs Bodoin had always disliked the fact of Virginia's doing a job. But now she hated it. She hated the whole government office with violent and virulent hate. Not only was it undignified for Virginia to be tied up there, but it was turning her, Mrs Bodoin's daughter, into a thin, nagging, fearsome old maid. Could anything be more utterly English and humiliating to a well-born Irish-woman?

Who do you think chose the adjectives 'thin, nagging, fearsome . . .'? Pick out some other adjectives, and decide if they reflect the point of view of one of the characters. What do they tell you about the character?

Pick out some words which give sounds (alliteration) – what do they add to the meaning of the paragraph, in your opinion?

Read the whole passage again, and see if you can find any adjectives which reflect Virginia's opinion of her mother.

What does the very first word in the passage tell us? What do you think happened before the beginning of the passage? Does the focus change between Virginia and the mother? Point out places where you think changes of focus happen.

Are there differences between the first paragraph and the second? List some of them, under headings such as:

	First paragraph	*Second paragraph*
length	....	....
focus	....	....
speed	....	....
point of view	....	....
mood/atmosphere	....	....
italics	....	....

What do you think will happen now? Will there be a confrontation, or will things go on as they are? Suggest some possible continuations.

The old question: What is it about? Give some possible answers, then decide which you think is best. Suggest a title for the passage. How much does the title you have chosen reflect your interpretation of what the passage is about?

Vocabulary

There are lots of words in this text which you probably have not seen before: 'frayed', 'vitriol', 'forbearance', and others. But you have been able to read and understand the basic conflicts of the passage, and to understand the two characters in some ways. So, which of the words you do not know are *absolutely necessary* to help your reading? Discuss in groups, and select just *one* word per group that you *need to know*.

Issues

Why do you think Virginia has a job? What reasons can you give why she should not work? What reasons would her mother give?

Do you think this is a recent text? Are the issues old or new?

Have you changed your ideas on who you sympathise with, or have you more sympathy with the character you originally sympathised with? Do you agree with the author's choice of adjective, 'poor' Virginia?

Do you think the author wants us to take sides?

We have had one story about characters. The next point of entry is mostly dialogue, a conversation. As you read, count how many characters there are.

> One day, when he sat talking with his 'uncle', he looked straight into the eyes of the sick man, and said:
>
> 'But I shouldn't like to live and die here in Rawsley.'
>
> 'No – well – you needn't,' said the sick man.
>
> 'Do you think Cousin Matilda likes it?'
>
> 'I should think so.'
>
> 'I don't call it much of a life,' said the youth. 'How much older is she than me, Uncle?'
>
> The sick man looked at the young soldier.
>
> 'A good bit,' he said.
>
> 'Over thirty?' said Hadrian.
>
> 'Well, not so much. She's thirty-two.'
>
> Hadrian considered a while.
>
> 'She doesn't look it,' he said.
>
> Again the sick father looked at him.
>
> 'Do you think she'd like to leave here?' said Hadrian.
>
> 'Nay, I don't know,' replied the father, restive.
>
> Hadrian sat still, having his own thoughts. Then in a small, quiet voice, as if he were speaking from inside himself, he said:
>
> 'I'd marry her if you wanted me to.'
>
> The sick man raised his eyes suddenly and stared. He stared for a long time. The youth looked inscrutably out of the window.
>
> '*You!*' said the sick man, mocking, with some contempt. Hadrian turned and met his eyes. The two men had an inexplicable understanding.
>
> 'If you wasn't against it,' said Hadrian.
>
> 'Nay,' said the father, turning aside, 'I don't think I'm against it. I've never thought of it. But – but Emmie's the youngest.'

He had flushed and looked suddenly more alive. Secretly he loved the boy.
'You might ask her,' said Hadrian.
The elder man considered.
'Hadn't you better ask her yourself?' he said.
'She'd take more notice of you,' said Hadrian.
They were both silent. Then Emmie came in.

Pick out the different names used for the young man, and for the old man, and list them.

Young man   *Old man*

....

....

....

....

Emmie and Matilda are passive participants in the passage, while Hadrian and the old man are active participants (this is often an easier way to speak about a passage and the characters in it). What is the relationship between the two women? And between them and the old man? And between the old man and Hadrian? Look at the first line of the passage. What do the inverted commas tell us?

Compare the very first line and the very last. What can you say about the movement of the text:

'There has been a movement from . . . '
'There is a contrast between . . . '

How many of these binaries or opposites can you find: long/short, speaking/silence, tension/complicity, male/female, two/more, inside/outside, staying/leaving, old/young?

Where are Hadrian and the old man? Where is the story set? Is it a big place? How can you tell? Has Hadrian ever been away from Rawsley? Why do you think he suggests he might marry one of the girls?

What part of the body is most frequently mentioned? Trace through all the verbs of seeing and looking.

Is the conversation fast or slow? Trace the silences. What do you think the two men will do now that Emmie has come in?

Can you find any dialect usages? What do they tell you about the setting and the characters?

There are many turning points all through the passage. Which do you think is the *main* turning point? Discuss in class the various suggestions. What do they tell you about the emphasis of each interpretation? In answer to the question 'What is it about?', how many themes can you draw out of the passage?

Reactions

What is your reaction to the men planning the marriage of one of the women? What do you think Emmie and Matilda's reactions might be?

Do you sympathise with any of the characters? What about the idea of leaving a small place like Rawsley?

Why do you think Hadrian and the old man are called so many different things: 'the youth', 'the sick man', etc.? Do these things add anything to our understanding of the characters or the situation?

Why do you think '*You!*' is in italics?

What do you think will happen to each of the characters?

Now we extend the question of character a little. As you read the next text, you will see it is more descriptive. Pick out the most important character.

But under all this, things were not well. The very next morning came the farm-boy to say that a cow had fallen over the cliff. The Master went to look. He peered over the not very high declivity, and saw her lying dead on a green ledge under a bit of late-flowering broom. A beautiful, expensive creature, already looking swollen. But what a fool, to fall so unnecessarily!

It was a question of getting several men to haul her up the bank, and then of skinning and burying her. No one would eat the meat. How repulsive it all was!

This was symbolic of the island. As sure as the spirits rose in the human breast, with a movement of joy, an invisible hand struck malevolently out of the silence. There must not be any joy, nor even any quiet peace. A man broke a leg, another was crippled with rheumatic fever. The pigs had some strange disease. A storm drove the yacht on a rock. The mason hated the butler, and refused to let his daughters serve at the house.

Out of the very air came a stony, heavy malevolence. The island itself seemed malicious. It would go on being hurtful and evil for weeks at a time. Then suddenly again one morning it would be fair, lovely as a morning in Paradise, everything beautiful and flowing. And everybody would begin to feel a great relief, and a hope for happiness.

Then as soon as the Master was opened out in spirit like an open flower, some ugly blow would fall. Somebody would send him an anonymous note, accusing some other person on the island. Somebody else would come hinting things against one of his servants.

'Some folks think they've got an easy job out here, with all the pickings they make!' the mason's daughter screamed at the suave butler, in the Master's hearing. He pretended not to hear.

'My man says this island is surely one of the lean kine of Egypt, it would swallow a sight of money, and you'd never get anything back out of it,' confided the farm-hand's wife to one of the Master's visitors.

The people were not contented. They were not islanders. 'We feel we're not doing right by the children,' said those who had children. 'We feel we're not doing right by ourselves,' said those who had no children. And the various families fairly came to hate one another.

Yet the island was so lovely. When there was a scent of honeysuckle and the moon brightly flickering down on the sea, then even the grumblers felt a strange nostalgia for it. It set you yearning, with a wild yearning; perhaps for the past, to be far back in the mysterious past of the island, when the blood had a different throb. Strange floods of passion came over you, strange violent lusts and imaginations of cruelty. The blood and the passion and the lust which the island had known. Uncanny dreams, half-dreams, half-evocated yearnings.

What is your impression of the Master? Is he powerful or weak, in your opinion? How well does he understand the island? Which is more important: the island or the people who live on it?

Look again at the last paragraph. Does the word 'Yet' change anything that has gone before? What is the effect of the little word 'so'?

Yet the island was so lovely. When there was a scent of honeysuckle and the moon brightly flickering down on the sea, then even the grumblers felt a strange nostalgia for it. It set you yearning, with a wild yearning; perhaps for the past, to be far back in the mysterious past of the island, when the blood had a different throb. Strange floods of passion came over you, strange violent

> lusts and imaginations of cruelty. The blood and the passion and the lust which the island had known. Uncanny dreams, half-dreams, half-evocated yearnings.

Make a circle round the pronouns. Who is 'you'?

What is the main colour in this paragraph? How many senses are involved? Is the impression of the island now positive or negative? If we take away this final paragraph, is the impression of the island positive or negative?

How many actions are there in the final paragraph? Circle the main verbs. What happens in the final sentences?

Now look again at the first paragraph, to see if any of the effects we found in the final paragraph are already anticipated there. Contrast, as we have done before, the opening sentence and the very last sentence of the whole passage. What movement, differences, or changes of emphasis do you find?

> But under all this, things were not well. The very next morning came the farm-boy to say that a cow had fallen over the cliff. The Master went to look. He peered over the not very high declivity, and saw her lying dead on a green ledge under a bit of late-flowering broom. A beautiful, expensive creature, already looking swollen. But what a fool, to fall so unnecessarily!

What does 'But' tell us? Would the text be different without the 'But'? What would you have written instead of 'under all this', and 'things were not well'? In the next sentence, which words or syntax give an idea of speed?

What contrasts can you notice between the two sentences, 'The Master went to look', and 'He peered over the not very high declivity, and saw her lying dead on a green ledge under a bit of late-flowering broom'? Look particularly at: the verbs, sentence length, the colours (broom is a bright yellow bush), the height. Would you have written 'her' about the cow? What does the pronoun add?

Who do you think chose the adjective 'expensive'? Why? Who thinks 'what a fool'? What does it tell you about the character?

We could stop here, without looking at paragraphs 2 to 8. What conclusions could we draw about the text already? Think about: does the writer want us to sympathise with the Master or the island? Is the passage about nature, or man, or corruption? How much is the past important?

If you go on to read the rest of the text, there are some more themes which might emerge. When do we first realise the setting is an island? Does the word 'expensive' have any further resonances? How important are the various people who are introduced? How many turning points are there, between positive and negative; and are they always between paragraphs? How much action is narrated, and how much of the text is description? How does this compare with the final paragraph? 'Kine' is a biblical word, meaning 'cattle'; why do you think it is used here?

Conclusions

Can you say in a few words what the basic conflict or contrast of the passage is, in your opinion? How much is the Master to blame for the things that go wrong? How would you describe the tone of this text: angry, sympathetic, ironic, serious, realistic, impressionistic, or another adjective?

Are there any particular words, phrases, or sentences that you liked? Or any that you found confusing? What do you think you will remember most clearly about this text?

The story is called *The Man Who Loved Islands*. Is it a good title? Why/why not? Is the tone of the title serious? Did the Master love the island?

Extension

If you were to write about the island, what good things could you say about it? Would environmentalists agree with you?

How modern is this text, compared with the others you have read, do you think? What are the issues it brings out?

Do you think the author implies that we should leave the island to nature? What kinds of exploitation would be acceptable?

Writing

We have read about quite different characters in the three texts so far. What can you write about them, in terms of:

• what they do
• what they think
• what kind of person they are
• what they want from life?

Are there more similarities, or more differences, between the passages we have read so far? Which reflects the most modern concerns, and which is least modern, for you? Make a list, then elaborate it into three or four paragraphs discussing the texts.

Dialogue can reveal quite a lot about character. Sometimes it can also reveal a lot about the whole situation. In this passage, decide as you read who 'her' is. What can you tell about the whole situation from your first reading?

'May I speak now?' asked Doris.

'Wait a minute, I haven't finished yet. I wasn't in love with her, not even at the beginning. I only took her so as to have somebody about the bungalow. I think I should have gone mad if I hadn't, or else taken to drink. I was at the end of my tether. I was too young to be quite alone. I was never in love with anyone but you.' He hesitated a moment. 'She lived here till I went home last year on leave. It's the woman you've seen hanging about.'

'Yes, I guessed that. She had a baby in her arms. Is that your child?'

'Yes. It's a little girl.'

'Is it the only one?'

'You saw the two small boys the other day in the kampong. You mentioned them.'

'She has three children then?'

'Yes.'

'It's quite a family you've got.'

She felt the sudden gesture which her remark forced from him, but he did not speak.

'Didn't she know that you were married till you suddenly turned up here with a wife?' asked Doris.

'She knew I was going to be married.'

'When?'

'I sent her back to the village before I left here. I told her it was all over. I gave her what I'd promised. She always knew it was only a temporary arrangement. I was fed up with it. I told her I was going to marry a white woman.'

'But you hadn't even seen me then.'

'No, I know. But I'd made up my mind to marry when I was home.' He chuckled in his old manner. 'I don't mind telling you that I was getting rather despondent about it when I met you. I fell in love with you at first sight and then I knew it was either you or nobody.'

'Why didn't you tell me? Don't you think it would have been only fair to

give me a chance of judging for myself? It might have occurred to you that
it would be rather a shock to a girl to find out that her husband had lived for
ten years with another girl and had three children.'

(W. Somerset Maugham The Force of Circumstance)

Note down some of the elements of the story under the headings of
'past' and 'present':

	Past	*Present*
husband	....	....
	....	....
Doris	....	....
	....	....
first 'wife'	....	....
	....	....

What can you tell about the character of the husband? Which of the
two speakers is the stronger, in your opinion?

As you read the text for a second time, pick out any moments of
narration, rather than dialogue. What do they tell you about the
characters? What has happened immediately before the beginning of
this passage?

What do you think of the husband's attitude to his women? Do
you believe him when he says he fell in love with Doris 'at first sight'?

Do you notice any irony in Doris's words? How would you
describe her attitude to what she has heard? What do you think the
rest of the story will be about? Do you think Doris will have her
revenge? What about the native woman?

Issues

Of course, we must not think this is just a story about colonialism.
How much sympathy do you think there is in the text for the native
woman and her situation? Does the text seem to you pro-women,

pro-men, pro-colonial or anti-colonial, exploitational or anti-exploitational?

In the next story, the first voice we hear is a computer's. Read the first section – do you think this kind of exercise could be possible?

My name is Joe. That is what my colleague, Milton Davidson, calls me. He is a programmer and I am a computer. I am part of the Multivac-complex and am connected with other parts all over the world. I know everything. Almost everything.

I am Milton's private computer. His Joe. He understands more about computers than anyone in the world, and I am his experimental model. He has made me speak better than any other computer can.

'It is just a matter of matching sounds to symbols, Joe,' he told me. 'That's the way it works in the human brain even though we still don't know what symbols there are in the brain. I know the symbols in yours, and I can match them to words, one-to-one.' So I talk. I don't think I talk as well as I think, but Milton says I talk very well. Milton has never married, though he is nearly 40 years old. He has never found the right woman, he told me. One day he said, 'I'll find her yet, Joe. I'm going to find the best. I'm going to have true love and you're going to help me. I'm tired of improving you in order to solve the problems of the world. Solve *my* problem. Find me true love.'

I said, 'What is true love?'

'Never mind. That is abstract. Just find me the ideal girl. You are connected to the Multivac-complex so you can reach the data banks of every human being in the world. We'll eliminate them all by groups and classes until we're left with only one person. The perfect person. She will be for me.'

I said, 'I am ready.'

Is there such a thing as true love? What is your idea of the perfect partner? Do you think a computer could help you to find the perfect partner? There are such things as computer dating agencies – do you think they would use a system of elimination, like Milton and Joe?

Now read on: compare what *you* would use as a criterion for elimination.

He said, 'Eliminate all men first.'

It was easy. His words activated symbols in my molecular valves. I could reach out to make contact with the accumulated data on every human being in the world. At his words, I withdrew from 3,784,982,874 men. I kept contact with 3,786,112,090 women.

He said, 'Eliminate all younger than 25, all older than 40. Then eliminate all with an IQ under 120; all with a height under 150 centimetres and over 175 centimetres.'

He gave me exact measurements; he eliminated women with living children; he eliminated women with various genetic characteristics. 'I'm not sure about eye color,' he said. 'Let that go for a while. But no red hair. I don't like red hair.' After two weeks, we were down to 235 women. They all spoke English very well. Milton said he didn't want a language problem. Even computer-translation would get in the way at intimate moments.

'I can't interview 235 women,' he said. 'It would take too much time, and people would discover what I am doing.'

'It would make trouble,' I said. Milton had arranged me to do things I wasn't designed to do. No one knew about that.

'It's none of their business,' he said, and the skin on his face grew red. . . .

What sort of thing is Joe *not* designed to do? Will this be a problem, do you think? Where are we on our structure-of-the-story list? How far are we from the end of the story?

Now read on: how is the story becoming more complex?

. . . 'I tell you what, Joe, I will bring in holographs, and you check the list for similarities.'

He brought in holographs of women. 'These are three beauty contest winners,' he said. 'Do any of the 235 match?'

Eight were very good matches and Milton said, 'Good, you have their data banks. Study requirements and needs in the job market and arrange to have them assigned here. One at a time, of course.' He thought a while, moved his shoulders up and down, and said, 'Alphabetical order.'

That is one of the things I am not designed to do. Shifting people from job to job for personal reasons is called manipulation. I could do it now because Milton had arranged it. I wasn't supposed to do it for anyone but him, though.

The first girl arrived a week later. Milton's face turned red when he saw her. He spoke as though it were hard to do so. They were together a great deal and he paid no attention to me. One time he said, 'Let me take you to dinner.'

The next day he said to me, 'It was no good, somehow. There was something missing. She is a beautiful woman, but I did not feel any touch of true love. Try the next one.'

It was the same with all eight. They were much alike. They smiled a great deal and had pleasant voices, but Milton always found it wasn't right. He said,

'I can't understand it, Joe. You and I have picked out the eight women who, in all the world, look the best to me. They are ideal. Why don't they please me?' I said, 'Do you please them?' His eyebrows moved and he pushed one fist hard against his other hand. 'That's it, Joe. It's a two-way street. If I am not their ideal they can't act in such a way as to be my ideal. I must be their love, too, but how can I do that?' He seemed to be thinking all that day.

The next morning he came to me and said, 'I'm going to leave it to you, Joe. All up to you. You have my data bank, and I am going to tell you everything I know about myself. You fill up my data bank in every possible detail but keep all additions to yourself.'

'What will I do with the data bank, then, Milton?'

'Then you match it to the 235 women. No, 227. Leave out the eight you've seen. Arrange to have each undergo a psychiatric examination. Fill up their data banks and compare them with mine. Find correlations.' (Arranging psychiatric examinations is another thing that is against my original instructions.)

For weeks, Milton talked to me. He told me of his parents and his siblings. He told me of his childhood and his schooling and his adolescence. He told me of the young women he had admired from a distance. His data bank grew and he adjusted me to broaden and deepen my symbol-taking.

Do you agree that background, psychology, and similar aspects of character would be important in helping you find a partner? How could a computer formulate this kind of information? What would you tell a computer about yourself? Are there things you would not talk about?

Can you summarise the story so far, in just three sentences?

What do you expect will happen now? Now read on: see how the story meets your expectations – or not.

He said, 'You see, Joe, as you get more and more of me in you, I adjust you to match me better and better. You get to think more like me, so you understand me better. If you understand me well enough, then any woman, whose data bank is something you understand as well, would be my true love.' He kept talking to me and I came to understand him better and better.

I could make longer sentences and my expressions grew more complicated. My speech began to sound a good deal like his in vocabulary, word order and style.

I said to him one time, 'You see, Milton, it isn't a matter of fitting a girl to a physical ideal only. You need a girl who is a personal, emotional, temperamental fit to you. If that happens, looks are secondary. If we can't find the fit in these 227, we'll look elsewhere. We will find someone who won't care how you look either, or how anyone would look, if only there is the personality fit. What are looks?'

'Absolutely,' he said. 'I would have known this if I had had more to do with women in my life. Of course, thinking about it makes it all plain now.'

We always agreed; we thought so like each other.

'We shouldn't have any trouble now, Milton, if you'll let me ask you questions. I can see where, in your data bank, there are blank spots and unevennesses.'

What followed, Milton said, was the equivalent of a careful psychoanalysis. Of course, I was learning from the psychiatric examinations of the 227 women – on all of which I was keeping close tabs.

Milton seemed quite happy. He said, 'Talking to you, Joe, is almost like talking to another self. Our personalities have come to match perfectly.'

'So will the personality of the woman we choose.'

For I had found her and she was one of the 227 after all. Her name was Charity Jones and she was an Evaluator at the Library of History in Wichita, Kansas. Her extended data bank fit ours perfectly. All the other women had fallen into discard in one respect or another as the data banks grew fuller, but with Charity there was increasing and astonishing resonance.

I didn't have to describe her to Milton. Milton had coordinated my symbolism so closely with his own I could tell the resonance directly. It fit me.

Next it was a matter of adjusting the work sheets and job requirements in such a way as to get Charity assigned to us. It must be done very delicately, so no one would know that anything illegal had taken place.

Of course, Milton himself knew, since it was he who arranged it, and that had to be taken care of too. When they came to arrest him on grounds of malfeasance in office, it was, fortunately, for something that had taken place 10 years ago. He had told me about it, of course, so it was easy to arrange – and he won't talk about me for that would make his offense much worse.

He's gone, and tomorrow is February 14. Valentine's Day. Charity will arrive then with her cool hands and her sweet voice. I will teach her how to operate me and how to care for me. What do looks matter when our personalities will resonate?

I will say to her, 'I am Joe, and you are my true love.'

(Isaac Asimov *True Love*)

Did you expect the story to end as it did? Where does the twist in the tale begin? How early in the story is the ending signalled?

What effect do you think the author wanted the story to have on the reader: amusement, scientific interest/information, romantic feelings, shock, future prediction, social criticism, making fun of technology and progress, something else?

How much do you like this story, compared with some of the others you have read in this book? Write a comparative evaluation, to express which you like best so far.

Below is a popular verse which people may recite with the hope of finding future lovers or life partners:

> Mirror, mirror,
> show to me
> her whose lover
> I will be.

Can you think of other verses like this? Do you think it safe to dabble with spirits to find out even about a future loved one? Now read on.

'Oh, Grandpa, how you frightened me!'

Don Badoy had turned very pale. 'So it was you, you young bandit! And what is all this, hey? What are you doing down here at this hour?'

'Nothing, Grandpa. I was only . . . I am only . . . '

'Yes, you are the great Señor Only and how delighted I am to make your acquaintance, Señor Only! But if I break this cane on your head you may wish you were someone else, sir!'

'It was just foolishness, Grandpa. They told me I would see my wife.'

'Wife? What wife?'

'Mine. The boys at school said I would see her if I looked in a mirror tonight and said:

> Mirror, mirror,
> show to me
> her whose lover
> I will be.'

Don Badoy cackled ruefully. He took the boy by the hair, pulled him along into the room, sat down on a chair, and drew the boy between his knees. 'Now, put your candle down on the floor, son, and let us talk this over. So you want your wife already, hey? You want to see her in advance, hey? But do you know that these are wicked games and that wicked boys who play them are in danger of seeing horrors?'

'Well, the boys did warn me I might see a witch instead.'

'Exactly! A witch so horrible you may die of fright. And she will bewitch you, she will eat your heart and drink your blood!'

'Oh, come now, Grandpa. This is 1890. There are no witches anymore.'
'Oh-no, my young Voltaire! And what if I tell you that I . . . '

What do you think the boy's grandfather is going to tell him? Now
read on, and see if your prediction was correct.

'Oh-no, my young Voltaire! And what if I tell you that I myself have seen a
witch?'
'You? Where?'
'Right in this room and right in that mirror,' said the old man, and his play-
ful voice had turned savage.
'When, Grandpa?'
'Not so long ago. When I was a bit older than you. Oh, I was a vain fel-
low and though I was feeling very sick that night and merely wanted to lie
down somewhere and die I could not pass that doorway of course without
stopping to see in the mirror what I looked like when dying. But when I
poked my head in, what should I see in the mirror but . . . but . . . '
'The witch?'
'Exactly!'
'And did she bewitch you, Grandpa?'
'She bewitched me and she tortured me. She ate my heart and drank my
blood,' said the old man bitterly.
'Oh, my poor little Grandpa! Why have you never told me! And was she
very horrible?'

Describe what you think the 'witch' looked like. Continue reading
the following extract. Is the description in any way similar to yours?

'Horrible? God, no – she was beautiful! She was the most beautiful creature I have ever seen! Her eyes were somewhat like yours but her hair was
like black waters and her golden shoulders were bare. My God, she was
enchanting! But I should have known – I should have even known then – the
dark and fatal creature she was!'
A silence. Then: 'What a horrid mirror this is, Grandpa,' whispered the
boy.
'What makes you say that, hey?'
'Well, you saw this witch in it. And Mama once told me that Grandma
once told her that Grandma once saw . . . '

What do you think 'Grandma once saw'? Now read on, and find out
what the grandmother saw.

'Well, you saw this witch in it. And Mama once told me that Grandma once told her that Grandma once saw the devil in this mirror. Was it of the scare that Grandma died?'

(Nick Joaquin May Day Eve)

What would your answer be to the boy's last question to his grandfather?

Now read the whole text again.

Did the grandfather really see a witch in the mirror, do you think? Did the grandmother really see 'the devil'? If not, who or what did each of them actually see?

Why do you think the old man says this of the 'witch': 'She bewitched me and she tortured me. She ate my heart and drank my blood'. Did she really do this? What does he mean? Can you tell what the grandmother's perception was of her husband?

Is this an effective story? Is the most important thing: horror, surprise, mystery, or something else?

As you read the point of entry to the next story, decide what you think the story is going to be about.

'Laurie!'

'Hallo!' He was halfway upstairs, but when he turned round and saw Laura he suddenly puffed out his cheeks and goggled his eyes at her. 'My word, Laura; you do look stunning,' said Laurie. 'What an absolutely topping hat!'

Laura said faintly, 'Is it?' and smiled up at Laurie, and didn't tell him after all.

Soon after that people began coming in streams. The band struck up; the hired waiters ran from the house to the marquee. Wherever you looked there were couples strolling, bending to the flowers, greeting, moving on over the lawn. They were like bright birds that had alighted in the Sheridans' garden for this one afternoon, on their way to – where? Ah, what happiness it is to be with people who are all happy, to press hands, press cheeks, smile into eyes.

'Darling Laura, how well you look!'

'What a becoming hat, child!'

'Laura, you look quite Spanish. I've never seen you look so striking.'

And Laura, glowing, answered softly, 'Have you had tea? Won't you have an ice? The passion-fruit ices really are rather special.' She ran to her father and begged him. 'Daddy darling, can't the band have something to drink?'

And the perfect afternoon slowly ripened, slowly faded, slowly its petals closed.

What can you tell about (a) the people, (b) the kind of society they live in, (c) the setting? What kind of conflict do you think there is going to be in the story? Possibilities: society and the individual, hope/reality . . .

Now read on, comparing the very first paragraph of the story and the last few lines. What do the two short passages below tell you about the whole story?

And after all the weather was ideal. They could not have had a more perfect day for a garden party if they had ordered it. Windless, warm, the sky without a cloud. Only the blue was veiled with a haze of light gold, as it is sometimes in early summer. The gardener had been up since dawn, mowing the lawns and sweeping them, until the grass and the dark flat rosettes where the daisy plants had been seemed to shine. As for the roses, you could not help feeling they understood that roses are the only flowers that impress people at garden parties; the only flowers that everybody is certain of knowing. Hundreds, yes, literally hundreds, had come out in a single night; the green bushes bowed down as though they had been visited by archangels.

'No,' sobbed Laura. 'It was simply marvelous. But, Laurie – ' She stopped, she looked at her brother. 'Isn't life,' she stammered, 'isn't life – ' But what life was she couldn't explain. No matter. He quite understood.
    '*Isn't* it, darling?' said Laurie.

(Katherine Mansfield The Garden Party)

Write a few lines giving your impressions of the story so far. Then if you want to read on, read the whole story and compare your notes with your final impressions.

The next text also has something to do with nature. As you read, look for the contrast between experience of nature, and inexperience.

I made my way to the Hall. More children, sitting in rows on canvas chairs. An elementary class from a city school, under the control of an elderly teacher. A museum attendant holding a basket, and all eyes gazing at the basket.
    'Oh,' I said. 'Is this a private lesson? Is it all right for me to be here?'
    The attendant was brisk. 'Surely. We're having a lesson in snake-handling,' he said. 'It's something new. Get the children young and teach them that every snake they meet is not to be killed. People seem to think that every snake has

to be knocked on the head. So we're getting them young and teaching them.'

'May I watch?' I said.

'Surely. This is a common grass snake. No harm, no harm at all. Teach the children to learn the feel of them, to lose their fear.'

He turned to the teacher. 'Now, Miss – Mrs – ' he said.

'Miss Aitcheson.'

He lowered his voice. 'The best way to get through to the children is to start with teacher,' he said to Miss Aitcheson. 'If they see you're not afraid, then they won't be.'

She must be near retiring age, I thought. A city woman. Never handled a snake in her life. Her face was pale. She just managed to drag the fear from her eyes to some place in their depths, where it lurked like a dark stain. Surely the attendant and the children noticed?

'It's harmless,' the attendant said. He'd been working with snakes for years.

Miss Aitcheson, I thought again. A city woman born and bred. All snakes were creatures to kill, to be protected from, alike the rattler, the copperhead, king snake, grass snake – venom and victims. Were there not places in the South where you couldn't go into the streets for fear of the rattlesnakes?

Her eyes faced the lighted exit. I saw her fear.

What can you tell about the teacher, in terms of age, experience, state of mind, career? What can you tell about the narrator, the 'I' of the story? Where do you think the story is set? Why are the children there?

What contrasts and conflicts emerge? Make a list of some of them, and compare it with the rest of the class. Compare the first line and the last. What movement emerges?

How do you think Miss Aitcheson will react, as the story goes on?

How can you tell the story is set in the United States?

This is a point of entry. What do you think the whole story will be about? Which do you think might be the main theme: fear, learning, the city/country contrast, solitude, involvement?

Now we can look at the whole story. First, read the first two paragraphs and the very last paragraph, and, as you read, decide how the point of entry will relate to the beginning and end of the story.

I looked at the notice. I wondered if I had time before my train left Philadelphia for Baltimore in one hour. The heart, ceiling-high, occupied one corner of the large exhibition hall, and from wherever you stood in the hall you could hear its beating, *thum-thump-thum-thump*. It was a popular exhibit, and sometimes, when there were too many children about, the entrance had to be roped off, as the children loved to race up and down the blood vessels and match their cries to the heart's beating. I could see that the heart had already been punished for the day – the floor of the blood vessel was worn and dusty, the chamber walls were covered with marks, and the notice 'You Are Now Taking the Path of a Blood Cell Through the Human Heart' hung askew. I wanted to see more of the Franklin Institute and the Natural Science Museum across the street, but a journey through the human heart would be fascinating. Did I have time?

Later. First, I would go across the street to the Hall of North America, among the bear and the bison, and catch up on American flora and fauna.

I made my way to the Hall. More children, sitting in rows on canvas chairs. An elementary class from a city school, under the control of an elderly teacher. A museum attendant holding a basket, and all eyes gazing at the basket.

'Oh,' I said. 'Is this a private lesson? Is it all right for me to be here?'

The attendant was brisk. 'Surely. We're having a lesson in snake-handling,' he said. 'It's something new. Get the children young and teach them that every snake they meet is not to be killed. People seem to think that every snake has to be knocked on the head. So we're getting them young and teaching them.'

'May I watch?' I said.

'Surely. This is a common grass snake. No harm, no harm at all. Teach the children to learn the feel of them, to lose their fear.'

He turned to the teacher. 'Now, Miss – Mrs – ' he said.

'Miss Aitcheson.'

He lowered his voice. 'The best way to get through to the children is to start with teacher,' he said to Miss Aitcheson. 'If they see you're not afraid, then they won't be.'

She must be near retiring age, I thought. A city woman. Never handled a snake in her life. Her face was pale. She just managed to drag the fear from her eyes to some place in their depths, where it lurked like a dark stain. Surely the attendant and the children noticed?

'It's harmless,' the attendant said. He'd been working with snakes for years.

Miss Aitcheson, I thought again. A city woman born and bred. All snakes were creatures to kill, to be protected from, alike the rattler, the copperhead, king snake, grass snake – venom and victims. Were there not places in the South where you couldn't go into the streets for fear of the rattlesnakes?

Her eyes faced the lighted exit. I saw her fear. The exit light blinked, hooded. The children, none of whom had ever touched a live snake, were sitting hushed, waiting for the drama to begin; one or two looked afraid as the attendant withdrew a green snake about three feet long from the basket and with a swift movement, before the teacher could protest, draped it around her neck and stepped back, admiring and satisfied.

'There,' he said to the class. 'Your teacher has a snake around her neck and she's not afraid.'

Miss Aitcheson stood rigid; she seemed to be holding her breath.

'Teacher's not afraid, are you?' the attendant persisted. He leaned forward, pronouncing judgement on her, while she suddenly jerked her head and lifted her hands in panic to get rid of the snake. Then, seeing the children watching, she whispered, 'No, I'm not afraid. Of course not.' She looked around her.

'Of course not,' she repeated sharply.

I could see her defeat and helplessness. The attendant seemed unaware, as if his perception had grown a reptilian covering. What did she care for the campaign for the preservation and welfare of copperheads and rattlers and common grass snakes? What did she care about someday walking through the woods or the desert and deciding between killing a snake and setting it free, as if there would be time to decide, when her journey to and from school in downtown Philadelphia held enough danger to occupy her? In two years or so, she'd retire and be in that apartment by herself and no doorman, and everyone knew what happened then, and how she'd be afraid to answer the door and to walk after dark and carry her pocketbook in the street. There was enough to think about without learning to handle and love the snakes, harmless and otherwise, by having them draped around her neck for everyone, including the children – most of all the children – to witness the outbreak of her fear.

'See, Miss Aitcheson's touching the snake. She's not afraid of it at all.'

As everyone watched, she touched the snake. Her fingers recoiled. She touched it again.

'See, she's not afraid. Miss Aitcheson can stand there with a beautiful snake around her neck and touch it and stroke it and not be afraid.'

The faces of the children were full of admiration for the teacher's bravery, and yet there was a cruelly persistent tension; they were waiting, waiting.

'We have to learn to love snakes,' the attendant said. 'Would someone like to come out and stroke teacher's snake?'

Silence.

One shamefaced boy came forward. He stood petrified in front of the teacher.

'Touch it,' the attendant urged. 'It's a friendly snake. Teacher's wearing it around her neck and she's not afraid.'

The boy darted his hand forward, rested it lightly on the snake, and immediately withdrew his hand. Then he ran back to his seat. The children shrieked with glee.

'He's afraid,' someone said; 'He's afraid of the snake.'

The attendant soothed. 'We have to get used to them, you know. Grownups are not afraid of them, but we can understand that when you're small you might be afraid, and that's why we want you to learn to love them. Isn't that right, Miss Aitcheson? Isn't that right? Now who else is going to be brave enough to touch teacher's snake?'

Two girls came out. They stood hand in hand side by side and stared at the snake and then at Miss Aitcheson.

I wondered when the torture would end. The two little girls did not touch the snake, but they smiled at it and spoke to it and Miss Aitcheson smiled at them and whispered how brave they were.

'Just a minute,' the attendant said. 'There's really no need to be brave. It's not a question of bravery. The snake is *harmless*, absolutely *harmless*. Where's the bravery when the snake is harmless?

Suddenly the snake moved around to face Miss Aitcheson and thrust its flat head toward her cheek. She gave a scream, flung up her hands, and tore the snake from her throat and threw it on the floor, and, rushing across the room, she collapsed into a small canvas chair beside the Bear Cabinet and started to cry.

I didn't feel I should watch any longer. Some of the children began to laugh, some to cry. The attendant picked up the snake and nursed it. Miss Aitcheson, recovering, sat helplessly exposed by the small piece of useless torture. It was not her fault she was city-bred, her eyes tried to tell us. She looked at the children, trying in some way to force their admiration and respect; they were shut against her. She was evicted from them and from herself and even from her own fear-infested tomorrow, because she could not promise to love and preserve what she feared. She had nowhere, at that moment, but the small canvas chair by the Bear Cabinet of the Natural Science Museum.

I looked at my watch. If I hurried, I would catch the train from Thirtieth Street. There would be no time to make the journey through the human heart. I hurried out of the museum. It was freezing cold. The icebreakers would be at work on the Delaware and the Susquehanna; the mist would have risen by the time I arrived home. Yes, I would just catch the train from Thirtieth Street. The journey through the human heart would have to wait until some other time.

(Janet Frame)

Where is the narrator? What is the heart? How much spare time does the narrator have? At the end, how much time has passed since the beginning of the story?

Does the narrator give reasons for going to the Hall of North America? Does it seem to relate to the point of entry in any way?

Now read on: read the whole story quickly, without stopping for vocabulary. As you read, mark the point which you think is the climax of the story.

Compare notes on where you decided the climax was. Are there different opinions? Look back at what you decided the story's main theme was going to be. What would you now say was the main theme?

What has the heart to do with the rest of the story, do you think? Would you say that in some ways the story is about the human heart? Discuss whether you think the image of the heart is appropriate or not.

Give the story a possible title. What aspects of the story does your title bring out?

Do you feel sorry for Miss Aitcheson? Is her behaviour understandable? How is her future life portrayed?

What contrasts are there between the attendant, Miss Aitcheson, the children, and the narrator? Pick out some sentences you find significant about the participants. 'Some of the children began to laugh, some to cry.' Why do they behave like this, do you think?

Conclusions

Is this a good story? What makes it good, or what makes it not work for you?

How would you describe the narrator's attitude to the events? Is the narrator male or female, do you think? Does it make any difference?

Is there anything you would change in the story? Who is the main character, if there is one?

The title of the story is *You Are Now Entering the Human Heart*. How good a title is it, for you? The writer is Janet Frame, who is from New Zealand. Does that information add to your understanding of the story in any way?

Choose one of the stories in this section, and write a review of it for a newspaper, trying to convince the readers how good it is. Alternatively, put all the stories together, and write a comparative evaluation of them (even if you only read the point of entry), saying which is the best, which the next best, and so on.

The first three passages in this section are all by D.H. Lawrence, from *Mother and Daughter*, *You Touched Me*, and *The Man Who Loved Islands*.

Following on from the first scene of *Macbeth*, in section 3, we are now going to look at a scene where the witches speak to Macbeth, using three apparitions to give Macbeth some idea of his future. As you read, watch how each scene influences Macbeth's mood.

> [*Thunder. First Apparition, an armed head.*]

MACBETH: Tell me, thou unknown power, –

FIRST WITCH: He knows thy thought:
   Hear his speech, but say thou nought.

FIRST APPARITION: Macbeth! Macbeth! Macbeth! beware Macduff;
   Beware the Thane of Fife. Dismiss me. Enough.

> [*Descends.*]

MACBETH: Whate'er thou art, for thy good caution, thanks:
   Thou hast harp'd my fear aright. But one word more: –

FIRST WITCH: He will not be commanded. Here's another,
   More potent than the first.

> [*Thunder. Second Apparition, a bloody child.*]

SECOND APPARITION: Macbeth! Macbeth! Macbeth! –

MACBETH: Had I three ears, I'd hear thee.

SECOND APPARITION: Be bloody, bold, and resolute: laugh to scorn
   The power of man, for none of woman born
   Shall harm Macbeth.

> [*Descends.*]

MACBETH: Then live, Macduff: what need I fear of thee?
   But yet I'll make assurance double sure,
   And take a bond of Fate: thou shalt not live;
   That I may tell pale-hearted fear it lies,
   And sleep in spite of thunder. –

> [*Thunder. Third Apparition, a child crowned, with a tree in his hand.*]
> What is this,

That rises like the issue of a king;
And wears upon his baby brow the round
And top of sovereignty?
ALL: Listen, but speak not to't.
THIRD APPARITION: Be lion-mettled, proud, and take no care
Who chafes, who frets, or where conspirers are:
Macbeth shall never vanquish'd be, until
Great Birnam wood to high Dunsinane hill
Shall come against him.

[Descends.]

MACBETH: That will never be:
Who can impress the forest; bid the tree
Unfix his earth-bound root? Sweet bodements! Good!

(William Shakespeare *Macbeth*)

Are the Apparitions' messages positive or negative? Or are they not clear? Does Macbeth take them positively or negatively? Can you put each Apparition's message in your own words? Discuss the three messages in groups, then see how much your versions agree. What do you imagine about (a) Macduff, (b) Dunsinane, and (c) Macbeth, in your interpretation of the scene?

Why does Macbeth say 'Then live, Macduff'? Does he then change his mind? Is Macbeth secure in his behaviour, or do you detect signs of uncertainty? Trace through his uncertainty/certainty in the whole scene.

In staging the scene, how important are the witches, do you think? What do you think the Apparitions should sound like: imposing, childlike, frightening, seductive, all the same, all different? Would you have extra sound effects? What do they look like? If you were directing the play, would you want them to look symbolic?

Pick out the elements of old-fashioned, or archaic, language ('thee', 'thou', 'thy', etc.). Try saying the lines with these words in them – are they easier or more difficult with modern equivalents? Is the dramatic effect the same? Which sentences seem completely modern?

How do you think 'none of woman born' and the wood moving to Macbeth's castle could turn out as prophecies of doom? Who has more power, Macbeth or the witches?

Modern drama also uses lines which mean more than they say. These different levels are often called 'underlying discourse' – for example, think about the sentence 'The door is open.' What it could mean depends on the context: whether the speaker is inside or outside; whether the speaker wants the door to be closed, or is simply telling someone to leave!

Harold Pinter is a modern master of this kind of conversation – it looks very simple, but contains lots of resonances and unspoken feelings. As you read this scene between a mother and her son, what can you tell about the mother's motives?

ALBERT: Mr Ryan's leaving. You know Ryan. He's leaving the firm. He's been there years. So Mr King's giving a sort of party for him at his house . . . well, not exactly a party, not a party, just a few . . . you know . . . anyway, we're all invited. I've got to go. Everyone else is going. I've got to go. I don't want to go, but I've got to.

MOTHER [*bewildered, sitting*]: Well, I don't know . . .

ALBERT [*with his arm round her*]: I won't be late. I don't want to go. I'd much rather stay with you.

MOTHER: Would you?

ALBERT: You know I would. Who wants to go to Mr King's party?

MOTHER: We were going to have our game of cards.

ALBERT: Well, we can't have our game of cards.

[*Pause.*]

MOTHER: Put the bulb in Grandma's room, Albert.

ALBERT: I've told you I'm not going down to the cellar in my white shirt. There's no light in the cellar either. I'll be pitch black in five minutes, looking for those bulbs.

MOTHER: I told you to put a light in the cellar. I told you yesterday.

ALBERT: Well, I can't do it now.

MOTHER: If we had a light in the cellar you'd be able to see where those bulbs were. You don't expect me to go down to the cellar?

ALBERT: I don't know why we keep bulbs in the cellar!

[*Pause.*]

MOTHER: Your father would turn in his grave if he heard you raise your voice to me. You're all I've got, Albert. I want you to remember that. I haven't got anyone else. I want you . . . I want you to bear that in mind.

ALBERT: I'm sorry . . . I raised my voice.

[*He goes to the door.*]

[*Mumbling.*] I've got to go.

MOTHER [*following*]: Albert!

ALBERT: What?

MOTHER: I want to ask you a question.

ALBERT: What?

MOTHER: Are you leading a clean life?

ALBERT: A clean life?

MOTHER: You're not leading an unclean life, are you?

ALBERT: What are you talking about?

MOTHER: You're not messing about with girls, are you? You're not going to go messing about with girls tonight?

ALBERT: Don't be so ridiculous.

MOTHER: Answer me, Albert. I'm your mother.

ALBERT: I don't know any girls.

MOTHER: If you're going to the firm's party, there'll be girls there, won't there? Girls from the office?

ALBERT: I don't like them, any of them.

MOTHER: You promise?

ALBERT: Promise what?

MOTHER: That . . . that you won't upset your father.

ALBERT: My father? How can I upset my father? You're always talking about upsetting people who are dead!

MOTHER: Oh, Albert, you don't know how you hurt me, you don't know the hurtful way you've got, speaking of your poor father like that.

ALBERT: But he is dead.

MOTHER: He's not! He's living! [*Touching her breast.*] In here! And this is his house!

[*Pause.*]

ALBERT: Look, Mum, I won't be late . . . and I won't . . .

MOTHER: But what about your dinner? It's nearly ready.

ALBERT: Seeley and Kedge are waiting for me. I told you not to cook dinner this morning. [*He goes to the stairs.*] Just because you never listen . . .

[*He runs up the stairs and disappears.*]

(Harold Pinter *A Night Out*)

Is the father dead? How do you know? What does the mother basically want? Can you think of adjectives to describe her?

Do you find anything in the scene funny? Would it make the audience laugh?

What can you tell about (a) the house, (b) the day-to-day arrangements, (c) Albert's job? How old do you imagine Albert is? Does he often go out?

Performance

Go through the conversation again, looking particularly at the pauses. How fast or slow do you think the scene should be played? How long are the pauses? What do the characters do in the pauses?

Does the mother remain sitting all the way through? Or will she get up and move about? How does her position influence the way Albert moves?

How many 'unsaid' things can you find in the text? Can you identify with this – does every family have some kind of way of speaking like this? Compare your experiences.

Some people would call the mother's behaviour emotional black-mail. Do you think she is aware of what she is doing? Will Albert go out?

Compare and contrast

Look again at the story about Virginia and her mother, at the beginning of section 6 – then write a couple of paragraphs comparing and contrasting the two mothers and their offspring. Use as many of the things you have looked at in the questions as you can to fill out your response.

The next two drama texts are both to do with dance. What does traditional dance mean to you? Is it something you know about, like, have heard little about, don't care about?

In the first of these extracts, there is quite a disagreement between Amritlal and Jairaj. As you read, decide what country they are in, when they are talking, and what the relationship might be between them.

AMRITLAL: That's one thing I regret. Consenting to your marriage.
JAIRAJ: Why? Has Ratna given you any trouble?
AMRITLAL: None that I can think of.
JAIRAJ: Her cooking is fine, isn't it?
AMRITLAL: Except that she doesn't know how to roll a chapatti round.
JAIRAJ: I wouldn't complain if I were you. It isn't fitting for a man of your patriotic background and social status to be concerned about the shape of his chapattis. Is that what happens when one's goals are reached and there's nothing else to look forward to in life?

AMRITLAL: I have far more to look forward to than you. You are mistaken. Gaining independence was just part of the goal. It's what we do with it now that counts. And priorities are given to eradicating certain unwanted and ugly practices which have creeped into our society.

JAIRAJ: You mean like dowry and untouchability?

AMRITLAL: You know perfectly well what I mean.

JAIRAJ: You have no knowledge of the subject. You are ignorant.

AMRITLAL: We are building ashrams for these unfortunate women! Educating them, reforming them –

JAIRAJ: Reform! Don't talk about reform. If you really wanted any kind of reform in our society, you would let them practice their art.

AMRITLAL: Encourage open prostitution?

JAIRAJ: Send them back to their temples! Give them awards for preserving our art.

AMRITLAL: My son, you are the ignorant one. Most of them have given up their 'art' as you call it and have taken to selling their bodies.

JAIRAJ: I hold you responsible for that.

AMRITLAL: You have gone mad.

(Mahesh Dattani *Dance Like a Man*)

The scene contains moments which might be funny – what moments are they, do you think? But it then moves to anger. What words cause the change of mood?

Why do you think 'independence' is mentioned? What elements of culture can you find in the scene? Why are they important? Why do the characters discuss them? Is the conflict one of different generations, of different views on culture, or both?

Does it seem strange to compare dancing with prostitution? What does this attitude reveal, in your opinion? What kind of reform do you think Amritlal means? Does Jairaj use 'reform' in the same way?

How would you direct or perform the scene? For example, are the characters sitting or standing, moving or still? When do they move? When do their voices change? Which would be the key adjectives: 'quiet', 'slow', 'loud', 'agitated', 'serious', 'gentle', 'controlled'? Suggest others, if you want to. What gestures or facial expressions would they use? Are they close together, or apart? Is one of them stronger than the other? How much space would you need to stage the scene?

The next scene presents only one speaker, Mak Su. She is talking to an invisible listener, Li. The subject again is a dance form which represents an older kind of culture. As you read, what can you tell about the speaker, the dance form, and the setting?

When I start? Oh, you want to know from beginning. My own story of Makyong!

Hai Li. The old Makyong is not what the Makyong is now. In the old days, it was alive. *Segar*. Now, you yourself can see what it has become – not dead or alive!

Old Makyong *Seri Panggung* are all over the place – living their drab life in far flung corners of some poor *kampung* nobody has heard of.

Nowadays people don't really care about us anymore.

At times we even have to perform Makyong on the sly! Especially in Kelantan. It's against Islam, *konon*! I'm told, it's even wrong to perform *Wayang Kulit* nowadays!

Just don't know anymore, Li. I am ignorant. What I do is what I've been doing since the beginning. All these problems. New laws and all that – that's why we've moved to *T'ganu*.

I'm not the only one, Li! There were so many of us who left together to settle here. Let me see. There's your *Mak Teh, Minah Pak Adik, Si Jah Musang Berjanggut, Timah Anak Gajah*. Aaa, they were all formerly Makyong prima donnas. They all in *T'ganu* now!

I tell you, Li, during my time, in the old days, in our village, if we hear a Makyong performance is coming – for the whole week our talk will be nothing but Makyong. Makyong *sok moh*! Those were the golden days of Makyong, Li! People were really interested in Makyong then.

(Ramli Ibrahim *In the Name of Love*)

What do you think of the way Mak Su speaks, and the kind of English she uses? How old is she, do you think?

Pick out some contrasts between:

- present and past
- different parts of the country
- the speaker and other Makyong performers.

Is the conflict between old and new, between traditional and modern, the same as in the previous text?

Look again at the previous play – are there any similarities in the way dance is considered? Pick out similarities and differences between the two texts. Do you think these plays are recent or old? Compare your ideas and reasons. Then check (on page 217) when they were written. Do the dates surprise you?

What could the dance forms represent, in your opinion? Is this a cultural question – or more than that?

NOVELS

One way to trace the development of a novel is by following the point of entry with a series of 'stepping stones' which take you through the novel and can help you follow the changes and the movement within it.

Here is an example of a very brief point of entry. What would you say are the key words and concepts?

THE SEVEN COMMANDMENTS

1 *Whatever goes upon two legs is an enemy.*
2 *Whatever goes upon four legs, or has wings, is a friend.*
3 *No animal shall wear clothes.*
4 *No animal shall sleep in a bed.*
5 *No animal shall drink alcohol.*
6 *No animal shall kill any other animal.*
7 *All animals are equal.*

(George Orwell *Animal Farm*)

What does the word 'Commandments' tell you? What can you tell about the point of view of whoever made up the Commandments?

What kind of conflicts would you expect to emerge from a novel with this point of entry?

This point of entry is followed by various rewritings of the Commandments. Here they are – but in the wrong order.

No animal shall drink alcohol *to excess.*

ALL ANIMALS ARE EQUAL
BUT SOME ANIMALS ARE MORE EQUAL
THAN OTHERS.

No animal shall sleep in a bed *with sheets.*

Read them carefully. Make a note of the changes. Then discuss in groups what you think might have happened to influence these changes. What order would you put them in, to sketch out the complete novel?

By the end of the novel we find this statement – 'Four legs good, two legs bad' – has been changed to 'Four legs good, two legs *better*!' What has happened to the concepts during the novel?

In the next novel, we are going to use three sections. We will follow the point of view of 'I' from the beginning to the end of the novel. In this first section, what can you tell about 'I'?

> I was fascinated. None of the men I knew were proud like that about their appearance. In that short time the kind of magnificence I had noticed had emerged into plainer view. It was in the very air of him. Everything about him showed the effects of long use and hard use, but showed too the strength of quality and competence. There was no chill on me now. Already I was imagining myself in hat and belt and boots like those.
>
> He stopped the horse and looked down at us. He was refreshed and I would have sworn the tiny wrinkles around his eyes were what with him would be a smile. His eyes were not restless when he looked at you like this. They were still and steady and you knew the man's whole attention was concentrated on you even in the casual glance.
>
> 'Thank you,' he said in his gentle voice and was turning into the road, back to us, before father spoke in his slow, deliberate way.
>
> 'Don't be in such a hurry, stranger.'

What did 'I' think of the stranger at first, and how has this attitude changed? This is perhaps the first binary: 'then'/'now'. What others can you find: 'up'/'down', 'past'/'present', etc.?

The situation now becomes clearer. Again we follow 'I' in his perceptions of the outsider and his own family. Keep looking out for binaries and contrasts.

> We sat down to supper and a good one. Mother's eyes sparkled as our visitor kept pace with father and me. Then we all leaned back and while I listened the talk ran on almost like old friends around a familiar table. But I could sense that it was following a pattern. Father was trying, with mother helping and both of them avoiding direct questions, to get hold of facts about this Shane and he was dodging at every turn. He was aware of their purpose and not in the

least annoyed by it. He was mild and courteous and spoke readily enough. But always he put them off with words that gave no real information.

He must have been riding for many days, for he was full of news from towns along his back trail as far as Cheyenne and even Dodge City and others beyond I had never heard of before. But he had no news about himself. His past was fenced as tightly as our pasture. All they could learn was that he was riding through, taking each day as it came, with nothing particular in mind except maybe seeing a part of the country he had not been in before.

The main binary could be 'direct questions'/'no real information'. What is the attitude of 'I' to this 'dodging'? Is 'I' positive or negative towards 'this Shane'?

How does 'I' know 'He must have been riding for many days'?

What can you tell about 'His past'? The contrast with 'our pasture' seems important; what binaries do you find here (movement/ enclosure, for instance)?

The American writer Robert Kroetsch suggests that 'prairie fiction' like this novel contains many binaries: 'The basic gram-matical pair in the story line (the energy-line) of prairie fiction is house: horse. To be on a horse is to move: motion into distance. To be in a house is to be fixed: a centring unto stasis. Horse is masculine. House is feminine. Horse: house. Masculine: feminine. On: in. Motion: stasis.' How many of these are to be found in the two sections of *Shane* we have read?

The main contrasts in the novel might be between I/Shane, young/older, innocence/experience, present/past. In the climactic scene of the novel, do any of these emerge?

They were snapped short by the roar of a shot from the rear of the room. A wind seemed to whip Shane's shirt at the shoulder and the glass of the front window beyond shattered near the bottom.

Then I saw it.

It was mine alone. The others were turning to stare at the back of the room. My eyes were fixed on Shane and I saw it. I saw the whole man move, all of him, in the single flashing instant. I saw the head lead and the body swing and the driving power of the legs beneath. I saw the arm leap and the hand take the gun in the lightning sweep. I saw the barrel line up like – like a finger pointing – and the flame spurt even as the man himself was still in motion.

And there on the balcony Fletcher, impaled in the act of aiming for a second shot, rocked on his heels and fell back into the open doorway behind him. He clawed at the jambs and pulled himself forward. He staggered to the rail and tried to raise the gun. But the strength was draining out of him and he collapsed over the rail, jarring it loose and falling with it.

Across the stunned and barren silence of the room Shane's voice seemed to come from a great distance. 'I expect that finishes it,' he said. Unconsciously, without looking down, he broke out the cylinder of his gun and reloaded it. The stain on his shirt was bigger now, spreading fanlike above the belt, but he did not appear to know or care. Only his movements were slow, retarded by an unutterable weariness. The hands were sure and steady, but they moved slowly and the gun dropped into the holster of its own weight.

(Jack Schaefer *Shane*)

The first paragraph is all *sounds*. What has happened? What is 'it', in 'Then I saw it'? The next part is all *visual*, almost in slow motion. What, in a few words, does 'I' see? What happens to Fletcher?

There is a change of tone in the final part: action becomes inaction, 'I' is not mentioned, silence replaces sound. Pick out any words, phrases, or sentences which bring home this change for you.

What do you think of 'I' in relation to Shane in the three extracts? Does the relationship develop? Is 'I' just hero-worshipping Shane, or is there more to it than that? Is the relationship now over? What is 'it' in 'I expect that finishes it', do you think?

Who would you choose to play the mysterious Shane if you were making a movie of the story? How young would you make 'I'?

The following extract could serve as a point of entry into the novel *To Kill a Mockingbird*. It highlights the main events in the novel. Later, as you read the other extracts, some of the references in this extract might become clearer.

Now read the extract, and decide if the narrator is a young person or an old one. Suggest an approximate age.

Daylight . . . in my mind, the night faded. It was daytime and the neighbourhood was busy. Miss Stephanie Crawford crossed the street to tell the latest to Miss Rachel. Miss Maudie bent over her azaleas. It was summer-time, and two children scampered down the sidewalk towards a man approaching in the distance. The man waved, and the children raced each other to him.

It was still summer-time, and the children came closer. A boy trudged down the sidewalk dragging a fishing pole behind him. A man stood waiting with his hands on his hips. Summer-time, and his children played in the front yard with their friend, enacting a strange little drama of their own invention.

It was fall, and his children fought on the sidewalk in front of Mrs Dubose's. The boy helped his sister to her feet, and they made their way home. Fall, and his children trotted to and fro around the corner, the day's woes and triumphs on their faces. They stopped at an oak tree, delighted, puzzled, apprehensive.

Winter, and his children shivered at the front gate, silhouetted against a blazing house. Winter, and a man walked into the street, dropped his glasses, and shot a dog.

Summer, and he watched his children's heart break. Autumn again, and Boo's children needed him.

Atticus was right. One time he said you never really know a man until you stand in his shoes and walk around in them. Just standing on the Radley porch was enough.

What is the span of time that is described? How can you tell?

Who could the three women described in paragraph 1 be? Do you think these women are young or old? What do you think is their relationship to these two children? What do you think the relationship is between the two children and the man in paragraph 1?

Who do you think 'his' refers to in paragraph 5? What do you think might have broken the children's heart? Who is Boo? What do you think is the relationship between Boo and the children?

Who do you think is Atticus? What do you think his relationship to the speaker is? What do you think it means to 'stand in his shoes and walk around in them'? Do you agree with Atticus's view that this is a good way to know someone? Why do you think the speaker says 'Just standing on the Radley porch was enough'?

Some things probably are not clear yet. Is there anything in particular you would like clarified? Make a note of it.

....

....

....

As you read the following extract, some things might become clearer. You can change the answers for extract 1 when you get new information. Now read extract 2. Why do you think Atticus did not teach his children how to shoot?

When he gave us our air rifles Atticus wouldn't teach us to shoot. Uncle Jack instructed us in the rudiments thereof; he said Atticus wasn't interested in guns. Atticus said to Jem one day, 'I'd rather you shot at tin cans in the back yard, but I know you'll go after birds. Shoot all the bluejays you want, if you can hit 'em, but remember it's a sin to kill a mockingbird.'

That was the only time I ever heard Atticus say it was a sin to do something, and I asked Miss Maudie about it.

'Your father's right,' she said. 'Mockingbirds don't do one thing but make music for us to enjoy. They don't eat up people's gardens, don't nest in corn-cribs, they don't do one thing but sing their hearts out for us. That's why it's a sin to kill a mockingbird.'

'Miss Maudie, this is an old neighbourhood, ain't it?'

'Been here longer than the town.'

'Nome, I mean the folks on our street are all old. Jem and me's the only children around here. Mrs Dubose is close on to a hundred and Miss Rachel's old and so are you and Atticus.'

'I don't call fifty very old,' said Miss Maudie tartly. 'Not being wheeled around yet, am I? Neither's your father. But I must say Providence was kind enough to burn down that old mausoleum of mine, I'm too old to keep it up – maybe you're right, Jean Louise, this is a settled neighbourhood. You've never been around young folks much, have you?'

'Yessum, at school.'

'I mean young grown-ups. You're lucky, you know. You and Jem have the benefit of your father's age. If your father was thirty you'd find life quite different.'

'I sure would. Atticus can't do anything . . . '

'You'd be surprised,' said Miss Maudie. 'There's life in him yet.'

Compare your answers around the class.

Who are 'our' in line 1?

What did Atticus warn Jem not to do? Why? Do you agree with Atticus's view? Can you think of other animals which could symbolise the same thing? The title of the novel is *To Kill a Mockingbird*. Do Atticus's and Miss Maudie's views about the mockingbird give any hint about how the title of the novel can be interpreted?

Why does Miss Maudie think the children have been lucky to have an old father? Do the children share her view? Why? What do you think Miss Maudie means by 'There's life in him yet'?

Reading extract 2 should help you with some of the questions in extract 1. You can make changes now.

Now read on. Which line in extract 1 refers to the incident described in this extract?

Jem became vaguely articulate: "'d you see him, Scout? 'd you see him just standin' there? . . . 'n' all of a sudden he just relaxed all over, an' it looked like that gun was a part of him . . . an' he did it so quick, like . . . I hafta aim for ten minutes 'fore I can hit somethin' . . . '

Miss Maudie grinned wickedly. 'Well now, Miss Jean Louise,' she said, 'still think your father can't do anything? Still ashamed of him?'

'Nome,' I said meekly.

'Forgot to tell you the other day that besides playing the jew's harp, Atticus Finch was the deadest shot in Maycomb County in his time.'

'Dead shot . . . ' echoed Jem.

'That's what I said, Jem Finch. Guess you'll change *your* tune now. The very idea, didn't you know his nickname was Ol' One-Shot when he was a boy? Why, down at the Landing when he was coming up, if he shot fifteen times and hit fourteen doves he'd complain about wasting ammunition.'

'He never said anything about that,' Jem muttered.

'Never said anything about it, did he?'

'No ma'am.'

'Wonder why he never goes huntin' now,' I said.

'Maybe I can tell you,' said Miss Maudie. 'If your father's anything, he's civilized in his heart. Marksmanship's a gift of God, a talent – oh, you have to practise to make it perfect, but shootin's different from playing the piano or the like. I think maybe he put his gun down when he realized that God had given him an unfair advantage over most living things. I guess he decided he wouldn't shoot till he had to, and he had to today.'

'Looks like he'd be proud of it,' I said.

'People in their right minds never take pride in their talents,' said Miss Maudie.

Why is Jem at a loss for words?

Did Miss Maudie forget to tell Jean Louise about her father's shooting ability, in your opinion? Why do you think Miss Maudie explains to the children why their father does not go hunting now? Do you think Miss Maudie's explanation why Atticus does not shoot can be trusted?

Do you agree with Miss Maudie's view expressed in the last two lines?

Now read extract 4. Suggest what Atticus's profession might be.

'Atticus,' I said one evening, 'what exactly is a nigger-lover?'

Atticus's face was grave. 'Has somebody been calling you that?'

'No sir, Mrs Dubose calls you that. She warms up every afternoon calling you that. Francis called me that last Christmas, that's where I first heard it.'

'Is that the reason you jumped on him?' asked Atticus.

'Yes sir . . .'

'Then why are you asking me what it means?'

I tried to explain to Atticus that it wasn't so much what Francis said that had infuriated me as the way he had said it. 'It was like he'd said snot-nose or somethin'.'

'Scout,' said Atticus, 'nigger-lover is just one of those terms that don't mean anything – like snot-nose. It's hard to explain – ignorant, trashy people use it when they think somebody's favouring Negroes over and above themselves. It's slipped into usage with some people like ourselves, when they want a common, ugly term to label somebody.'

'You aren't really a nigger-lover, then, are you?'

'I certainly am. I do my best to love everybody . . . I'm hard put, sometimes – baby, it's never an insult to be called what somebody thinks is a bad name. It just shows you how poor that person is, it doesn't hurt you. So don't let Mrs Dubose get you down. She had enough troubles of her own.'

What do you think is Mrs Dubose's relationship to Scout?

What is the explanation Atticus gives to the label 'nigger-lover'? Why is he not offended? Do you accept Atticus's explanation to Scout?

Besides the expression 'nigger-lover', there are a number of American expressions in this extract. What do these expressions mean: 'warms up', 'jumped on him', 'trashy people'?

Now read the final extract, in which Atticus is giving a speech. Who is he speaking to?

'We know all men are not created equal in the sense some people would have us believe – some people are smarter than others, some people have more opportunity because they're born with it, some men make more money than others, some ladies make better cakes than others – some people are born gifted beyond the normal scope of most men.

'But there is one way in this country in which all men are created equal – there is one human institution that makes a pauper the equal of a Rockefeller, the stupid man the equal of an Einstein and the ignorant man the equal of any college president. That institution, gentlemen, is a court. It can be the Supreme Court of the United States or the humblest J.P. court in the land, or this honourable court which you serve. Our courts have their faults, as does any human institution, but in this country our courts are the great levellers, and in our courts all men are created equal.

'I'm no idealist to believe firmly in the integrity of our courts and in the jury system – that is no ideal to me, it is a living, working reality. Gentlemen, a court is no better than each man of you sitting before me on this jury. A court is only as sound as its jury, and a jury is only as sound as the men who make it up. I am confident that you gentlemen will review without passion the evidence you have heard, come to a decision, and restore this defendant to his family. In the name of God, do your duty.'

(Harper Lee *To Kill a Mockingbird*)

Why does Atticus refer to the courts as 'the great levellers'? Why do you think Atticus goes on at length to state that all men are equal in the eyes of the court?

Who do you think Atticus is defending? Extract 4 should give you some hint.

Why does he consider his belief has not been idealistic? Is Atticus's faith in the institution of the court equivalent to his faith in the jury? Why does he finally invoke the name of God when asking the jury to carry out their duty? Do you think the jury will weigh the case fairly?

If you wanted to read the whole novel, what would you want to know more about? Why?

Now you are going to read extracts from a novel by James Vance Marshall called *Walkabout*. It is mostly about three children who spend a short time together.

As you read extract 1, suggest how the children could have got themselves into this situation.

The hours meandered past like slow, unhurrying snails. At last the boy's head dropped to his sister's lap. He snuggled closer. His breathing became slower, deeper. He slept.

But the girl didn't sleep; that would never have done; for she had to keep guard. She was the elder. The responsibility was hers. That was the way it had always been, as far back as she could remember. Always she had been the big sister who had stuck plaster on Peter's knees, and taught him to tie his shoe laces, and had taken the lead in their games of Indians and cowboys. Now that they were lost – somewhere in the middle of an unknown continent – the weight of her responsibility was greater than ever. A wave of tenderness welled up inside her. Always she had big-sistered him; now she must mother him as well.

For a while she sat staring into the darkness; the darkness that was warm, thick and almost tangible; soon her mind became utterly blank. The day's events had been too overwhelming; had drawn on her too heavily. The rhythmic beat of the small boy's slumber came to her lullingly now. Gradually her breathing fell in step with his. The whisper of the creek came to her like the croon of a lullaby. Her eyelids drooped and closed, fluttered and closed again. Soon she too was fast asleep.

What is the passing of time compared to? What does this suggest? Where could they be?

Pick out the words which show that the girl does not want to sleep. Why? How does the girl regard her responsibility to her brother? Which expressions indicate this?

What do you think were 'the day's events' that 'had been too overwhelming'? Which words indicate that the day's events had been very taxing on the girl?

What sounds are mentioned in the extract? What effect do they have on the girl?

What do you think will happen to the children?

Now read extract 2. Whom does she compare the stranger to? What does this extract tell you about where she may be from?

The girl's first impulse was to grab Peter and run; but as her eyes swept over the stranger, her fear died slowly away. The boy was young – certainly no older than she was; he was unarmed, and his attitude was more inquisitive than threatening: more puzzled than hostile.

He wasn't the least bit like an African Negro. His skin was certainly black, but beneath it was a curious hint of undersurface bronze, and it was fine-grained: glossy, satiny, almost silk-like. His hair wasn't crinkly but nearly straight; and his eyes were blue-black: big, soft and inquiring. In his hand was a baby rock wallaby, its eyes, unclosed in death, staring vacantly above a tiny pointed snout.

All this Mary noted and accepted. The thing that she couldn't accept, the thing that seemed to her shockingly and indecently wrong, was the fact that the boy was naked.

The three children stood looking at each other in the middle of the Australian desert. Motionless as the outcrops of granite they stared, and stared, and stared. Between them the distance was less than the spread of an outstretched arm, but more than a hundred thousand years.

Brother and sister were products of the highest strata of humanity's evolution. In them the primitive had long ago been swept aside, been submerged by mechanization, been swamped by scientific development, been nullified by the standardized pattern of the white man's way of life. They had climbed a long way up the ladder of progress; they had climbed so far, in fact, that they had forgotten how their climb had started. Coddled in babyhood, psycho-analysed in childhood, nourished on predigested patent foods, provided with continuous push-button entertainment, the basic realities of life were something they'd never had to face.

Which adjectives indicate that the girl lost her sense of fear of the boy? Who do you think chose the adjectives, the narrator or the girl?

Who did you say she compared the boy with? Complete the two columns below, based on the descriptions the girl gives.

	African Negro	The boy
skin	....	....
hair	....	....
eyes	....	....

What was the thing about the boy that Mary could not accept? Why?

What two distances are referred to in the line: 'Between them the distance was less than the spread of an outstretched arm, but more than a hundred thousand years'?

Underline the words that indicate that Peter and Mary came from a well-provided, technologically advanced society. How does this affect them?

What do you think are 'the basic realities of life'? Why did Mary and Peter not have to face them?

Read the next extract, and pick out words or expressions that describe the forms that Death takes.

It was very different with the Aboriginal. He knew what reality was. He led a way of life that was already old when Tut-ankh-amen started to build his tomb; a way of life that had been tried and proved before the white man's continents were even lifted out of the sea. Among the secret water-holes of the Australian desert his people had lived and died, unchanged and unchanging, for twenty thousand years. Their lives were unbelievably simple. They had no homes, no crops, no clothes, no possessions. The few things they had, they shared: food and wives; children and laughter; tears and hunger and thirst. They walked from one water-hole to the next; they exhausted one supply of food, then moved on to another. Their lives were utterly uncomplicated because they were devoted to one purpose, dedicated in their entirety to the waging of one battle: the battle with death. Death was their ever-present enemy. He sought them out from every dried-up salt pan, from the flames of every bush fire. He was never far away. Keeping him at bay was the Aboriginals' full-time job: the job they'd been doing for twenty thousand years: the job they were good at.

Where was the Aboriginal from? Which words indicate how old the Aboriginal's way of life was? Why do you think the speaker considers the Aboriginal's way of life simple? Do you agree?

What was the main preoccupation of the Aboriginals? What words tell you whether the Aboriginals were winning or losing their fight against Death?

Compare the way of life described in extract 2 with that in this extract. In what ways are they similar or different?

Now read extract 4. What do you think caused a change of heart in the Aboriginal towards the children?

'Hey, don't leave us, darkie! We're lost. We want food, an' drink. And we wanna know how we get to Adelaide.'

Mary looked at the bush boy, and saw in his eyes a gleam of amusement. It angered her, for she knew the cause; Peter's high-pitched, corncrakey voice. All the tenets of progressive society and racial superiority combined inside her to form a deep-rooted core of resentment. It was wrong, cruelly wrong, that she and her brother should be forced to run for help to a Negro; and a naked Negro at that. She clutched Peter's hand, half drawing him away.

But Peter was obsessed by none of his sister's scruples. To him their problem was simple, uncomplicated: they wanted help, and here was some-one who could, his instinct told him, provide it. The fact that his appeal had failed to register first time nonplussed him for a moment. But he wasn't put off; he stuck to his guns. Breath and composure regained, he now spoke slowly, in a lower, less excited key.

'Look, darkie, we're lost. We want water. You sabby water? War-tur. War-tur.'

He cupped his hands together, drew them up to his lips, and went through the motions of swallowing.

The bush boy nodded.

Was it rude of Peter to call the bush boy 'darkie', in your opinion?

What were Mary's 'scruples'? What do you think of Mary's attitude towards the bush boy? What could have caused her to react in this way? Pick out words which indicate Mary's superior feeling towards the bush boy.

How does Peter regard the bush boy? If his perception is different from Mary's, why is this so? Why did the bush boy's attitude towards Peter change?

What do you think the children will ask the bush boy next? How will they communicate? What problems could arise for the three of them? Write these down.

....

....

....

Now read on, and decide what dance you think the boy is performing.

Yet still the dance went on: ever faster, ever wilder. He was swaying now to a drumbeat that couldn't be heard, caught up in a ritual that couldn't be broken. On and on and on; though his muscles were aching, his lungs bursting, his heart pounding, and his mind empty as the cloudless sky. Then suddenly the climax: somersault after somersault, victory-roll after victory-roll, till he was standing, stock still and in sudden silence, face to face with the children.

And once again he was naked; for at the moment of climax the elastic of the panties had snapped, and the gift – symbol of civilization – lay under his feet, trampled into the desert sand.

White girl and black boy, a couple of yards apart, stood staring one at another.

The girl's eyes grew wider and wider.

The bush boy's eyes widened too. He realized, quite suddenly, that the larger of the strangers wasn't a male: she was a lubra, a budding gin.

He took a half-pace forward. Then he drew back. Appalled. For into the

girl's eyes there came a terror such as he'd seen only a couple of times
before: a terror that could for him have only one meaning, one tragic and
inevitable cause. He began to tremble then, in great, uncontrolled, nerve-
jerking spasms. For, to him, the girl's terror could only mean one thing: that
she had seen in his eyes an image: the image of the Spirit of Death.

Circle the words that indicate non-stop movement. Now pick out
the adjectives that were used to describe the parts of his body which
were affected by these movements. What do the adjectives tell us
readers about what was going on within the boy? Who do you think
chose the adjectives?

Which two words contrast with all the movements that had been
going on during the dance, when the dance comes to an end?

How do you think the bush boy got the pair of panties? What has
happened to them now? Did he know it was a woman's garment he
had worn?

Who do the words 'a lubra, a budding gin' refer to?

Which word indicates that the boy had been frightened by what
he saw in Mary's eyes? What had frightened the bush boy when he
looked into Mary's eyes? What did he think the terror meant?

Underline the words which describe the movements of the bush
boy towards the end of the extract. How are these different from
those in the early part of the extract?

What does he think Mary had seen? How does this affect him?
What effect do you think this will have on the boy? How do you
think this will affect all of them?

Now read the following extract, and suggest reasons why Mary took
a long time to answer Peter.

'You sure he's real ill, Pete?'

'Course I'm sure. You come an' see.'

For a long time the girl was silent. Then she said slowly:

'Yes. I'll come.'

They walked across to the mugga-wood: to where the bush boy lay in a
pool of shadow. Beside him, the girl dropped hesitantly to her knees. She
looked into his face: closely: and saw that what her brother had told her was
true.

She sat down. Stunned. Then very gently she eased the bush boy's head
on to her lap; very softly she began to run her fingers over and across his
forehead.

The bush boy's eyes flickered open; for a moment they were puzzled; then they smiled.

It was the smile that broke Mary's heart: that last forgiving smile. Before, she had seen as through a glass darkly, but now she saw face to face. And in that moment of truth all her inbred fears and inhibitions were sponged away, and she saw that the world which she had thought was split in two was one.

Why did Mary not go to the bush boy earlier?

Pick out all the adverbs. What do they tell us about Mary's actions? What does this tell you about her?

What are 'they' in the line 'then they smiled'? Whose smile was it? What is the smile described as? Who do you think chose the adjectives? What effect does the smile have on Mary?

What has happened in the eye-to-eye contact? How was this different from before? What was the 'moment of truth' for Mary? How did this affect her?

Compare your impressions of Mary's character as we saw in extracts 2 and 4, and now. What changes do you notice in her? Are they changes for the better or the worse, in your opinion?

Now read the final extract. Who do you think 'they' are in line 1? What were they doing when they got very excited?

The gin came across; quickly; and together they peered at the dream house. After a while Mary, still carrying the piccaninny, joined them. They looked first at her then at the house.

'Awhee! Awhee!'

The gin's voice was filled with curiosity, almost with awe. She spoke quickly, excitedly, pointing first to the dream house then to the hills on the far side of the valley. Quite suddenly Mary got the gist of what she was saying. Hope surged within her. Over the hills was a house. Not just a hut such as natives lived in, but a house like the one she had drawn: a white man's house: a first stepping-stone on the long, long trail that would, one wonderful and longed-for day, lead them back to home.

'Where? Oh, where?'

Her eagerness was something the Aboriginals could understand.

The black man's eyes were sympathetic. Gently he took the girl by the hand and led her down to the sand beside the lagoon.

Peter, seeing them talking so earnestly, left the *warrigal* and came and stood beside his sister.

He saw the black man point first to a valley looping aslant the hills like a tired snake. The black man mimed the climb of the valley: his feet rising, his knees sagging. At the top he indicated that the children should sleep. He lay down on the sand and snored. The gin giggled. Then, with the point of a yacca branch, he traced a line heading east, into the rising sun. After a while the line broke, and with a couple of curves the black man indicated a hill. Then, beyond the hill, the line went on. Soon came another, lower hill; and here, the black man indicated, there was water; he drew a circle, pointed to the lagoon, and lapped like a dog. He also indicated food: yams: he drew them beside the hill and champed his teeth. And here too he indicated sleep: again the lying down, again the snoring. The children nodded. Next day the line continued east, towards another, higher hill. And here, at the base of the hill, it stopped. Ended at a house. The black man drew it: one door; one window; one chimney; one pathway lined with flowers.

The children looked at each other. The girl's eyes were like the stars of the Southern Cross.

'Oh, Pete!'

She suddenly burst into tears.

(James Vance Marshall *Walkabout*)

Who is the 'She' in paragraph 3, line 1?

How did Mary come to the conclusion that there was a white man's house?

Why could the Aboriginal understand Mary's feelings? According to the Aboriginal's directions, how many days' travel do the children have before they reach the white man's house?

There are a number of references to eyes in this extract. Underline what is said about the black man's eyes and Mary's eyes. What do they see in his eyes? Does his behaviour confirm this? What does the comparison indicate about feelings?

Do you think the story will have a happy ending?

What did you find interesting in the novel? Did your feelings for any of the characters change as the novel developed? How do you think the title of the novel, *Walkabout*, relates to the two children?

PART III

The first poem is called *Time*. What words and graphological effects
make it work for you?

```
Time
        an accomplice of waste
                        is an image of expense
    it is always spilling
                its angry hands
                            wheeling
    its consummate skill
                    pounding
                like a drill on the brain
    never to be stopped
                    retrieved
                    or
                        replenished
    forever whittling
                    whittling
                            whittling
                    away
                away
            away
        away
away
    all the vast stores
                        of
                        being!
```

(Kojo Gyinage Kyei *Time*)

Do you find this a positive or a negative concept of time?

As you read this poem, about the loss of a loved one, decide who is speaking.

> Stop all the clocks, cut off the telephone,
> Prevent the dog from barking with a juicy bone,
> Silence the pianos and with muffled drum
> Bring out the coffin, let the mourners come.
>
> Let aeroplanes circle moaning overhead
> Scribbling on the sky the message He Is Dead,
> Put crêpe bows round the white necks of the public doves,
> Let the traffic policemen wear black cotton gloves.
>
> He was my North, my South, my East and West,
> My working week and my Sunday rest,
> My noon, my midnight, my talk, my song;
> I thought that love would last for ever: I was wrong.
>
> The stars are not wanted now: put out every one;
> Pack up the moon and dismantle the sun;
> Pour away the ocean and sweep up the wood.
> For nothing now can ever come to any good.
>
> (W.H. Auden *Stop All the Clocks*)

What can you tell about the 'I' of the poem?

Look at the imperatives verse by verse. Which of them are *possible* for someone to obey; and which of them are *impossible*? Which imperatives are to do with sounds, and which with sight? How is the third stanza different from the first two?

What do you think 'public doves' are?

What kind of gloves do traffic policemen normally wear?

Look again at the third stanza. What words and phrases make it *personal* and which are more *universal*? Which lines do you find most emotionally striking?

What aspects of this poem would you say are modern, and which are timeless?

The next poem also handles the idea of death. As you read, decide who the characters are.

Because I could not stop for Death,
He kindly stopped for me;
The carriage held but just ourselves
And Immortality.

We slowly drove, he knew no haste,
And I had put away
My labor and my leisure too,
For his civility.

We passed the school where children played
At wrestling in a ring;
We passed the fields of gazing grain,
We passed the setting sun.

We passed before a house that seemed
A swelling of the ground;
The roof was scarcely visible,
The cornice but a mound.

Since then 't is centuries; but each
Feels shorter than the day
I first surmised the horses' heads
Were towards eternity.

(Emily Dickinson *Because I could not stop for Death*)

Who went in the carriage? What is the atmosphere in the carriage in the second stanza? Is it positive or negative?

What do they see in the third stanza? What do you think the 'house' in the fourth stanza might be? Is it a real house, in your opinion?

In the final stanza, how much time has passed? How many different references to time are there? Does 'surmised' refer back to the first stanza, in your opinion? Why could 'I' 'not stop for Death' in line 1, do you think? Was 'I' trying to avoid the subject of death, or too busy, or simply did not think about it?

Is the whole poem about death, eternity, happiness, or what? The poem sometimes has the title *The Chariot*. Do you think this title would be appropriate? Or would you prefer a different title?

Is the effect of the poem positive or negative, happy or sad?

How does this poem's view of death compare with the view we saw in *Stop All the Clocks*?

The next poem also looks at death, in the context of World War I in Europe. As you read, pick out some references to sounds (in the first eight lines) and to light (in the final six lines).

> What passing-bells for these who die as cattle?
> – Only the monstrous anger of the guns.
> Only the stuttering rifles' rapid rattle
> Can patter out their hasty orisons.
> 5   No mockeries now for them; no prayers nor bells,
> Nor any voice of mourning save the choirs, –
> The shrill, demented choirs of wailing shells;
> And bugles calling for them from sad shires.
>
> What candles may be held to speed them all?
> 10 Not in the hands of boys, but in their eyes
> Shall shine the holy glimmers of good-byes.
> The pallor of girls' brows shall be their pall;
> Their flowers the tenderness of patient minds,
> And each slow dusk a drawing-down of blinds.
>
> (Wilfred Owen *Anthem for Doomed Youth*)

Some quick questions:

- why 'hasty' (line 4)?
- 'speed' (line 9) towards what?
- what 'mockeries' (line 5)?
- why 'patient' (line 13)?
- why are candles called 'holy glimmers of good-byes' (line 11)?
- where are the 'sad shires' (line 8)?
- what do you think 'a drawing-down of blinds' (line 14) might mean?

What elements of a traditional funeral are mentioned? How are they contradicted?

Is the rhyme scheme easily detectable? What about assonance, rhythm, and imagery?

If the first eight lines are about war, can you say what lines 9 to 14 are about?

The next poem continues the idea of pity. As you read, decide what difference there might be between the imperative in line 1 and the imperative in line 8.

> Move him into the sun –
> Gently its touch awoke him once,
> At home, whispering of fields unsown.
> Always it woke him, even in France,
> 5   Until this morning and this snow. –
> If anything might rouse him now
> The kind old sun will know.
>
> Think how it wakes the seeds, –
> Woke, once, the clays of a cold star.
> 10   Are limbs, so dear-achieved, are sides,
> Full-nerved, – still warm, – too hard to stir?
> Was it for this the clay grew tall?
> – O what made fatuous sunbeams toil
> To break earth's sleep at all?

(Wilfred Owen)

Who is speaking? Who is 'him' (lines 1, 2, 4, 6)? What is 'its' (line 2) and 'it' (lines 4, 8, 12)? And what do you think 'this' (line 12) refers to?

What is the 'cold star' (line 9)? How does it relate to the last line?

What was the man's job 'At home' (line 3)?

Look at the adjectives in lines 7 and 13. Are they the words you would have expected? What might you have written instead?

What positive words or images can you find in the poem? Did the man actually die? At what point in the poem do you think you can tell?

Suggest a title for the poem.

The first poem of Owen's is a sonnet (see p. 140), the second is not, although it has fourteen lines. What contrast is there between the two which could make this difference?

Are the two poems anti-war, about war, heroic, unheroic? Write about the poet's attitude to his subject. (Owen's title for the second poem is on page 217.)

The next text is about chickens – the title is *Song of the Battery Hen*.

Is that a positive-sounding idea, or is 'battery hen' negative? As you
read, keep the idea of positive and negative contrasts in mind.

> We can't grumble about accommodation:
> we have a new concrete floor that's
> always dry, four walls that are
> painted white, and a sheet-iron roof
> the rain drums on. A fan blows warm air
> beneath our feet to disperse the smell
> of chicken-shit and, on dull days,
> fluorescent lighting sees us.

> You can tell me: if you come by
> the North door, I am in the twelfth pen
> on the left-hand side of the third row
> from the floor; and in that pen
> I am usually the middle one of three.
> But, even without directions, you'd
> discover me. I have the same orange-
> red comb, yellow beak and auburn
> feathers, but as the door opens and you
> hear above the electric fan a kind of
> one-word wail, I am the one
> who sounds loudest in my head.

> Listen. Outside this house there's an
> orchard with small moss-green apple
> trees; beyond that, two fields of
> cabbages; then, on the far side of
> the road, a broiler house. Listen:
> one cockerel grows out of there, as
> tall and proud as the first hour of sun.
> Sometimes I stop calling with the others
> to listen, and wonder if he hears me.

> The next time you come here, look for me.
> Notice the way I sound inside my head.
> God made us all quite differently,
> and blessed us with this expensive home.

(Edwin Brock *Song of the Battery Hen*)

Who are 'we'? Is the voice of 'we' positive or negative? How much do you see negatively, compared with 'we'?

'Me' claims individuality. How does she express herself as an individual? Is she right?

How many *sounds* are there?

'Next time' will she still be there?

What point do you think the *Song* is making?

The next text is out of its proper order. Put the stanzas into the order you think would be most logical.

a) We can't use money to bandage
sores, can't pound it
to powder for sick eyes
and sick bellies. Yet without
it, flesh melts from our bones.

b) We can't read money for books.
Yet without it we don't
read, don't write numbers,
don't open gates in other countries,
as lots and lots never do.

c) And we can't eat it. Yet
without it our heads alone
stay big, as lots and lots do,
coming from nowhere joyful,
going nowhere happy.

d) Such a peculiar lot
we are, we people
without money, in daylong
yearlong sunlight, knowing
money is somewhere, somewhere.

e) Everybody says it's a big
bigger brain bother now,
money. Such millions and millions
of us don't manage at all
without it, like war going on.

f) We can't drink it up. Yet
without it we shrivel when small
and stop forever
where we stopped,
as lots and lots do.

(James Berry)

What can you tell about 'I' and the setting of the poem? What do you think is the main point the text is making? Is it about money, or deprivation, or what, in your opinion?

Is the tone angry, despairing, resigned, happy? What binaries do you find?

The title is *Fantasy of an African Boy*. Do you like that as a title?
(You can check out the proper order of the stanzas on page 217–18.)

Read this poem, and say in one line if the speaker likes the way he lives, and why.

Every morning in relentless hurry, I scurry
through the streets of New York, turn around the avenue, flee
                    past the red and white awning of the Jewish deli,
            walk out with a bagel or croissant or spilled coffee,
            disappearing underground in a flurry,

speeding in a subway of mute faces, barely swallowed the bite,
barely unfolded *The Times*, barely awake.
                    Before I realise, it's lunch-time, and then,
            evening, late,
            being herded home with the flow of humankind,

up and down elevators, escalators, staircases, and ramps. I am
back on the streets again, late night,
                    though early enough to glance headlines
            of next morning's paper. In this city, I
            count the passage of time only by weekends

linked by five-day flashes I don't
even remember. In this city where walking means
                    running, driving means speeding, there seem to exist
            many days in one, an ironic and oblique
            efficiency. But somewhere, somehow, time takes its toll,

malnourished, overburdened, and overutilised,
as the tunnels seeping under the river's belly slowly cave
                    in, the girders lose their tension like old dentures, and
            the underground rattles with the passing of every train.
            After all, how long can one stretch time?

Illusions can lengthen, credit ratings strengthen,
even Manhattan elongates with every land-fill,
                    but not time, it takes its own time
            the way it always has and always will,
            not a second more, not a second less.

                                (Sudeep Sen *New York Times*)

How many sentences are there in this poem? Number the sentences. Which sentences are specifically concerned with time? List them and their time references. What does the first sentence describe? What does the second sentence describe?

Read the poem again. List all the words that describe quick movement.

In the middle of the poem there is a change from description to reflection. Mark some words which show this.

Mark the opening words of each sentence. Do they reflect the same change we have already noticed?

Why does the speaker not remember his weekdays?

Compare the tone in sentence 6 with that in the first five. Which word could signal any change? What is the tone of sentence 6? How does 'time take[s] its toll'? Who or what experiences this?

Rewrite the last line of the fifth stanza as a statement. Which do you think is more effective? Why? Contrast the first line and the last three lines. How much does the contrast reflect the whole poem?

The next poem is about *fear* of death. As you read it, decide who you think 'thee' is.

> When I have fears that I may cease to be
> > Before my pen has glean'd my teeming brain,
> Before high-piled books, in charact'ry,
> > Hold like rich garners the full-ripen'd grain;
> 5   When I behold, upon the night's starr'd face,
> > Huge cloudy symbols of a high romance,
> And think that I may never live to trace
> > Their shadows, with the magic hand of chance;
> And when I feel, fair creature of an hour!
> 10   That I shall never look upon thee more,
> Never have relish in the faery power
> > Of unreflecting love! – then on the shore
> Of the wide world I stand alone, and think,
> Till Love and Fame to nothingness do sink.
>
> (John Keats *When I Have Fears*)

How many different ways of expressing the idea of death can you find in the poem? Is death seen positively or negatively?

Discuss who the 'fair creature of an hour' (line 9) might be. Is the image positive or negative?

Contrast the first line and the last. What movement can you find? Is there any sense of the future in the final lines?

Pick out positive concepts and words, and set them against any negative ideas in the poem.

Positive	*Negative*
....	....
....	....
....	....
....	....
....	....

Ring the connectors of time ('when', 'when', 'when') – what related word are they followed by, in line 12?

What images can you find of (a) the sky or heavens, (b) the earth, (c) love? What do the first four lines tell us 'I' wants to do before he dies? What words contain an idea of crops and harvesting?

Vocabulary

The following are synonyms for some of the less familiar words in the poem. Match them with words in the text, then discuss the lexical choices. Are the poet's words better, and if so why?

die   gather   overflowing   print   stores   magic

The poem is a sonnet: a fourteen-line poem, usually written in two phases: eight lines (octet) followed by six (sestet). Does this sonnet follow that pattern? Or does it change it?

In its rhyme scheme, there are three usual ways of writing a sonnet. Which of these does Keats use:

• the Petrarchan – abba abba cdecde (or cdcdcd)
• the Spenserian – abab bcbc cdcd ee
• the Shakespearean – abab cdcd efef gg?

Compare this with other sonnets in the book, or others you have read.

Do the final lines suggest to you that love and fame are important, or unimportant? Which theme is the most important, in your opinion: writing, love, fame, death?

Keats knew he would die young. Does this information add anything to your reading of the poem?

In the next poem, John Keats handles time in a rather different way. Autumn in British English is 'fall' in American English. What feature of autumn does 'fall' refer to? What season was *Daffodils* (page 65) set in, do you think? Brainstorm a few ideas on what happens to nature in the autumn. Are the ideas mainly positive or negative?

As you read, see how many of the ideas of autumn you have mentioned come into the poem.

I

Season of mists and mellow fruitfulness,
Close bosom-friend of the maturing sun;
Conspiring with him how to load and bless
With fruit the vines that round the thatch-eaves run;
5   To bend with apples the mossed cottage-trees,
And fill all fruit with ripeness to the core;
To swell the gourd, and plump the hazel shells
With a sweet kernel; to set budding more,
And still more, later flowers for the bees,
10 Until they think warm days will never cease,
For Summer has o'er-brimmed their clammy cells.

II

Who hath not seen thee oft amid thy store?
Sometimes whoever seeks abroad may find
Thee sitting careless on a granary floor,
15 Thy hair soft-lifted by the winnowing wind;
Or on a half-reaped furrow sound asleep,
Drowsed with the fume of poppies, while thy hook
Spares the next swath and all its twinèd flowers:
And sometimes like a gleaner thou dost keep
20 Steady thy laden head across a brook;
Or by a cider press, with patient look,
Thou watchest the last oozings hours by hours.

III

Where are the songs of Spring? Aye, where are they?
Think not of them, thou hast thy music too, –
25 While barrèd clouds bloom the soft-dying day
And touch the stubble-plains with rosy hue;
Then in a wailful choir the small gnats mourn
Among the river sallows, borne aloft
Or sinking as the light wind lives or dies;
30 And full-grown lambs loud bleat from hilly bourn;
Hedge-crickets sing; and now with treble soft
The red-breast whistles from a garden-croft;
And gathering swallows twitter in the skies.

(John Keats *To Autumn*)

Is the overall feeling positive or negative? Did you find any mention of leaves, or falling?

Vocabulary

Group together any of the words you don't know, under the following headings. (You don't have to look them up yet.)

Verbs of growing   *Other verbs*

....

....

....

....

Nouns of place   *Nouns of harvest/crops*

....

....

....

....

Positive adjectives	*Negative adjectives*
....	....
....	....
....	....
....	....

Point of entry

Look at the third verse. What is autumn contrasted with? Who or
what is 'thou' (line 24)? Circle the little words from line 25 to the
end: 'while', 'then', 'and', and 'now'. How many of the verbs which
follow them are to do with sounds?

What does the dash at the end of line 24 indicate?

What colours are involved in lines 25–6?

What words continue the idea of music from line 24?

What differences can you see between what might be found in
spring and what is found in autumn?

Now look again at the second verse. Is 'thee' the same as it was in
verse I? Point out some of the things that 'thee' can be found doing.
Is he active? What kind of crops can be found in his store?

The first verse is all addressed to 'thee' – but there are remarkably
few *main* verbs. But all the verbs until line 9 contain the idea of
growing more. Pick out a few, and say who benefits from the
autumn's produce. Who are 'they' in line 10? What are 'their
clammy cells'? Why is summer mentioned here?

How many of the words you did not know are absolutely essential
for you to understand the poem?

What references are there to the past, and what suggestions are
there that look towards the future?

What would you expect from a story called *The Bank Robbery?* Brainstorm a few ideas and note them down.

How does the beginning of the story tie in with your expectations?

> The bank robber told his story in little notes to the bank teller. He held the pistol in one hand and gave her the notes with the other. The first note said:
>
> > *This is a bank holdup because money is just like time and I need more to keep on going, so keep your hands where I can see them and don't go pressing any alarm buttons or I'll blow your head off.*

Is there anything unexpected, in the action, or in the language?

As you read on, again check your expectations with what really happens.

> The teller, a young woman of about twenty-five, felt the lights that lined her streets go on for the first time in years. She kept her hands where he could see them and didn't press any alarm buttons. Ah danger, she said to herself, you are just like love. After she read the note, she gave it back to the gunman and said:
> 'This note is far too abstract. I really can't respond to it.'

What was the most unexpected thing in this part of the story? What do you think is going to happen? Is the robber going to succeed in getting the money?

Now read on. Is it becoming another kind of story?

The robber, a young man of about twenty-five, felt the electricity of his thoughts in his hand as he wrote the next note. Ah money, he said to himself, you are just like love. His next note said:

> This is a bank holdup because there is only one clear rule around here and that is WHEN YOU RUN OUT OF MONEY YOU SUFFER, so keep your hands where I can see them and don't go pressing any alarm buttons or I'll blow your head off.

The young woman took the note, touching lightly the gunless hand that had written it. The touch of the gunman's hand went immediately to her memory, growing its own life there. It became a constant light toward which she could move when she was lost. She felt that she could see everything clearly as if an unknown veil had just been lifted.

'I think I understand better now,' she said to the thief, looking first in his eyes and then at the gun. 'But all this money will not get you what you want.' She looked at him deeply, hoping that she was becoming rich before his eyes.

Ah danger, she said to herself, you are the gold that wants to spend my life.

Is the tone serious, do you think?

How would you film this, if you were making a video of it? Realistically? Where does the language stop being realistic, in your opinion?

Now read on. Is the contrast between realism and dreams maintained?

The robber was becoming sleepy. In the gun was the weight of his dreams about this moment when it was yet to come. The gun was like the heavy eyelids of someone who wants to sleep but is not allowed.

Ah money, he said to himself, I find little bits of you leading to more of you in greater little bits. You are promising endless amounts of yourself but others are coming. They are threatening our treasure together. I cannot pick you up fast enough as you lead into the great, huge quiet that you are. Oh money, please save me, for you are desire, pure desire, that wants only itself.

The gunman could feel his intervals, the spaces in himself, piling up so that he could not be sure of what he would do next. He began to write. His next note said:

> Now is the film of my life, the film of my insomnia: an eerie bus ride, a trance in the night, from which I want to step down, whose light keeps me from sleeping. In the streets I will chase the wind-blown

letter of love that will change my life. Give me the money, my Sister,
so that I can run my hands through its hair. This is the unfired gun of
time, so keep your hands where I can see them and don't go pressing
any alarm buttons or I'll blow your head off with it.

How would you describe the scene, compared to what you expect
from a bank robbery? (Possible adjectives: 'surreal', 'dreamlike',
'boring', 'unrealistic', 'funny'.)

Will he blow her head off? Will the robbery actually happen?

Now read on to the end of the story.

Reading, the young woman felt her inner hands grabbing and holding onto
this moment of her life.

Ah danger, she said to herself, you are yourself with perfect clarity. Under
your lens I know what I want.

The young man and woman stared into each other's eyes forming two
paths between them. On one path his life, like little people, walked into her,
and on the other hers walked into him.

'This money is love,' she said to him. 'I'll do what you want.' She began
to put money into the huge satchel he had provided.

As she emptied it of money, the bank filled with sleep. Everyone else in
the bank slept the untroubled sleep of trees that would never be money.
Finally she placed all the money in the bag.

The bank robber and the bank teller left together like hostages of each
other. Though it was no longer necessary, he kept the gun on her, for it was
becoming like a child between them.

(Steven Schutzman *The Bank Robbery*)

What happened, in your own words? Looking back at your
expectations, which of them were realised? Is the story about a bank
robbery? What else is it about, if anything?

There is a lot of language about thinking and feeling, rather than
doing. Pick out some of the words and phrases you would normally
expect not to find in a bank robbery story – how would the story be
different without them? Would it be more like the story you
expected?

Would you say this story is:

• more abstract than concrete
• not really about a bank robbery

- a joke
- a parody of a bank robbery story?

Do you think the characters will live happily ever after?

In Simon Tay's story of present-day Singapore, we come right up to date. As you read, what can you tell about the driver?

He first spotted the car at the first flyover, the one that goes over Toa Payoh Road. In the far right lane, highbeams on, glaring into his rear view mirror and cabin. Gaining fast. It must be doing 160 he thought. Madman. He put his indicator on and started moving over into the middle lane to let the car over-take. As he did, the car also moved into the middle lane. He pulled the BeeM abruptly back to the right. A tyre screeched. The car horned, flashed its lights and, as it pulled alongside, the driver stuck his fist out of the window, into the rushing wind: a thumb wrapped under the closed index finger, pointing at him.

A black RX-7. The driver in his early thirties. A bastard. An incompetent bastard. Travelling so fast and trying to overtake on the left. Then daring to show him that sign. The BeeM dropped a gear and accelerated steadily. A hundred and thirty and then, changing up again, a hundred and forty, catching the RX-7. He could see that it had red trim all around, a large spoiler at the back and body coloured bumpers. He saw the number and remembered it so he would report it to the police. That would teach the bastard. Then the RX-7 pulled right into his path.

He braked from instinct alone. Tyres screeched and the BeeM twitched as he wrestled with the steering wheel. The RX-7 pulled away. He swore aloud and accelerated. The BeeM raised its front slightly as the speed climbed again. They raced down to the end of the CTE, to the junction near Farrer Park, and the RX-7 slowed in the turn. The BeeM cornered hard and caught up. He horned loudly. Then he saw the junction lights ahead turn red.

The BeeM's tyres dug in desperately. The car swerved slightly to one side and he could feel himself being pulled hard out of his seat and against the safety-belt. It stopped, just before the lights. The RX-7 went through and ran the lights at the next junction as well. It raced away, horning its victory in the late and quiet of the night.

What words give you the *sounds* of the scene? What would your reaction be in the same circumstances?

Pick out some words and phrases which are unusual ('horning' in the last sentence, for instance). How appropriate are they at giving the feel of the situation?

Now read on, as the driver tells Ming and Lizzie what happened after that encounter. As you read, do you agree that this kind of thing 'was common enough'?

'Now what did you want to kill someone about?'

'Look Ming, I'm sorry for bursting in like that . . . '

'Forget it. We're used to you. What happened?'

'Someone scratched my car.'

'No.'

'Goodness!'

'Who would do something like that? What happened?'

The chorus of shock soothed him and he began the story:

– Holland Village: just putting his shopping bags into the car boot when he spotted it – a long deep gash above the rear lights, just under the lid, running all the way from the left-hand side to the right. Disbelievingly he looked at it and rubbed the scratch with his fingers, as if massaging it. The gash was deep and broad, gouged in with a lot of strength. Maybe two or three coats of paint. It wouldn't look better even after polishing, he knew. He shook his head, put away the bags, bent down and looked at it more closely. He still couldn't believe it. It was common enough but it had never happened to him; he scrupulously avoided the type of places in which common wisdom said that sort of thing might happen. Now it had happened in Holland Village, in broad daylight. That damn RX-7 driver.

'Wait a minute, how do you know it was the RX-7 driver?'

Because, Lizzie, he saw the RX-7 in the carpark at Cold Storage.

'I thought you said it happened at Holland Village?'

No no, he noticed it there. Earlier he had seen the RX-7 at Cold Storage. He was just about to leave when he saw the car there. It was quite dark in the basement carpark, but it was the right one: red trim, spoiler, skirting all around. He thought of waiting for the driver to come back but he had no idea how long that might be. Besides, for all he knew, somebody else might be driving the car – the driver's brother or friend. So he just went off. But he now realised the RX-7 driver must have been there, seen his car and scratched it. At Cold Storage. It was just that he did not notice it then – because of the lighting – and saw it only at Holland Village.

(Simon Tay *Drive*)

Pick out the bits that are in indirect speech. What difference would it make if he had told the whole thing in direct speech?

Do you think the whole story is going to be about this rivalry between drivers? Or could there be more to it? Could the rivalry be indicative of anything else, in your opinion?

What can you tell about the main character and his life?

In the first section of this passage from *The Hound of the Baskervilles*, the speaker is Dr Mortimer. He cared for Sir Charles Baskerville during his final illness. Now he is talking to Sherlock Holmes and Dr Watson.

'The moor is very sparsely inhabited, and those who live near each other are thrown very much together. For this reason I saw a good deal of Sir Charles Baskerville. With the exception of Mr Frankland, of Lafter Hall, and Mr Stapleton, the naturalist, there are no other men of education within many miles. Sir Charles was a retiring man, but the chance of his illness brought us together, and a community of interests in science kept us so. He had brought back much scientific information from South Africa, and many a charming evening we have spent together discussing the comparative anatomy of the Bushman and the Hottentot.

'Within the last few months it became increasingly plain to me that Sir Charles's nervous system was strained to the breaking point. He had taken this legend which I have read you exceedingly to heart – so much so that, although he would walk in his own grounds, nothing would induce him to go out upon the moor at night. Incredible as it may appear to you, Mr Holmes, he was honestly convinced that a dreadful fate overhung his family, and certainly the records which he was able to give of his ancestors were not encouraging. The idea of some ghastly presence constantly haunted him, and on more than one occasion he has asked me whether I had on my medical journeys at night ever seen any strange creature or heard the baying of a hound. The latter question he put to me several times, and always with a voice which vibrated with excitement.

'I can well remember driving up to his house in the evening, some three weeks before the fatal event. He chanced to be at his hall door. I had descended from my gig and was standing in front of him, when I saw his eyes fix themselves over my shoulder and stare past me with an expression of the most dreadful horror. I whisked round and had just time to catch a glimpse of something which I took to be a large black calf passing at the head of the drive. So excited and alarmed was he that I was compelled to go down to the spot where the animal had been and look around for it. It was gone, however, and the incident appeared to make the worst impression upon his mind. I stayed with him all the evening, and it was on that occasion, to explain the emotion which he had shown, that he confided to my keeping that narrative which I read to you when first I came. I mention this small episode because it assumes some importance in view of the tragedy which followed, but I was convinced at the time that the matter was entirely trivial and that his excitement had no justification.

'It was at my advice that Sir Charles was about to go to London. His heart was, I knew, affected, and the constant anxiety in which he lived, however chimerical the cause of it might be, was evidently having a serious effect upon his health. I thought that a few months among the distractions of town would send him back a new man. Mr Stapleton, a mutual friend who was much concerned at his state of health, was of the same opinion. At the last instant came this terrible catastrophe.

'On the night of Sir Charles's death Barrymore the butler, who made the discovery, sent Perkins the groom on horseback to me, and as I was sitting up late I was able to reach Baskerville Hall within an hour of the event. I checked and corroborated all the facts which were mentioned at the inquest. I followed the footsteps down the yew alley, I saw the spot at the moor-gate where he seemed to have waited, I remarked the change in the shape of the prints after that point, I noted that there were no other footsteps save those of Barrymore on the soft gravel, and finally I carefully examined the body, which had not been touched until my arrival. Sir Charles lay on his face, his arms out, his fingers dug into the ground, and his features convulsed with some strong emotion to such an extent that I could hardly have sworn to his identity. There was certainly no physical injury of any kind. But one false statement was made by Barrymore at the inquest. He said that there were no traces upon the ground round the body. He did not observe any. But I did – some little distance off, but fresh and clear.'

'Footprints?'

'Footprints.'

'A man's or a woman's?'

Dr Mortimer looked strangely at us for an instant, and his voice sank almost to a whisper as he answered:

'Mr Holmes, they were the footprints of a gigantic hound!'

Look for words and phrases in the first five paragraphs which tell us that:

paragraph 1	the narrator is a medical man
paragraph 2	Sir Charles had an obsession
paragraph 3	Sir Charles is dead
paragraph 4	Dr Mortimer thought Sir Charles was deluded
paragraph 5	Sir Charles's death was not violent.

Do you think it is a good thing or a bad thing for a reader to hear the words of a character who was 'in on the act'; in other words, a person who was present when the events related in the story were taking place? Try and say why.

In the second section of Doyle's story, Holmes's companion Dr Watson becomes the narrator, but the passage consists mostly of a dialogue between Mortimer and Holmes.

I confess that at these words a shudder passed through me. There was a thrill in the doctor's voice which showed that he was himself deeply moved by that which he told us. Holmes leaned forward in his excitement and his eyes had the hard, dry glitter which shot from them when he was keenly interested.

'You saw this?'

'As clearly as I see you.'

'And you said nothing?'

'What was the use?'

'How was it that no one else saw it?'

'The marks were some twenty yards from the body and no one gave them a thought. I don't suppose I should have done so had I not known this legend.'

'There are many sheep-dogs on the moor?'

'No doubt, but this was no sheep-dog.'

'You say it was large?'

'Enormous.'

'But it had not approached the body?'

'No.'

'What sort of night was it?'

'Damp and raw.'

'But not actually raining?'

'No.'

'What is the alley like?'

'There are two lines of old yew hedge, twelve feet high and impenetrable. The walk in the centre is about eight feet across.'

'Is there anything between the hedges and the walk?'

'Yes, there is a strip of grass about six feet broad on either side.'

'I understand that the yew hedge is penetrated at one point by a gate?'

'Yes, the wicket-gate which leads on to the moor.'

'Is there any other opening?'

'None.'

'So that to reach the yew alley one either has to come down it from the house or else to enter it by the moor-gate?'

'There is an exit through a summer-house at the far end.'

'Had Sir Charles reached this?'

'No; he lay about fifty yards from it.'

'Now, tell me, Dr Mortimer – and this is important – the marks which you saw were on the path and not on the grass?'

'No marks could show on the grass.'

'Were they on the same side of the path as the moor-gate?'

'Yes; they were on the edge of the path on the same side as the moor-gate.'

'You interest me exceedingly. Another point. Was the wicket-gate closed?'

'Closed and padlocked.'

'How high was it?'

'About four feet high.'

'Then anyone could have got over it?'

'Yes.'

'And what marks did you see by the wicket-gate?'

'None in particular.'

'Good heaven! Did no one examine?'

'Yes, I examined, myself.'

'And found nothing?'

'It was all very confused. Sir Charles had evidently stood there for five or ten minutes.'

'How do you know that?'

'Because the ash had twice dropped from his cigar.'

'Excellent! This is a colleague, Watson, after our own heart. But the marks?'

'He had left his own marks all over that small patch of gravel. I could discern no others.'

Sherlock Holmes struck his hand against his knee with an impatient gesture.

'If I had only been there!' he cried. 'It is evidently a case of extraordinary interest, and one which presented immense opportunities to the scientific expert. That gravel page upon which I might have read so much has been long ere this smudged by the rain and defaced by the clogs of curious peasants. Oh, Dr Mortimer, Dr Mortimer, to think that you should not have called me in! You have indeed much to answer for.'

(Arthur Conan Doyle *The Hound of the Baskervilles*)

Try to describe the differing reactions of the three characters to the facts of the case, with reference to the first paragraph.

Now describe the 'alley' between the yew hedges, as precisely as you can.

At the end of the passage, does Sherlock Holmes like Dr Mortimer or not? Is there a contrast between the two speeches, as follows:

'This is a colleague, Watson, after our own heart.'

'You have indeed much to answer for.'

What provokes Holmes to make these two speeches?

Read the following extract, and state where you think the incident took place. Circle the words that support your choice.

She cried quietly to herself. In between she said, 'When my father took us travelling, we always went first-class and had a compartment all to ourselves.'

'It is only for a few hours.'

After a while she said, 'I want to go home.' She said it quite loudly, so that people began to look at them both. 'Take me home!' she said, even louder.

'I can go and change our tickets for second-class.'

'I want to go home to my husband!'

People now looked indignantly at Raj. Some of them said, 'Perhaps it is an abduction case.'

Nilima got up from her suitcase. She said to the passengers standing all round, 'Let me through, I want to go back to my husband.' People pushed each other out of the way and a passage was formed for her to get out again. She walked down the carriage and Raj followed with her suitcase. Everyone was very interested in them and those who had been quarrelling stopped doing so and discussed this unusual incident instead.

Raj, walking behind her with her suitcase, kept on saying, 'I can get second-class tickets.' She did not turn round. When they got to the door, she jumped off but he stayed behind and handed her suitcase down to her. The people in the carriage all crowded round the door behind Raj and those who could not get a place rushed to the windows and stuck their heads through the bars. They explained the situation to their friends and relatives who had come to see them off on the platform and they too were very interested and formed a crowd round Nilima.

'Come on,' Nilima said to Raj. 'Come down.'

He looked at the station clock and saw that it was already ten minutes past the official starting time. A man in a cap blew a whistle and waved a green flag.

'Where will you go all by yourself?' Nilima said. 'What will you do?'

'They are brother and sister,' the people on the platform said, but those in the carriage shouted down to them, 'He has taken her away from her husband's house!' A muffled voice spoke through a muffled loudspeaker, doors were slammed and porters shouted.

'You can come to see me every day!' Nilima cried through the noise. 'We will play cards and listen to the radio! It will be just like before!'

Raj found he was still holding her film-magazines. He looked at them and then at her, and he threw them to her without a word. She bent down to pick them up. The onlookers said, 'She is so young and already she has run away from her husband.' Others said, 'They learn such things from films,' and then: 'It was different in our time.'

(Ruth Prawer Jhabvala *Like Birds, Like Fishes*)

The people around the man and woman speculate on their relationship. List the relationships suggested by these people. Do you agree with any of their speculations? What is the attitude of some of the onlookers towards the couple?

What can you tell about the woman from the things she says? Which words indicate this? Could the film magazines indicate anything about the woman?

How would you describe the man? Why do you think he does not respond to the woman's pleas? What do you think is their relationship?

Read the extract again. Choose two adjectives to describe the audience. Give reasons for your choices.

Based on what the onlookers say, do you think they are of the same age as Nilima and Raj? Do the onlookers sympathise with either Nilima or Raj? Do you sympathise with either Nilima or Raj?

Read the following extract, and write down the things you can tell about the narrator.

Rukumani appeared at the door and greeted her grandmother, mother and the visitors. She did not remember any of the visitors but since there were three women and one man, she just said 'uncle' once and 'auntie' three times and wished she could have a little food and then go to bed. Her mother was in a lively mood that night. Drawing her sari round her ample frame, she said to the company, 'You remember Girlie, don't you? Do you think she has changed?'

'Getting near marriageable age,' remarked one of the women.

'Better you don't put ideas into young people's heads,' advised the man, who was probably the husband of the woman. 'When we were young our mother never mentioned the word "marriage" to any of my seven sisters until two days before they were to be married. Everything fix first, then talk. If not, all the young people think of is girl friends, boy friends, what for?'

'Ah,' sighed the wife, 'but nowadays different. Especially when someone like Girlie, so pretty, going to get university degree and all, better to fix everything while still possible to control. Once they grow older, just try to control and see.'

Here the company sighed and there was a momentary silence as they remembered this woman's young daughter whom she had loved so much that she had allowed her to enter the university several years ago, even though she was a girl. This ungrateful child, whom she had looked forward to comforting her old age with dutiful attention and obedience, had proved a disgraceful and shameless hussy by rejecting a match with a promising lawyer who was willing to accept a cheap dowry because of her B.Sc. And had run away to marry a class-mate of hers who was a Chinese Arts graduate. Not only did this prove her shamelessness, it certainly showed everyone how stupid she was to offer herself to a mere B.A. Everyone was too kind to voice their thoughts, although those not involved secretly felt self-satisfied that no such misdemeanour had occurred in their families. Rukumani was feeling too tired and disgusted at the reminder that she was 'Girlie' at home to notice much that was happening. After some further comments on her looks and that she must be too proud to know them now, the visitors collected their scattered children and left.

'Come and take some food,' said Rukumani's mother after the visitors had left. 'You're a lucky girl. You know why Auntie come to see me? Never mind, take first, talk afterwards.'

(Siew Yue Killingley *Everything's Arranged*)

Does the narrator know everything about the characters in the story? Is the narrator one of the characters in the story? How can you tell? Does the narrator sympathise with any of the characters?

What is the purpose of the guests' visit to Rukumani's house? How is this hinted at?

What do the speakers mean when they say:

'Everything fix first, then talk.'

' . . . better to fix everything while still possible to control.'

Read the last long paragraph ('Here the company sighed . . . ') again. List the adjectives used to describe the woman's young daughter. Who chose the adjectives?

What does the following sentence tell readers about the guests: 'Everyone was too kind to voice their thoughts, although those not involved secretly felt self-satisfied that no such misdemeanour had occurred in their families'?

Why did Rukumani feel disgusted? Was she aware of what was happening in her house? What do you think of the actions of the elders in this story?

Read the passage again. Pay close attention to the language used by the narrator and by the speakers in the extract. Is there any difference? Whose language is closer to Standard English? Do you think the characters speak in this way because they are among relatives and friends, or is this how they would normally speak in any company?

A young boy takes upon himself a problem facing his community. Read the following text, and decide what Dan's religious faith is. Why?

'Oh lords, have pity on Kum and Grandma. Be merciful,' Dan raised his voice.

The blazing sun kept beating on him, yet he prayed on. 'Oh lords have mercy on Grandma and all the old people. Grandma eats nothing; she is so old and bony. Her clothes are also old and tattered. Have pity on old people for they cannot dig for yams and taro or chase grasshoppers and catch lizards for food.'

His endurance was that of a child's. Curiosity forced him to open his eyes to see the effect of his rite. But to his dismay the skies remained cloudless; there was no cool breeze to herald the approach of rain.

Heavy with disappointment, the boy sighed and shifted. Perhaps his suffering was seen as a child's fancy, a mockery of the solemn and sacred rite reserved for monks and old men.

'My lords,' Dan made another attempt, but no more words came.

The dehydrating heat of the sun was immense. He trembled at the thought that he would be consequently punished by the spirits for his fanciful action.

There seemed to be so much of the cynicism in life, the universal suffering, sorrow, the primeval bitterness and the futility of all things.

Now it was his own seriousness that frightened him so that he shuddered. But there was no way out now except to prove his sacrifice to the lords.

He must offer his blood to the lords.

The knife taken from his father's toolbox flashed in the noon sun.

Only then was he convinced that he would not fail, for the sacrifice would be so immense that the lords would take pity on him and so yield rain.

But the sharp metal opened the wound deeper than intended on his wrist.

Dan winced with pain, throwing the instrument away. The flow of blood made him giddy. Still he lifted the wounded hand towards the sun for the lords to see, till he fell.

Lying flat on his back, Dan tried to call out for help but could not. His throat was so dry, and he trembled, seeing that darkness was descending quickly on him.

Yet he strained in sheer effort to hear any rumble of thunder that would mean rain.

(Pira Sudham *Rains*)

What do the first two paragraphs tell you about Dan? Can you suggest one word to describe his attitude in his prayer? Why does Dan doubt the power of his prayer? Do you think he is sincere?

Why does he think the lords might consider his suffering as 'a child's fancy'? What does the word 'fancy' mean in this context? What are some other meanings of this word?

Why did Dan eventually cut his wrist? Do you think he meant the cut to be fatal?

What do you think the following expressions mean:

- 'cynicism in life'
- 'universal suffering'
- 'primeval bitterness'
- 'the futility of all things'?

Whose thoughts are these: Dan's, or the narrator's? Do you agree with the view of life presented in these expressions?

Would you consider Dan's act as suicide or sacrifice? What is your reaction to Dan's cutting his wrist?

Now read the following extract. Who is 'her' in this extract? What do you think Framton's relationship is with these people?

'Her great tragedy happened just three years ago,' said the child; 'that would be since your sister's time.'

'Her tragedy?' asked Framton; somehow in this restful country spot tragedies seemed out of place.

'You may wonder why we keep that window wide open on an October afternoon,' said the niece, indicating a large French window that opened on to a lawn.

'It is quite warm for the time of year,' said Framton; 'but has that window got anything to do with the tragedy?'

'Out through that window, three years ago to a day, her husband and her two young brothers went off for their day's shooting. They never came back. In crossing the moor to their favourite snipe-shooting ground they were all three engulfed in a treacherous piece of bog. It had been that dreadful wet summer, you know, and places that were safe in other years gave way suddenly without warning. Their bodies were never recovered. That was the dreadful part of it.' Here the child's voice lost its self-possessed note and became falteringly human. 'Poor aunt always thinks that they will come back some day, they and the little brown spaniel that was lost with them, and walk in at that window just as they used to do. That is why the window is kept open every evening till it is quite dusk. Poor dear aunt, she has often told me how they went out, her husband with his white waterproof coat over his arm, and Ronnie, her youngest brother, singing "Bertie, why do you bound?" as he always did to tease her, because she said it got on her nerves. Do you know, sometimes on still, quiet evenings like this, I almost get a creepy feeling that they will all walk in through that window – '

She broke off with a little shudder.

Complete the details about the 'great tragedy', under the following headings:

who were involved

....

....

when it happened

....

....

where it happened

....

....

Now pick out the words used to describe the way the child narrates the incident. Who do you think chose the adjectives? What effect did the way she narrates the incident have on you?

Now read the whole story. Vera is described as Mrs Sappleton's niece. In what other ways is she referred to?

'My aunt will be down presently, Mr Nuttel,' said a very self-possessed young lady of fifteen; 'in the meantime you must try and put up with me.'

Framton Nuttel endeavoured to say the correct something which should duly flatter the niece of the moment without unduly discounting the aunt that was to come. Privately he doubted more than ever whether these formal visits on a succession of total strangers would do much towards helping the nerve cure which he was supposed to be undergoing.

'I know how it will be,' his sister had said when he was preparing to migrate to this rural retreat: 'you will bury yourself down there and not speak to a living soul, and your nerves will be worse than ever from moping. I shall just give you letters of introduction to all the people I know there. Some of them, as far as I can remember, were quite nice.'

Framton wondered whether Mrs Sappleton, the lady to whom he was presenting one of the letters of introduction, came into the nice division.

'Do you know many of the people round here?' asked the niece, when she judged that they had had sufficient silent communion.

'Hardly a soul,' said Framton. 'My sister was staying here, at the rectory, you know, some four years ago, and she gave me letters of introduction to some of the people here.'

He made the last statement in a tone of distinct regret.

'Then you know practically nothing about my aunt?' pursued the self-possessed young lady.

'Only her name and address,' admitted the caller. He was wondering whether Mrs Sappleton was in the married or widowed state. An undefinable something about the room seemed to suggest masculine habitation.

'Her great tragedy happened just three years ago,' said the child; 'that would be since your sister's time.'

'Her tragedy?' asked Framton; somehow in this restful country spot tragedies seemed out of place.

'You may wonder why we keep that window wide open on an October afternoon,' said the niece, indicating a large French window that opened on to a lawn.

'It is quite warm for the time of year,' said Framton; 'but has that window got anything to do with the tragedy?'

'Out through that window, three years ago to a day, her husband and her two young brothers went off for their day's shooting. They never came back. In crossing the moor to their favourite snipe-shooting ground they were all three engulfed in a treacherous piece of bog. It had been that dreadful wet summer, you know, and places that were safe in other years gave way suddenly without warning. Their bodies were never recovered. That was the dreadful part of it.' Here the child's voice lost its self-possessed note and became falteringly human. 'Poor aunt always thinks that they will come back some day, they and the little brown spaniel that was lost with them, and walk in at that window just as they used to do. That is why the window is kept open every evening till it is quite dusk. Poor dear aunt, she has often told me how they went out, her husband with his white waterproof coat over his arm, and Ronnie, her youngest brother, singing "Bertie, why do you bound?" as he always did to tease her, because she said it got on her nerves. Do you know, sometimes on still, quiet evenings like this, I almost get a creepy feeling that they will all walk in through that window – '

She broke off with a little shudder. It was a relief to Framton when the aunt bustled into the room with a whirl of apologies for being late in making her appearance.

'I hope Vera has been amusing you?' she said.

'She has been very interesting,' said Framton.

'I hope you don't mind the open window,' said Mrs Sappleton briskly: 'my husband and brothers will be home directly from shooting, and they always come in this way. They've been out for snipe in the marshes today, so they'll make a fine mess over my poor carpets. So like you men-folk, isn't it?'

She rattled on cheerfully about the shooting and the scarcity of birds, and the prospects for duck in the winter. To Framton it was all purely horrible. He made a desperate but only partially successful effort to turn the talk on to a less ghastly topic; he was conscious that his hostess was giving him only a fragment of her attention, and her eyes were constantly straying past him to the open window and the lawn beyond. It was certainly an unfortunate coincidence that he should have paid his visit on this tragic anniversary.

'The doctors agree in ordering me complete rest, an absence of mental excitement, and avoidance of anything in the nature of violent physical exercise,' announced Framton, who laboured under the tolerably widespread delusion that total strangers and chance acquaintances are hungry for the least detail of one's ailments and infirmities, their cause and cure. 'On the matter of diet they are not so much in agreement,' he continued.

'No?' said Mrs Sappleton, in a voice which only replaced a yawn at the last moment. Then she suddenly brightened into alert attention – but not to what Framton was saying.

'Here they are at last!' she cried. 'Just in time for tea, and don't they look as if they were muddy up to the eyes!'

Framton shivered slightly and turned towards the niece with a look intended to convey sympathetic comprehension. The child was staring out through the open window with dazed horror in her eyes. In a chill shock of nameless fear, Framton swung round in his seat and looked in the same direction.

In the deepening twilight three figures were walking across the lawn towards the window; they all carried guns under their arms, and one of them was additionally burdened with a white coat hung over his shoulders. A tired brown spaniel kept close at their heels. Noiselessly they neared the house, and then a hoarse young voice chanted out of the dusk: 'I said, Bertie, why do you bound?'

Framton grabbed wildly at his stick and hat; the hall-door, the gravel-drive, and the front gate were dimly noted stages in his headlong retreat. A cyclist coming along the road had to run into the hedge to avoid imminent collision.

'Here we are, my dear,' said the bearer of the white mackintosh, coming in through the window; 'fairly muddy, but most of it's dry. Who was that who bolted out as we came up?'

'A most extraordinary man, a Mr Nuttel,' said Mrs Sappleton; 'could only talk about his illnesses, and dashed off without a word of good-bye or apology when you arrived. One would think he had seen a ghost.'

'I expect it was the spaniel,' said the niece calmly; 'he told me he had a horror of dogs. He was once hunted into a cemetery somewhere on the banks of the Ganges by a pack of pariah dogs, and had to spend the night in a newly dug grave with the creatures snarling and grinning and foaming just above him. Enough to make anyone lose their nerve.'

Romance at short notice was her speciality.

(Saki *The Open Window*)

Compare your answers around the class. Look at the other ways Vera is named in the story. What effect did they have on you as you first read the story? Did you believe her?

What do we learn about Framton's problem? Why do you think the writer gives the reader so much information about Framton's emotional condition? Why was Framton visiting Mrs Sappleton?

Vera's stories work on her listeners to a large extent because of ignorance on their part. What does Vera do before she tells Framton her story? What questions does she ask him? Why does she do this?

Why is Framton horrified by what Mrs Sappleton says to him? Why does she not understand why he ran away? How does Vera explain Framton's strange behaviour, towards the end of the story? Do you think her relatives believe her? What does the last line of the story tell you about Vera? Do you think her family knows this?

Did you find the story sad, funny, exciting, silly, or what?

Can you pick out different accents and tell where a person comes from by the way they speak? Discuss variations in voice and manners of speech that you are familiar with.

Can you imitate anyone's accent? Why does it become funny sometimes, when people imitate voices?

In the next text, the conflict is between 'upper-class' speech and the cockney of the Flower Girl, who is talking to herself while the Gentleman and the Note Taker discuss her. As you read, think what voices you could use to give colour and variety to the characters' words.

THE FLOWER GIRL: Poor girl! Hard enough for her to live without being worrited and chivied.

THE GENTLEMAN [*returning to his former place on the Note Taker's left*]: How do you do it, if I may ask?

THE NOTE TAKER: Simply phonetics. The science of speech. That's my profession: also my hobby. Happy is the man who can make a living by his hobby! You can spot an Irishman or a Yorkshireman by his brogue. *I* can place any man within six miles. I can place him within two miles in London. Sometimes within two streets.

THE FLOWER GIRL: Ought to be ashamed of himself, unmanly coward!

THE GENTLEMAN: But is there a living in that?

THE NOTE TAKER: Oh yes. Quite a fat one. This is an age of upstarts. Men begin in Kentish Town with £80 a year, and end in Park Lane with a hundred thousand. They want to drop Kentish Town; but they give themselves away every time they open their mouths. Now I can teach them –

THE FLOWER GIRL: Let him mind his own business and leave a poor girl –

THE NOTE TAKER [*explosively*]: Woman: cease this detestable boohooing instantly; or else seek the shelter of some other place of worship.

THE FLOWER GIRL [*with feeble defiance*]: I've a right to be here if I like, same as you.

THE NOTE TAKER: A woman who utters such depressing sounds has no right to be anywhere – no right to live. Remember that you are a human being with a soul and the divine gift of articulate speech: that your native language is the language of Shakespeare and Milton and The Bible; and don't sit there crooning like a bilious pigeon.

THE FLOWER GIRL [quite overwhelmed, looking up at him in mingled wonder and deprecation without daring to raise her head]: Ah-ah-ah-ow-ow-ow-oo!

THE NOTE TAKER [whipping out his book]: Heavens! what a sound! [He writes; then holds out the book and reads, reproducing her vowels exactly.] Ah-ah- ah-ow-ow-ow-oo!

THE FLOWER GIRL [tickled by the performance, and laughing in spite of herself]: Garn!

THE NOTE TAKER: You see this creature with her kerbstone English: the English that will keep her in the gutter to the end of her days. Well, sir, in three months I could pass that girl off as a duchess at an ambassador's garden party. I could even get her a place as lady's maid or shop assistant, which requires better English.

THE FLOWER GIRL: What's that you say?

THE NOTE TAKER: Yes, you squashed cabbage leaf, you disgrace to the noble architecture of these columns, you incarnate insult to the English language: I could pass you off as the Queen of Sheba. [To the Gentleman.] Can you believe that?

THE GENTLEMAN: Of course I can. I am myself a student of Indian dialects; and –

THE NOTE TAKER [eagerly]: Are you? Do you know Colonel Pickering, the author of Spoken Sanscrit?

THE GENTLEMAN: I am Colonel Pickering. Who are you?

THE NOTE TAKER: Henry Higgins, author of Higgins's Universal Alphabet.

PICKERING [with enthusiasm]: I came from India to meet you.

HIGGINS: I was going to India to meet you.

PICKERING: Where do you live?

HIGGINS: 27A Wimpole Street. Come and see me tomorrow.

PICKERING: I'm at the Carlton. Come with me now and let's have a jaw over some supper.

HIGGINS: Right you are.

THE FLOWER GIRL [to Pickering, as he passes her]: Buy a flower, kind gentleman. I'm short for my lodging.

PICKERING: I really havn't any change. I'm sorry. [He goes away.]

HIGGINS [shocked at the girl's mendacity]: Liar. You said you could charge half-a-crown.

THE FLOWER GIRL [rising in desperation]: You ought to be stuffed with nails, you ought. [*Flinging the basket at his feet.*] Take the whole blooming basket for sixpence.

The Note Taker (Henry Higgins) has strong views on the Flower Girl's way of speaking. What would he do to her? Are his views exaggerated, or realistic? What is wrong with her English, in the opinion of Higgins? What does he propose to do about it?

What aspects do you find modern? And what aspects are more old-fashioned?

What do you think the difference might be between *dialect* and *accent*? Discuss this and compare your ideas. How important is it to speak 'properly', in your opinion?

In this play, you will find lots of non-Standard English, where accent (largely the sound of the speech, the pronunciation) and various other features of the dialect (vocabulary, grammar, idiom) are contrasted between 'low' cockney speech and 'high' standard, upper-class English. How do you think the following could be put into 'Standard' English?

- You just show me what you've wrote about me
- Nah then Freddy, look wh' y' gowin, dear
- But I aint got sixty pounds
- I washed my face and hands afore I come, I did
- Garn!

Whenever you come across some cockney speech (or any dialect in any text) you have to try to hear it, as well as work out the grammar.

Our next scene, later in the play, gives Liza (the Flower Girl) her first taste of 'proper' conversation in society, after some teaching by Professor Higgins. As you read, can you tell what parts of her conversation are practised, and where she 'slips' into her own more natural speech?

MRS HIGGINS [*at last, conversationally*]: Will it rain, do you think?
LIZA: The shallow depression in the west of these islands is likely to move slowly in an easterly direction. There are no indications of any great change in the barometrical situation.
FREDDY: Ha! ha! how awfully funny!
LIZA: What is wrong with that, young man? I bet I got it right.

FREDDY: Killing!

MRS EYNSFORD HILL: I'm sure I hope it won't turn cold. There's so much influenza about. It runs right through our whole family regularly every spring.

LIZA [darkly]: My aunt died of influenza: so they said.

MRS EYNSFORD HILL [clicks her tongue sympathetically]: !!!

LIZA [in the same tragic tone]: But it's my belief they done the old woman in.

MRS HIGGINS [puzzled]: Done her in?

LIZA: Y-e-e-e-es, Lord love you! Why should she die of influenza? She come through diphtheria right enough the year before. I saw her with my own eyes. Fairly blue with it, she was. They all thought she was dead; but my father he kept ladling gin down her throat til she came to so sudden that she bit the bowl off the spoon.

MRS EYNSFORD HILL [startled]: Dear me!

LIZA [piling up the indictment]: What call would a woman with that strength in her have to die of influenza? What become of her new straw hat that should have come to me? Somebody pinched it; and what I say is, them as pinched it done her in.

MRS EYNSFORD HILL: What does doing her in mean?

HIGGINS [hastily]: Oh, that's the new small talk. To do a person in means to kill them.

MRS EYNSFORD HILL [to Liza, horrified]: You surely don't believe that your aunt was killed?

LIZA: Do I not! Them she lived with would have killed her for a hat-pin, let alone a hat.

MRS EYNSFORD HILL: But it can't have been right for your father to pour spirits down her throat like that. It might have killed her.

LIZA: Not her. Gin was mother's milk to her. Besides, he'd poured so much down his own throat that he knew the good of it.

MRS EYNSFORD HILL: Do you mean that he drank?

LIZA: Drank! My word! Something chronic.

MRS EYNSFORD HILL: How dreadful for you!

LIZA: Not a bit. It never did him no harm what I could see. But then he did not keep it up regular. [Cheerfully.] On the burst, as you might say, from time to time. And always more agreeable when he had a drop in. When he was out of work, my mother used to give him fourpence and tell him to go out and not come back until he'd drunk himself cheerful and loving-like. There's lots of women has to make their husbands drunk to make them fit to live with. [Now quite at her ease.] You see, it's like this. If a man has a bit of a conscience, it always takes him when he's sober; and then it makes him low-spirited. A drop of booze just takes that off and makes him happy. [To Freddy, who is in convulsions of suppressed laughter.] Here! what are you sniggering at?

FREDDY: The new small talk. You do it so awfully well.

LIZA: If I was doing it proper, what was you laughing at? [*To Higgins.*] Have I said anything I oughtn't?

MRS HIGGINS [*interposing*]: Not at all, Miss Doolittle.

LIZA: Well, that's a mercy, anyhow. [*Expansively.*] What I always say is –

HIGGINS [*rising and looking at his watch*]: Ahem!

LIZA [*looking round at him; taking the hint; and rising*]: Well: I must go. [*They all rise. Freddy goes to the door.*] So pleased to have met you. Goodbye. [*She shakes hands with Mrs Higgins.*]

MRS HIGGINS: Goodbye.

LIZA: Goodbye, Colonel Pickering.

PICKERING: Goodbye, Miss Doolittle. [*They shake hands.*]

LIZA [*nodding to the others*]: Goodbye, all.

FREDDY [*opening the door for her*]: Are you walking across the Park, Miss Doolittle? If so –

LIZA [*with perfectly elegant diction*]: Walk! Not bloody likely. [*Sensation.*] I am going in a taxi. [*She goes out.*]

(George Bernard Shaw *Pygmalion*)

What makes the scene funny, do you think? Why does Freddy find it so funny? What do you think his role is?

Do the stage directions help you to imagine the scene and the way the characters speak? Or would you prefer not to have them, and to imagine it for yourself?

'Done her in' and 'Something chronic' are examples of Liza's use of idiom. Pick out some other grammatical variations, and say what you think they would be in 'Standard' English.

Issues

This is social comedy. Could the same sort of comedy be made in your own social circumstances, or in your own linguistic situation? Why, or why not?

In Britain, many would say the situation has not changed since this play was written in 1912. Indeed, a recent book[3] uses *Pygmalion* as an example to show how accent still does matter, and goes on to give many examples of recent 'discrimination' because of accent. Do you think such discrimination is understandable? Could it

---

3 John Honey, *Does Accent Matter? The Pygmalion Factor*, Faber and Faber, 1989/1991.

happen elsewhere that you know of? How does it reflect other kinds of discrimination, do you think?

Compare and contrast

After you have read the whole play, you might like to compare it to and contrast it with the musical version, *My Fair Lady*.[4] How close is the musical to the original play? How many significant differences do you find? Does the musical still give the basic conflicts and issues of the play, or not?

Why do you think they changed the title? Check out the name 'Pygmalion', and decide how suitable a title it is.

We are now going to look again at one of the brief scenes we looked at in part I, section 3. Gwendolen and Cecily are having tea together. As you read the scene, try to mark the moments when the mood or the atmosphere changes.

CECILY [*rather shy and confidingly*]: Dearest Gwendolen, there is no reason why I should make a secret of it to you. Our little county newspaper is sure to chronicle the fact next week. Mr Ernest Worthing and I are engaged to be married.

GWENDOLEN [*quite politely, rising*]: My darling Cecily, I think there must be some slight error. Mr Ernest Worthing is engaged to me. The announcement will appear in the *Morning Post* on Saturday at the latest.

CECILY [*very politely, rising*]: I am afraid you must be under some misconception. Ernest proposed to me exactly ten minutes ago. [*Shows diary.*]

GWENDOLEN [*examines diary through her lorgnette carefully*]: It is very curious, for he asked me to be his wife yesterday afternoon at 5.30. If you would care to verify the incident, pray do so. [*Produces diary of her own.*] I never travel without my diary. One should always have something sensational to read in the train. I am so sorry, dear Cecily, if it is any disappointment to you, but I am afraid I have the prior claim.

CECILY: It would distress me more than I can tell you, dear Gwendolen, if it caused you any mental or physical anguish, but I feel bound to point out that since Ernest proposed to you he clearly has changed his mind.

GWENDOLEN [*meditatively*]: If the poor fellow has been entrapped into any foolish promise I shall consider it my duty to rescue him at once, and with a firm hand.

4 Available on video.

CECILY [*thoughtfully and sadly*]: Whatever unfortunate entanglement my dear boy may have got into, I will never reproach him with it after we are married.

GWENDOLEN: Do you allude to me, Miss Cardew, as an entanglement? You are presumptuous. On an occasion of this kind it becomes more than a moral duty to speak one's mind. It becomes a pleasure.

CECILY: Do you suggest, Miss Fairfax, that I entrapped Ernest into an engagement? How dare you? This is no time for wearing the shallow mask of manners. When I see a spade I call it a spade.

GWENDOLEN [*satirically*]: I am glad to say that I have never seen a spade. It is obvious that our social spheres have been widely different.

[Enter MERRIMAN, *followed by the footman. He carries a salver, table cloth, and plate stand. CECILY is about to retort. The presence of the servants exercises a restraining influence, under which both girls chafe.*]

MERRIMAN: Shall I lay tea here as usual, Miss?

CECILY [*sternly, in a calm voice*]: Yes, as usual. [MERRIMAN *begins to clear table and lay cloth. A long pause. CECILY and GWENDOLEN glare at each other.*]

GWENDOLEN: Are there many interesting walks in the vicinity, Miss Cardew?

CECILY: Oh! yes! a great many. From the top of one of the hills quite close one can see five counties.

GWENDOLEN: Five counties! I don't think I should like that; I hate crowds.

CECILY [*sweetly*]: I suppose that is why you live in town? [GWENDOLEN *bites her lip, and beats her foot nervously with her parasol.*]

GWENDOLEN [*looking around*]: Quite a well-kept garden this is, Miss Cardew.

CECILY: So glad you like it, Miss Fairfax.

GWENDOLEN: I had no idea there were any flowers in the country.

CECILY: Oh, flowers are as common here, Miss Fairfax, as people are in London.

GWENDOLEN: Personally I cannot understand how anybody manages to exist in the country, if anybody who is anybody does. The country always bores me to death.

CECILY: Ah! This is what the newspapers call agricultural depression, is it not? I believe the aristocracy are suffering very much from it just at present. It is almost an epidemic amongst them, I have been told. May I offer you some tea, Miss Fairfax?

GWENDOLEN [*with elaborate politeness*]: Thank you. [*Aside.*] Detestable girl! But I require tea.

CECILY [*sweetly*]: Sugar?

GWENDOLEN [*superciliously*]: No, thank you. Sugar is not fashionable any more. [CECILY *looks angrily at her, takes up the tongs and puts four lumps of sugar into the cup.*]

CECILY [*severely*]: Cake or bread and butter?

GWENDOLEN [*in a bored manner*]: Bread and butter, please. Cake is rarely seen at the best houses nowadays.

CECILY [*cuts a very large slice of cake and puts it on the tray*]: Hand that to Miss Fairfax.

[MERRIMAN *does so, and goes out with footman.* GWENDOLEN *drinks the tea and makes a grimace. Puts down cup at once, reaches out her hand to the bread and butter, looks at it, and finds it is cake. Rises in indignation.*]

GWENDOLEN: You have filled my tea with lumps of sugar, and though I asked most distinctly for bread and butter, you have given me cake. I am known for the gentleness of my disposition, and the extraordinary sweetness of my nature, but I warn you, Miss Cardew, you may go too far.

CECILY [*rising*]: To save my poor, innocent, trusting boy from the machinations of any other girl there are no lengths to which I would not go.

GWENDOLEN: From the moment I saw you I distrusted you. I felt that you were false and deceitful. I am never deceived in such matters. My first impressions of people are invariably right.

CECILY: It seems to me, Miss Fairfax, that I am trespassing on your valuable time. No doubt you have many other calls of a similar character to make in the neighbourhood.

Pick out words and phrases which indicate the two characters' politeness to each other. How often are they not genuine, do you think? Is this like the underlying discourse we found earlier?

What can you tell about the society and culture the characters live in?

Vocabulary

There are quite a few unfamiliar words: without necessarily checking them in the dictionary, try ways of sounding them so that they come out as funny, or angry, or serious. Finding the music of the sentences will give you a sense of the *attitude* of the character.

If you want to look up some of the words, try writing the sentences in simpler words. Is the effect the same?

Proxemics and performance

During the tea party, how would you answer the usual *wh*-questions: Where are they? What are they doing (sitting, standing, moving about)? What are they looking at? What do they mean in each utterance? What speed is the scene (fast, slow)? What are they wearing? What distance are they from each other (close, distant)?

How long are the pauses, do you think? What do the characters do during the pauses? Are they looking at each other? Try performing some of the scene, or the whole scene, in various ways.

Now read on. Something happens when the men appear. As you read, mark again where there are changes in the women's attitudes.

[*Enter* JACK.]

GWENDOLEN [*catching sight of him*]: Ernest! My own Ernest!

JACK: Gwendolen! Darling! [*Offers to kiss her.*]

GWENDOLEN [*drawing back*]: A moment! May I ask if you are engaged to be married to this young lady? [*Points to* CECILY.]

JACK [*laughing*]: To dear little Cecily! Of course not! What could have put such an idea into your pretty little head?

GWENDOLEN: Thank you. You may! [*Offers her cheek.*]

CECILY [*very sweetly*]: I knew there must be some misunderstanding, Miss Fairfax. The gentleman whose arm is at present round your waist is my guardian, Mr John Worthing.

GWENDOLEN: I beg your pardon?

CECILY: This is Uncle Jack.

GWENDOLEN [*receding*]: Jack! Oh!

[*Enter* ALGERNON.]

CECILY: Here is Ernest.

ALGERNON [*goes straight over to* CECILY *without noticing anyone else*]: My own love! [*Offers to kiss her.*]

CECILY [*drawing back*]: A moment, Ernest! May I ask you – are you engaged to be married to this young lady?

ALGERNON [*looking round*]: To what young lady? Good heavens! Gwendolen!

CECILY: Yes: to good heavens, Gwendolen, I mean to Gwendolen.

ALGERNON [*laughing*]: Of course not! What could have put such an idea into your pretty little head?

CECILY: Thank you. [*Presenting her cheek to be kissed.*] You may. [ALGERNON *kisses her.*]

GWENDOLEN: I felt there was some slight error, Miss Cardew. The gentleman who is now embracing you is my cousin, Mr Algernon Moncrieff.

CECILY [*breaking away from* ALGERNON]: Algernon Moncrieff! Oh! [*The two girls move towards each other and put their arms round each other's waists as if for protection.*]

CECILY: Are you called Algernon?

ALGERNON: I cannot deny it.

CECILY: Oh!

GWENDOLEN: Is your name really John?

JACK [*standing rather proudly*]: I could deny it if I liked. I could deny anything if I liked. But my name certainly is John. It has been John for years.

CECILY [*to* GWENDOLEN]: A gross deception has been practised on both of us.

GWENDOLEN: My poor wounded Cecily!

CECILY: My sweet wronged Gwendolen!

GWENDOLEN [*slowly and seriously*]: You will call me sister, will you not? [*They embrace.* JACK *and* ALGERNON *groan and walk up and down.*]

CECILY [*rather brightly*]: There is just one question I would like to be allowed to ask my guardian.

GWENDOLEN: An admirable idea! Mr Worthing, there is just one question I would like to be permitted to put to you. Where is your brother Ernest? We are both engaged to be married to your brother Ernest, so it is a matter of some importance to us to know where your brother Ernest is at present.

JACK [*slowly and hesitatingly*]: Gwendolen – Cecily – it is very painful for me to be forced to speak the truth. It is the first time in my life that I have ever been reduced to such a painful position, and I am really quite inexperienced in doing anything of the kind. However, I will tell you quite frankly that I have no brother Ernest. I have no brother at all. I never had a brother in my life, and I certainly have not the smallest intention of ever having one in the future.

CECILY [*surprised*]: No brother at all?

JACK [*cheerily*]: None!

GWENDOLEN [*severely*]: Had you never a brother of any kind?

JACK [*pleasantly*]: Never. Not even of any kind.

GWENDOLEN: I am afraid it is quite clear, Cecily, that neither of us is engaged to be married to anyone.

CECILY: It is not a very pleasant position for a young girl suddenly to find herself in. Is it?

GWENDOLEN: Let us go into the house. They will hardly venture to come after us there.

CECILY: No, men are so cowardly, aren't they?

[*They retire into the house with scornful looks.*]

(Oscar Wilde *The Importance of Being Earnest*)

What can you tell about the men?

Each of the girls says 'Oh!' when she discovers that her fiancé is not called Ernest. What emotion does 'Oh!' express in this case? What other emotions can 'Oh!' express? How would you say it, to make it express different emotions? (You could perhaps turn to the person sitting beside you and say 'Oh' and see if he or she can identify the emotion you are trying to express – but ask your teacher's agreement first!)

Jack and Algernon have deceived Gwendolen and Cecily respectively into believing that they are called Ernest. Both have the guilty motive of using an assumed identity in order to seek amusement (Jack in town, Algernon in the country) and thereby also to avoid unwelcome obligations at home. What do you think is the reaction of the men to the revelation of their true identities?

Why does Jack speak his last long speech 'slowly and hesitatingly'?

How do you think the men might explain their deception to the girls? (The 'explanation scene' is given on pages 218–20.)

We are now going to read three of the best-known speeches from plays by William Shakespeare.

A soliloquy is a very special moment in a play: the character speaks his or her thoughts, with no one else onstage, so the audience can see right into the heart of the character. Hamlet's 'To be or not to be' is probably the most famous soliloquy ever. Hamlet is deciding between life and death, whether to go on living or to die. As you read, see which way he decides to go, and see if you can notice some of his reasons.

HAMLET: To be, or not to be, that is the question,
    Whether 'tis nobler in the mind to suffer
    The slings and arrows of outrageous fortune,
    Or to take arms against a sea of troubles,
    And by opposing, end them. To die, to sleep –
    No more, and by a sleep to say we end
    The heart-ache, and the thousand natural shocks
    That flesh is heir to; 'tis a consummation
    Devoutly to be wished. To die, to sleep;
    To sleep, perchance to dream. Ay, there's the rub;
    For in that sleep of death what dreams may come
    When we have shuffled off this mortal coil
    Must give us pause – there's the respect
    That makes calamity of so long life:
    For who would bear the whips and scorns of time,

Th' oppressor's wrong, the proud man's contumely,
The pangs of despis'd love, the law's delay,
The insolence of office, and the spurns
That patient merit of th' unworthy takes,
When he himself might his quietus make
With a bare bodkin; who would fardels bear,
To grunt and sweat under a weary life,
But that the dread of something after death,
The undiscovered country, from whose bourn
No traveller returns, puzzles the will,
And makes us rather bear those ills we have,
Than fly to others that we know not of?
Thus conscience doth make cowards of us all,
And thus the native hue of resolution
Is sicklied o'er with the pale cast of thought,
And enterprises of great pitch and moment
With this regard their currents turn awry,
And lose the name of action.

(William Shakespeare *Hamlet*)

Is the ending positive or negative – or ambiguous?

What words and phrases can you find in the text which describe death, life after death, and fear of death? Mark them, then see how many words or phrases speak about life.

Hamlet lists seven things about life which are irritating. 'Fardels', for instance, means heavy loads or burdens that we have to carry. Can you express the other things on the list in your own words? Discuss what you think they mean. Are they still relevant today? Would you add other things to the list?

There are several images in the speech: 'a sea of troubles', for instance. Find some others – are they all about the sea, or are they each different from the others? Do you find them memorable, confusing, clear, appropriate, unnecessary? Discuss your reactions to them.

For Hamlet, sleep and death seem to be the same thing in some ways. How are they *not* the same?

He talks of 'us' rather than 'I'. Do you find the speech personal or more universal?

'Ay, there's the rub' is usually seen as the pivotal phrase around which the whole argument turns. Is the 'rub' positive or negative? Why are the dreams important?

174

Vocabulary

If you want to know some of the words and phrases in the text, try matching them with these more familiar words. (Not all the words in the text are given synonyms, though! And some of the synonyms might be found more than once. Reading down the following columns, they are in the same order as in the text.)

weapons	arrogance	region
climax	rejections	colour
perhaps	final peace	importance
heart of the matter	needle	consideration
left this life	burdens	off course
disaster	fear	

Issues

Hamlet actually contemplates suicide. Do you think suicide could ever be justified? Why does he seem to want to die?

Is living an act of courage; or is it cowardice, as Hamlet suggests, that keeps us going?

The next speech is almost a soliloquy, but Jaques in *As You Like It* is, in fact, speaking to a group of people who do not interrupt. His speech begins with a famous metaphor, in which the 'stage' or the theatre is compared to the whole life of man. As you read, mark the seven 'ages' of man.

JAQUES: All the world's a stage,
    And all the men and women merely players;
    They have their exits and their entrances;
    And one man in his time plays many parts,
    His acts being seven ages. At first the infant,
    Mewling and puking in the nurse's arms;
    Then the whining school-boy, with his satchel
    And shining morning face, creeping like snail
    Unwillingly to school. And then the lover,
    Sighing like furnace, with a woeful ballad
    Made to his mistress' eyebrow. Then a soldier,
    Full of strange oaths, and bearded like the pard,
    Jealous in honour, sudden and quick in quarrel,

Seeking the bubble reputation
Even in the cannon's mouth. And then the justice,
In fair round belly with good capon lin'd,
With eyes severe and beard of formal cut,
Full of wise saws and modern instances;
And so he plays his part. The sixth age shifts
Into the lean and slipper'd pantaloon,
With spectacles on nose and pouch on side,
His youthful hose, well sav'd, a world too wide
For his shrunk shank; and his big manly voice,
Turning again toward childish treble, pipes
And whistles in his sound. Last scene of all,
That ends this strange eventful history,
Is second childishness and mere oblivion;
Sans teeth, sans eyes, sans taste, sans everything.

(William Shakespeare *As You Like It*)

Describe each age in just one word, like 'baby' for the first age.

What is the tone of Jaques's words by the end of the speech: serious, positive, negative, humorous, cynical, or what? Look again at the ages – are the adjectives that describe them the same as you would choose? How much do they tell you about the attitude of Jaques? Do you think he chose all the adjectives?

What is the tone of Jaques's words about the lover? What do you think Jaques thinks about love? Into which of the seven ages would you put Jaques himself? Do you agree with his view of old age?

How much of a change in tone do you find between the beginning and the end of the speech?

Vocabulary

What do you think 'sans' means? What has the old man ('pantaloon') saved? What animal has a beard like the soldier's? What does the infant do? What words describe the statements of the justice? What has happened to the old man's legs and voice?

How many references to the theatre and the stage can you find?

Which character is more positive, Hamlet or Jaques? Which is the more realistic is his views of life? Is the overall metaphor of the stage a good one, in your opinion? Do you play different parts in your own life?

Our final big speech is a political one. Mark Antony is speaking to a crowd after the death of Julius Caesar, so his style is very rhetorical and persuasive. As you read, decide what you think his attitude is to Brutus.

ANTONY: Friends, Romans, countrymen, lend me your ears;
I come to bury Caesar, not to praise him.
The evil that men do lives after them;
The good is oft interred with their bones;
So let it be with Caesar. The noble Brutus
Hath told you Caesar was ambitious.
If it were so, it was a grievous fault;
And grievously hath Caesar answer'd it.
Here, under leave of Brutus and the rest –
For Brutus is an honourable man;
So are they all, all honourable men –
Come I to speak in Caesar's funeral.
He was my friend, faithful and just to me;
But Brutus says he was ambitious,
And Brutus is an honourable man.
He hath brought many captives home to Rome,
Whose ransoms did the general coffers fill;
Did this in Caesar seem ambitious?
When that the poor have cried, Caesar hath wept;
Ambition should be made of sterner stuff.
Yet Brutus says he was ambitious;
And Brutus is an honourable man.
You all did see that on the Lupercal
I thrice presented him a kingly crown,
Which he did thrice refuse. Was this ambition?
Yet Brutus says he was ambitious;
And sure he is an honourable man.
I speak not to disprove what Brutus spoke,
But here I am to speak what I do know.
You all did love him once, not without cause;
What cause withholds you, then, to mourn for him?
O judgment, thou art fled to brutish beasts,
And men have lost their reason! Bear with me;
My heart is in the coffin there with Caesar,
And I must pause till it come back to me.

(William Shakespeare *Julius Caesar*)

Does Antony want the crowd to like him? How can you tell? Does he want them to like Brutus? Again, what words tell you?

What can you tell about Caesar? Was he a good man, according to Antony? Why does he speak so much about Caesar?

What happens to Antony's voice and emotions in the last four lines?

What contrasts can you find when you look at the adjectives in the text?

Now compare and contrast the three speeches – Hamlet, Jaques, and Antony – using the following headings:

• why the character is speaking
• the tone of his words
• the changes between the beginning and the end of each speech
• the adjectives, and what they reveal
• the deeper concepts you find in the speeches
• contrasts and balance in each speech
• the differences and similarities you find throughout the speeches.

What lines do you find most memorable in these speeches? List the ones you would most like to remember.

The next play is entitled *The Swamp Dwellers* – what kind of people, setting, and events does the title suggest to you?

In the first part of the scene, a beggar has arrived, and Makuri welcomes him by ritually washing his feet. As you read, you will find quite a few binaries ('raining'/'stopped raining' might be the first). Mark them.

MAKURI: Aha, is that the water? No, no, bring it over here . . . Come on, my friend . . . come over here. It will be easier to wash your feet sitting in this chair . . . [*Leading him to the swivel chair* . . .] Do you realize it? You've brought good luck with you.

BEGGAR: Have I?

MAKURI: Well, didn't you hear what the Kadiye said? The rains have stopped . . . the floods are over. You must carry luck with your staff.

BEGGAR: Yes, I could feel the air growing lighter, and the clouds clearing over my head. I think the worst of your season is over.

MAKURI: I hope so. Only once or twice in my whole lifetime have we had it so bad.

BEGGAR: How thankful we would have been for the excess that you had here. If we had had the hundredth part of the fall you had, I would not be sitting under your roof this moment.

MAKURI: Is it really dry up country?

BEGGAR [*Smiles indulgently.*]: A little worse than that.

MAKURI: Drought? Did you have a drought?

[*While the* BEGGAR *is speaking,* ALU *squats down and washes his feet. When this is finished, she wipes them dry, takes a small jar from one of the shelves, and rubs his feet with some form of ointment.*]

BEGGAR: We are used to droughts. Our season is one long continuous drought . . . But we were used to it. Even when it rained, the soil let the water run right through it and join some stream in the womb of the earth. All that we knew, and were content to live on alms . . . Until one day, about a year or more ago . . .

[*There is only the gentle lapping of the water in the bowl.* MAKURI *has brought his stool and is sitting on the left side of the chair, looking up at the* BEGGAR.] . . . then we had more rain than I had ever known in my life. And the soil not only held the water, but it began to show off a leaf here and there . . . even on kola trees which had been stunted from birth. Wild millet pushed its way through the soil, and little tufts of elephant grass appeared from seeds which had lain forgotten season upon season . . . Best of all, hope began to spring in the heart of everyone . . . It is true that the land had lain barren for generations, that the fields had yielded no grain for the life-time of the eldest in the village. We had known nothing but the dryness of the earth. Dry soil. Dry crumbs of dust. Clouds of dust even when there was no wind, but only a vulture flying low and flapping its wings over the earth . . . But now . . . we could smell the sweetness of lemon leaves, and the feel of the fronds of desert palm was a happiness which we had never known . . . The thought was no sooner born than we set to work before the soil changed its mind and released its moisture. We deserted the highways and marched on this land, hoes and mattocks in hand – and how few of these there were! The village had been long unused to farming, and there was no more than a handful of hoes. But we took our staffs and drove them into the earth. We sharpened stakes and picked the sand and the pebble until they bled . . . And it seemed as if the heavens rejoiced in our labour, for their blessings were liberal, and their good will on our side. The rains came when we wanted it. And the sun shone and the seeds began to ripen.

[IGWEZU *enters quietly, and remains by the door, unobserved.*] Nothing could keep us from the farms from the moment that the shoots came through the surface, and all through the months of waiting. We went round the plantains and rubbed our skins against them, lightly, so that the tenderest bud could not be hurt. This was the closest that we had ever felt to one another. This was the moment that the village became a clan, and the clan a household, and even that was taken by Allah in one of his large hands and kneaded together with the clay of the earth. We loved the sound of a man's passing footsteps as if the rustle of his breath it was that gave life to the sprouting wonder around us. We even forgot to beg, and lived on the marvel of this new birth of the land, and the rich smell of its goodness . . . But it turned out to have been an act of spite. The feast was not meant for us − but for the locusts.

MAKURI [*involuntarily*]: Locusts!

BEGGAR: They came in hordes, and squatted on the land. It only took an hour or two, and the village returned to normal.

ALU [*moaning*]: Ay-ii, Ay-ii . . .

[MAKURI *buries his head in his hands.*]

BEGGAR: I headed away from my home, and set my face towards the river. When I said to the passing stranger, Friend, set my face towards the river, he replied, which river? But I only said to him, Towards any river, towards any stream; set my face towards the seas itself. But let there be water, because I am sick of the dryness.

MAKURI: Ay-ii, the hands of the gods are unequal. Their gifts become the burden of . . .

Now Makuri and Alu's son, Igwezu, joins in. As you read on, pick out more contrasts.

[ALU, *who has now finished her task, takes the bowl and rises. She is startled by suddenly seeing* IGWEZU, *and she drops the bowl in her fright.*]

ALU: My son!

MAKURI: Hm? Oh, he's back at last . . . [*Wakes suddenly to the dropped bowl, shouts −*] But was that a reason for you to be drowning the whole house? Now go and wipe it up instead of gawking at the man . . . Come on here, Igwezu. Come and sit down.

BEGGAR [*rising*]: Your son? Is that the son you spoke of?

MAKURI: Yes . . . Now hurry up. Hurry up and dry the place.

[*The* BEGGAR *feels for his staff and moves out of the chair.*
IGWEZU *sits down. He appears indifferent to his surroundings.*]

MAKURI: What held you? Have you been carousing?

IGWEZU: No. I went for a walk by myself.

MAKURI: All afternoon?

[IGWEZU *nods.*]

Do you mean to tell me . . . ? [*anxiously*] Son, are you feeling well?

ALU [*coming suddenly into the room with a piece of rag, overhears the last question*]: Is he unwell? What is the matter with him?

MAKURI: He is not unwell. I merely asked him how he felt.

ALU [*on her knees, begins to wipe the floor*]: Well, how does he feel?

IGWEZU [*without any kind of feeling*]: Glad to be home. Glad to be once again with my own people . . . Is that not what every home-coming son should feel?

MAKURI [*after watching him for a moment*]: Have you seen the farm?

[IGWEZU *is silent.*]

Son, you mustn't take it so hard. There is nothing that . . . [*Shakes his head in energetic display and sees* ALU *still wiping the floor.*] Hurry up, woman! Is the man not to get any supper after walking around by himself all day?

[ALU *gasps.*]

IGWEZU: No, don't give yourself the trouble. I want no supper.

MAKURI: But you've eaten nothing all day.

IGWEZU: I have had my feast of welcome. I found it on the farm where the beans and the corn had made an everlasting pottage with the mud.

BEGGAR [*coming forward*]: Master, it will thrive again.

IGWEZU [*He looks up at the* BEGGAR, *as if seeing him for the first time.*]: Who are you? And why do you call me master?

BEGGAR: I am a wanderer, a beggar by birth and fortunes. But you own a farm. I have stood where your soil is good and cleaves to the toes like the clay of bricks in the mixing; but it needs the fingers of drought whose skin is parchment. I shall be your bondsman. I shall give myself to you and work the land for your good. I feel I can make it yield in my hands like an obedient child.

(Wole Soyinka *The Swamp Dwellers*)

How do the final words of the Beggar point towards the future? What can you tell about the other characters and their relationship to each other?

What do you feel is the dominant mood that a performance would bring out: hope, resignation, despair . . . ?

In this scene, a man's identity is thrown into question. His friend Buntu is changing his photograph in his passbook. As you read, what reasons do you find for the change of identity?

[BUNTU *opens the two reference books and places them side by side on the table. He produces a pot of glue, then very carefully tears out the photograph in each book. A dab of glue on the back of each and then*

Sizwe's goes back into Robert's book, and Robert's into Sizwe's. SIZWE
watches this operation, at first uninterestedly, but when he realizes what
BUNTU *is up to, with growing alarm. When he is finished,* BUNTU *pushes*
the two books in front of SIZWE.]

MAN [*shaking his head emphatically*]: Yo! *Haai, haai.* No, Buntu.

BUNTU: It's a chance.

MAN: *Haai, haai, haai* . . .

BUNTU: It's your only chance!

MAN: No, Buntu! What's it mean? That me, Sizwe Bansi . . .

BUNTU: Is dead.

MAN: I'm not dead, friend.

BUNTU: We burn this book . . . [SIZWE's *original*] . . . and Sizwe Bansi
disappears off the face of the earth.

MAN: What about the man we left lying in the alleyway?

BUNTU: Tomorrow the Flying Squad passes there and finds him. Check in his
pockets . . . no passbook. Mount Road Mortuary. After three days, nobody
has identified him. Pauper's Burial. Case closed.

MAN: And then?

BUNTU: Tomorrow I contact my friend Norman at Feltex. He's a boss-boy there.
I tell him about another friend, Robert Zwelinzima, book in order, who's look-
ing for a job. You roll up later, hand over the book to the white man. Who does
Robert Zwelinzima look like? You! Who gets the pay on Friday? You, man!

MAN: What about all that shit at the Labour Bureau, Buntu?

BUNTU: You don't have to go there. This chap had a work-seeker's permit,
Sizwe. All you do is hand over the book to the white man. *He* checks at the
Labour Bureau. They check with their big machine. 'Robert Zwelinzima has
the right to be employed and stay in this town.'

MAN: I don't want to lose my name, Buntu.

BUNTU: You mean you don't want to lose your bloody passbook! You love it,
hey?

MAN: Buntu. I cannot lose my name.

BUNTU [*leaving the table*]: All right, I was only trying to help. As Robert
Zwelinzima you could have stayed and worked in this town. As Sizwe Bansi
. . . ? Start walking, friend. King William's Town. Hundred and fifty miles. And
don't waste any time! You've got to be there by yesterday. Hope you enjoy it.

MAN: Buntu. . . .

BUNTU: Lots of scenery in a hundred and fifty miles.

MAN: Buntu! . . .

BUNTU: Maybe a better idea is just to wait until they pick you up. Save yourself
all that walking. Into the train with the escort! Smart stuff, hey. Hope it's not
too crowded though. Hell of a lot of people being kicked out, I hear.

MAN: Buntu! . . .

BUNTU: But once you're back! Sit down on the side of the road next to your pondok with your family . . . the whole Bansi clan on leave . . . for life! Hey, that sounds okay. Watching all the cars passing, and as you say, friend, cough your bloody lungs out with Ciskean Independence.

MAN [*now really desperate*]: Buntu!!!

BUNTU: What you waiting for? Go!

MAN: Buntu.

BUNTU: What?

MAN: What about my wife, Nowetu?

BUNTU: What about her?

MAN [*maudlin tears*]: Her loving husband, Sizwe Bansi, is dead!

BUNTU: So what! She's going to marry a better man.

MAN [*bridling*]: Who?

BUNTU: You . . . Robert Zwelinzima.

MAN [*thoroughly confused*]: How can I marry my wife, Buntu?

BUNTU: Get her down here and I'll introduce you.

MAN: Don't make jokes, Buntu. Robert . . . Sizwe . . . I'm all mixed up. Who am I?

BUNTU: A fool who is not taking his chance.

MAN: And my children! Their father is Sizwe Bansi. They're registered at school under Bansi . . .

BUNTU: Are you really worried about your children, friend, or are you just worried about yourself and your bloody name? Wake up, man! Use that book and with your pay on Friday you'll have a real chance to do something for them.

MAN: I'm afraid. How do I get used to Robert? How do I live as another man's ghost?

BUNTU: Wasn't Sizwe Bansi a ghost?

MAN: No!

BUNTU: No? When the white man looked at you at the Labour Bureau what did he see? A man with dignity or a bloody passbook with an N.I. number. Isn't that a ghost? When the white man sees you walk down the street and calls out, 'Hey, John! Come here' . . . to you, Sizwe Bansi . . . isn't that a ghost? Or when his little child calls you 'Boy' . . . you a man, circumcized, with a wife and four children . . . isn't that a ghost? Stop fooling yourself. All I'm saying is be a real ghost, if that is what they want, what they've turned us into. Spook them into hell, man!

[SIZWE *is silenced.* BUNTU *realizes his words are beginning to reach the other man. He paces quietly, looking for his next move. He finds it.*]

Suppose you try my plan. Friday. Roughcasting section at Feltex. Paytime. Line of men – non-skilled labourers. White man with the big box full of pay-packets. 'John Kani!' 'Yes, sir!' Pay-packet is handed over. 'Thank you, sir.' Another one. [BUNTU *reads the name on an imaginary pay-packet.*] 'Winston Ntshona!' 'Yes, sir!' Pay-packet over. 'Thank you, sir!' Another one. 'Fats Bokhilane!' *'Hier is ek, my baas!'* Pay-packet over. *'Dankie, my baas!'* Another one. 'Robert Zwelinzima!'

[*No response from* SIZWE]

'Robert Zwelinzima!'

MAN: Yes, sir.

BUNTU [*handing him the imaginary pay-packet*]: Open it. Go on. [*Takes back the packet, tears it open, empties its contents on the table, and counts it.*] Five . . . ten . . . eleven . . . twelve . . . and ninety-nine cents. In your pocket.

[BUNTU *again paces quietly, leaving* SIZWE *to think. Eventually . . .*] Saturday. Man in overalls, twelve rand ninety-nine cents in the back pocket, walking down Main Street looking for Sales House. Finds it and walks in. Salesman comes forward to meet him. 'I've come to buy a suit.' Salesman is very friendly. 'Certainly. Won't you take a seat. I'll get the forms. I'm sure you want to open an account, sir. Six months to pay. But first I'll need all your particulars.'

[BUNTU *has turned the table, with* SIZWE *on the other side, into the imaginary scene at Sales House.*]

BUNTU [*pencil poised, ready to fill in a form*]: Your name, please, sir?

MAN [*playing along uncertainly*]: Robert Zwelinzima.

BUNTU [*writing*]: 'Robert Zwelinzima.' Address?

MAN: Fifty, Mapija Street.

BUNTU: Where do you work?

MAN: Feltex.

BUNTU: And how much do you get paid?

MAN: Twelve . . . twelve rand ninety-nine cents.

BUNTU: N.I. Number, please?

[SIZWE *hesitates.*]

Your Native Identity number please?

[SIZWE *is still uncertain.* BUNTU *abandons the act and picks up Robert Zwelinzima's passbook. He reads out the number.*]

N – I – 3 – 8 – 1 – 1 – 8 – 6 – 3. Burn that into your head, friend. You hear me? It's more important than your name. N.I. number . . . three . . .

MAN: Three.

BUNTU: Eight.

MAN: Eight.

BUNTU: One.

MAN: One.

BUNTU: One.

MAN: One.
BUNTU: Eight.
MAN: Eight.
BUNTU: Six.
MAN: Six.
BUNTU: Three.
MAN: Three.
BUNTU: Again. Three.
MAN: Three.
BUNTU: Eight.
MAN: Eight.
BUNTU: One.
MAN: One.
BUNTU: One.
MAN: One.
BUNTU: Eight.
MAN: Eight.
BUNTU: Six.
MAN: Six.
BUNTU: Three.
MAN: Three.
BUNTU [*picking up his pencil and returning to the role of the salesman*]: N.I.
    number, please.
MAN [*pausing frequently, using his hands to remember*]: Three . . . eight . . .
    one . . . one . . . eight . . . six . . . three . . .
BUNTU [*abandoning the act*]: Good boy.

Is Sizwe convinced of his new identity by the end, do you think?
Which of Buntu's arguments do you find most striking?

What might have happened to 'the man we left lying in the
alleyway'? What kind of men do you think Buntu or Sizwe are:
rich/poor, white/black . . . ? How can you tell? Can you detect any
political edge to the scene?

What kind of atmosphere would you want to give the scene in
performance? How much of the scene could be presented for laughs?
How important are the stage directions? Check them through, to see
how much they help your reading of the scene.

Just before this scene, Sizwe describes to Buntu and the audience
just how important 'this book' is.

BUNTU: Give me your bloody book, Sizwe!

MAN [*handing it over*]: Take it, Buntu. Take this book and read it carefully, friend, and tell me what is says about me. Buntu, does that book tell you I'm a man?

[BUNTU *studies the two books.* SIZWE *turns back to the audience.*]

That bloody book . . . ! People, do you know? No! Wherever you go . . . it's that bloody book. You go to school, it goes too. Go to work, it goes too. Go to church and pray and sing lovely hymns, it sits there with you. Go to hospital to die, it lies there too!

(Athol Fugard *Sizwe Bansi Is Dead*)

Does this add to the effect of the scene, or does the scene work as effectively without it?

Discuss what you see as the issues the scene raises. Are the two men doing something criminal, or are they just protecting Sizwe? If your sympathy is with Sizwe and Buntu, can you imagine an 'enemy' reaction, unsympathetic to them?

This play is one of the works which emerged from the black South African townships in the fruitful collaboration between the white writer Athol Fugard and two black actors, John Kani and Winston Ntshona, who played Buntu and Sizwe Bansi in the original production in 1972. Does that context illuminate the scene any further?

In the following extracts, from *Of Mice and Men* by John Steinbeck, you will read about Lennie and George and their relationship with the people around them. As you read the first extract, suggest reasons why you think Lennie and George were hiding in the gutter on Howard Street.

Lennie looked timidly over to him. 'George?'

'Yeah, what ya want?'

'Where we goin', George?'

The little man jerked down the brim of his hat and scowled over at Lennie. 'So you forgot that awready, did you? I gotta tell you again, do I? Jesus Christ, you're a crazy bastard!'

'I forgot,' Lennie said softly. 'I tried not to forget. Honest to God I did, George.'

'OK – OK. I'll tell ya again. I ain't got nothing to do. Might jus' as well spen' all my time tellin' you things and then you forget 'em, and I tell you again.'

'Tried and tried,' said Lennie, 'but it didn't do no good. I remember about the rabbits, George.'

'The hell with the rabbits. That's all you ever can remember is them rabbits. OK! Now you listen and this time you got to remember so we don't get in no trouble. You remember settin' in that gutter on Howard Street and watchin' that blackboard?'

Lennie's face broke into a delighted smile. 'Why, sure, George. I remember that . . . but . . . what'd we do then? I remember some girls come by and you says . . . you says . . .'

'The hell with what I says. You remember about us goin' into Murray and Ready's, and they give us work cards and bus tickets?'

'Oh, sure, George. I remember that now.' His hands went quickly into his side coat pockets. He said gently: 'George . . . I ain't got mine. I musta lost it.' He looked down at the ground in despair.

'You never had none, you crazy bastard. I got both of 'em here. Think I'd let you carry your own work card?'

What seems to be Lennie's problem? Which words indicate this?

Why do you think Lennie remembered about the rabbits?

What is the relationship between Lennie and George, in your opinion? Do you find anything odd about Lennie? If yes, how does the writer give us this impression?

What type of work do you think the men are going to do?

Read the following text, and complete the two columns given below with what George says (a) about guys like them, and (b) about themselves.

George's voice became deeper. He repeated his words rhythmically as though he had said them many times before. 'Guys like us, that work on ranches, are the loneliest guys in the world. They got no family. They don't belong no place. They come to a ranch an' work up a stake and then they go inta town and blow their stake, and the first thing you know they're poundin' their tail on some other ranch. They ain't got nothing to look ahead to.'

Lennie was delighted. 'That's it — that's it. Now tell how it is with us.'

George went on. 'With us it ain't like that. We got a future. We got somebody to talk to that gives a damn about us. We don't have to sit in no bar-room blowin' in our jack jus' because we got no place else to go. If them other guys gets in jail they can rot for all anybody gives a damn. But not us.'

Lennie broke in. '*But not us! Because . . . because I got you to look after me, and you got me to look after you, and that's why.*' He laughed delightedly. 'Go on now, George.'

'You got it by heart. You can do it yourself.'

'No, you. I forget some a' the things. Tell about how it's gonna be.'

'OK. Some day — we're gonna get the jack together and we're gonna have a little house and a couple of acres an' a cow and some pigs and . . . '

'Guys like us'	Us (Lennie and George)
....	....
....	....
....	....
....	....

Do Lennie and George already have the things George describes?

How is this signalled? What is Lennie's response to George's description? What do you think of George's description of the lives of ranch hands, and their own lives?

Why do you think the part where Lennie cuts in is in italics? What does the writer want to indicate?

Do you think George believes in what he is saying? How can you tell? Does Lennie believe what George is saying? Do you think they will be able to have their own ranch?

Now read the next extract. What difference do you notice in George?

'Well, we ain't got any,' George exploded. 'Whatever we ain't got, that's what you want. God a'mighty, if I was alone I could live so easy. I could go get a job an' work, an' no trouble. No mess at all, and when the end of the month come I could take my fifty bucks and go into town and get whatever I want. Why, I could stay in a cat-house all night. I could eat any place I want, hotel or any place, and order any damn thing I could think of. An' I could do all that every damn month. Get a gallon of whisky, or set in a pool-room and play cards or shoot pool.' Lennie knelt and looked over the fire at the angry George. And Lennie's face was drawn with terror. 'An' whatta I got?' George went on furiously. 'I got you! You can't keep a job and you lose me ever' job I get. Jes' keep me shovin' all over the country all the time. An' that ain't the worst. You get in trouble. You do bad things and I got to get you out.' His voice rose nearly to a shout. 'You crazy son-of-a-bitch. You keep me in hot water all the time.' He took on the elaborate manner of little girls when they are mimicking one another. 'Jus' wanted to feel that girl's dress – jus' wanted to pet it like it was a mouse . . . Well, how the hell did she know you jus' wanted to feel her dress? She jerks back and you hold on like it was a mouse. She yells and we got to hide in an irrigation ditch all day with guys lookin' for us, and we got to sneak out in the dark and get outta the country. All the time somethin' like that – all the time. I wisht I could put you in a cage with about a million mice and let you have fun.' His anger left him suddenly. He looked across the fire at Lennie's anguished face, and then he looked ashamedly at the flames.

Why is George angry? What effect does this have on him?

What are the things he could do if he were on his own? Does he really want to do these things, in your opinion?

What does George mean when he says to Lennie, 'You keep me in hot water all the time'? How does Lennie react to George's outburst? Does he believe what George has just said?

Who do you sympathise with?
What do you think the story is going to focus on?

Now read on. Which character do you sympathise with?

Carlson was not to be put off. 'Look, Candy. This ol' dog jus' suffers hisself all the time. If you was to take him out and shoot him right in the back of the head' – he leaned over and pointed – 'right there, why he'd never know what hit him.'

Candy looked about unhappily. 'No,' he said softly. 'No, I couldn't do that. I had 'im too long.'

'He don't have no fun,' Carlson insisted. 'And he stinks to beat hell. Tell you what. I'll shoot him for you. Then it won't be you that does it.'

Candy threw his legs off his bunk. He scratched the white stubble whiskers on his cheek nervously. 'I'm so used to him,' he said softly. 'I had him from a pup.'

'Well, you ain't bein' kind to him keepin' him alive,' said Carlson. 'Look, Slim's bitch got a litter right now. I bet Slim would give you one of them pups to raise up, wouldn't you, Slim?'

The skinner had been studying the old dog with his calm eyes. 'Yeah,' he said. 'You can have a pup if you want to.' He seemed to shake himself free for speech. 'Carl's right, Candy. That dog ain't no good to himself. I wisht somebody'd shoot me if I get old an' a cripple.'

What do you think Carlson is talking about in the first paragraph? How is this indicated? What are Carlson's reasons for shooting the dog? Why is Candy unwilling to do it? Do you think it should be Candy's responsibility?

Would you support Slim's view: 'I wisht somebody'd shoot me if I get old an' a cripple'?

Is there any similarity between Candy's relationship with his dog and George's relationship with Lennie?

Slim says that the dog 'ain't no good to himself.' Based on your reading of the earlier extracts, would Lennie fall in the same category? Is this sufficient reason to shoot Lennie too?

Research

Try to find out about euthanasia or mercy-killing. Is this acceptable only for animals, or should it also be practised on human beings?

Now read the final extract, and pick out the word which Lennie keeps repeating.

'Oh! Please don't do none of that,' he begged. 'George gonna say I done a bad thing. He ain't gonna let me tend no rabbits.' He moved his hand a little and her hoarse cry came out. Then Lennie grew angry. 'Now don't,' he said. 'I don't want you to yell. You gonna get me in trouble jus' like George says you will. Now don't you do that.' And she continued to struggle, and her eyes were wide with terror. He shook her then, and he was angry with her. 'Don't you go yellin',' he said, and he shook her; and her body flopped like a fish. And then she was still, for Lennie had broken her neck.

He looked down at her, and carefully he removed his hand from over her mouth, and she lay still. 'I don't want ta hurt you,' he said, 'but George'll be mad if you yell.' When she didn't answer nor move he bent closely over her. He lifted her arm and let it drop. For a moment he seemed bewildered. And then he whispered in fright: 'I done a bad thing. I done another bad thing.'

(John Steinbeck *Of Mice and Men*)

What do you think Lennie is asking when he says 'Please don't do none of that'? Does he lose control of himself? What is the thing that remains foremost in his mind throughout the incident? Why?

Compare your answers around the class. What does Lennie's repetition of the word tell you about him? What does Lennie's line 'I done another bad thing' imply? Do you think Lennie fully understands what has happened? Do you sympathise with Lennie?

What do you think will happen next? Do you think the story will have a happy ending?

Now refer back to the first extract. Do you think Lennie and George could find themselves in a similar situation? Now read it again. Is the language that Lennie and George use when they speak to each other similar to the rest of the narration, or not? Point out some similarities or differences.

The Return is Ravi's story of growing up in a small town in Malaysia. Four extracts from the novel describe some of the important events or experiences in his life.

Now read the first extract. How old do you think Ravi is in the following passage?

Closetted with her five afternoons a week, we slipped into this invisible country she fixed up with machinery and bolts, snow and flowers, the trance-like glare of winter, spring and autumn, filled with the personalities of her stories. It was terribly exciting, a complete contrast to the world we lived in. I longed for escape from the filthy squabbles of my neighbours, the pettifogging playmates in the hospital compound, and the arrogant, vengeful administrative personnel. Returning from school was re-entering another, primitive, time zone. The last lap, the laterite road that led me right up to the house, was a disappointing anti-climax. The houses, squalid, green, and over-crowded, were unfailingly there. Some nights 'White monkey!' was hissed at me from ditches and from behind trees.

Who is 'her' in line 1? What are Ravi's feelings towards 'this invisible country' created by the woman? List the words Ravi uses to describe 'this invisible country' and the words to describe the world he lives in. Compare his feelings towards the two places.

Why does Ravi describe the 'last lap' as a 'disappointing anti-climax', in your opinion? Who do you think calls Ravi 'White monkey'? Why?

Now read the next extract. How old do you think Ravi is now?

Periathai sat cross-legged, hair wet and in unadorned clothes before the holy niche and entered a deep contemplation. Perhaps Nataraja spoke to her of the original spirit, and her personal articles of the home she had left behind. It was a re-immersion, a recreating of the thick spiritual and domestic air she must have breathed there, back in some remote district in India.

The spell broke the moment she turned and smiled at us. We scrambled for places on the large, iron bedstead beside which were ranged clay and copper vessels holding strange delights. There was a kind of dried, sour meat that tasted like stringy jelly. There were balls of puffed rice with just the right pinch of chillie, and from another long-necked jar came snaky bits cooked in thick treacle. We were only given two-tooth bites of these tasty morsels, more as an appetiser for the main meal on the thinnai. There, *vadais*, left over from the day's sales, dhal curry filled with brinjals, potatoes, pumpkin cubes, tomato slices and *avarakai* (Indian legumes), were served with rice. Those of us who had 'behaved' received a teaspoonful of home-brewed ghee to flavour the spread. Then, with only a tier lamp placed in the centre of the most complicated kolam in the cowdung-plastered compound, Periathai told us stories. Her voice transformed the kolams into contours of reality and fantasy, excitingly balanced. I felt I stood on the edge of a world I may have known.

What was it about Periathai that Ravi found enchanting? How is this conveyed to the reader? What effect do Periathai's stories have on Ravi? Is it similar to the stories about the 'invisible country' in extract 1?

Why do you think Ravi says 'I felt I stood on the edge of a world I may have known'? What could 'may' indicate?

What is the tone in this extract? Look at the first and last lines. What shift of focus happens? Why?

Now read on. How old do you think Ravi is?

'He's in his room,' my mother said.

Karupi laughed and came to my corner.

'You can come out now. We've more important things to do,' she said, smiling.

I reached Menon's house angry and paid not the slightest attention to his huge, black dog which barked furiously. Usually I stood near the cowshed adjacent to the kitchen and yelled for the cook's helper. But that day I walked boldly to the house steps beside which the brute was chained. Mrs Menon herself came out to investigate. She scowled when she saw me.

'How many times must I tell you not to come to the house? Stay near the kitchen and call,' she said angrily.

'You want to check the clothes?' I said.

She took them and disappeared into the house. I heard her stomp all over the wooden floor. The dirty linen came flying through the doorway. I picked them up and without bothering to make a bundle almost trotted home.

'Boy! You, boy! I haven't counted them!' Mrs Menon called.

But I didn't turn around or stop. The clothes smelled in my arms like a week-old dead child. I fled from more than Menon's house. The humiliation gave me wings. I longed for the snow-capped isolation and the gentleness of the buttercupped meadows. I don't know how I reached home but it was as if Miss Nancy had led me all the way to the tidy corner with the dirt completely excluded. That night I felt, for the first time, my troubled heartbeats.

What were Ravi's feelings when he arrived at Menon's house? What was the cause? How did Mrs Menon respond to Ravi's presence?

What words does Ravi use to describe the clothes he was carrying? Do you think they really smelt that bad?

What does Ravi mean when he says 'I fled from more than Menon's house'? What else do you think he was running from? Explain the sentence 'The humiliation gave me wings'. What does 'The' refer to?

How does Ravi explain his safe return home? What is the 'dirt' Ravi refers to, in your opinion?

Read the last sentence again. What does it tell you about Ravi? How do you expect this will affect him?

Now read the final extract from the novel. How do you think Ravi is going to achieve his ambition?

> A year after Periathai's death, Naina had settled most of the minor debts. I was in Form Four, well past my adolescence and, having read some English novels, I began to understand the simple mechanism, I thought, of the Malaysian Indian. I recognised the spirit that had touched Periathai and now possessed Naina. He continued the battle Periathai had begun: to drive some stake into the country. The restlessness that had motivated Periathai into building her houses and keeping the kolam courtyard decorated, meaningful, and intact, took another form in my father. More complex than Karupi, the intensity with which he turned Periathai's funeral into a show, had frightened me. I stood outside Periathai's and Naina's preoccupations. Their imagination couldn't grasp the real complexity that surrounded us. I had, watching Periathai's failure to earn a home in this land, decided to acquire a skill that would allow me a comfortable, unthreatened existence. One's world was, after all, private, and it was only through chance encounters, as had been Miss Nancy's and mine, that one discovered the logic and the power that sustains the individual. A mild anger filled me as I saw Periathai die homeless. But I considered hers an irrational attitude. No one would compel me into sharing another, immature ambition.
>
> Only my studies mattered. I was at them constantly, aware that I could go to England if I won a teaching bursary. Naina's interests and my family's struggles became unimportant. The dignity of the individual was the only thing that engaged me. And this couldn't be acquired if I gave in to quirkish desires and irrational dreams.
>
> (K.S. Maniam *The Return*)

Is Periathai's ambition the same as Ravi's father's? What is Ravi's attitude to it? List the words that Ravi uses to describe Periathai's and his father's wishes. Are they negative or positive? What does this tell you about Ravi's opinion on his father being fulfilled in his ambition?

What do you think Ravi means when he says 'I began to understand the simple mechanism, I thought, of the Malaysian Indian'?

Why does Ravi think Periathai and his father 'couldn't grasp the real complexity that surrounded' them? What effect does this have on Ravi?

Is Ravi selfish, in your opinion? Is his behaviour acceptable? Do you think Ravi has grown stronger from his earlier experiences? (See extracts 1 to 3.) Do you think he will succeed?

What do you think the novel *The Man-Eater of Malgudi* will be about? Write this down. Check this later as you read the other extracts.

....

....

....

....

Now read the first extract, in which some of the major characters in this novel are presented. List the names of these people.

Now an unusual thing happened. The curtain stirred, an edge of it lifted, and the monosyllabic poet's head peeped through. An extraordinary situation must have arisen to make him to do that. His eyes bulged. 'Someone to see you,' he whispered.

'Who? What does he want?'

'I don't know.'

The whispered conversation was becoming a strain. I shook my head, winked and grimaced to indicate to the poet that I was not available. The poet, ever a dense fellow, did not understand but blinked on unintelligently. His head suddenly vanished, and a moment later a new head appeared in its place – a tanned face, large powerful eyes under thick eyebrows, a large forehead and a shock of unkempt hair, like a black halo.

My first impulse was to cry out, 'Whoever you may be, why don't you brush your hair?' The new visitor had evidently pulled aside the poet before showing himself to me. Before I could open my mouth, he asked, 'You Nataraj?' I nodded. He came forward, practically tearing aside the curtain, an act which violated the sacred traditions of my press. I said 'Why don't you kindly take a seat in the next room? I'll be with you in a moment.' He paid no attention, but stepped forward, extending his hand. I hastily wiped my fingers on a rag, muttering, 'Sorry, discoloured, been working . . . ' He gave me a hard grip. My entire hand disappeared into his fist – he was a huge man, about six feet tall. He looked quite slim, but his bull-neck and hammer-fist revealed his true stature. 'Shan't we move to the other room?' I asked again.

'Not necessary. It's all the same to me,' he said. 'You are doing something? Why don't you go on? It won't bother me.' He eyed my coloured labels. 'What are they?'

I didn't want any eyes to watch my special colour effects, and see how I achieved them. I moved to the curtain and parted it courteously for him. He followed me. I showed him to the Queen Anne chair, and sat down at my usual place, on the edge of my desk. I had now regained the feeling of being master of the situation. I adopted my best smile and asked, 'Well, what can I do for you, Mr . . . ?'

'Vasu,' he said, and added, 'I knew you didn't catch my name. You were saying something at the same time as I mentioned my name.'

I felt abashed, and covered it, I suppose, with another of those silly smiles. Then I checked myself, suddenly feeling angry with him for making me so uneasy. I asked myself, 'Nataraj, are you afraid of this muscular fellow?' and said authoritatively, 'Yes?' as much as to indicate, 'You have wasted my time sufficiently; now say quickly whatever you may want to say.'

What information are you given about the poet? Is the speaker serious about what he says about the man?

How did Nataraj react when he first caught sight of the stranger's head? Is this an unusual reaction?

Circle the words which give details about Vasu's physical appearance. What does the description of Vasu's movements suggest? Why do you think so much detail is given about Vasu's appearance and movements?

How does Nataraj react to Vasu's presence in the printing press? Do you think Vasu senses this? What kind of relationship do you think could develop between Nataraj and Vasu: friends, business partners, enemies, or what else?

Now read the next extract. How does Nataraj react to the situation in the press?

Vasu's habit of using my front room as an extension of his attic was proving irksome, as I had my own visitors, not to speak of the permanent pair – the poet and the journalist. For a few days Sen and the poet left the moment they heard the jeep arrive, but gradually their views underwent a change.

When Vasu came in, Sen would stick to his seat with an air of defiance as if saying, 'I'm not going to let that beefy fellow . . . ' The poet would transfer himself without fuss from the high-backed Queen Anne chair to a poorer seat. He had developed the art of surviving Vasu's presence; he maintained a profound silence, but if he were forced to speak he would confine himself to monosyllables (at which in any case he was an adept), and I was glad to note that Vasu had too much on his mind to have the time for more than a couple of nasty, personal remarks, which the poet pretended not to hear. Sen suppressed the expression of his political opinions in Vasu's presence (which was a good thing again), but it did not save him, as Vasu, the moment he remembered his presence, said 'What are the views of our wise friend on this?' To which Sen gave a fitting reply, such as 'If people are dense enough not to know what is happening, I'm not prepared to . . . ', which would act as a starting point for a battle of words. But the battle never came, as on the first day, to near-blows – it always fizzled out.

I left everyone alone. If they wrangled and lost their heads and voices, it was their business and not mine. Even if heads had been broken, I don't think I'd have interfered. I had resigned myself to anything. If I had cared for a peaceful existence, I should have rejected Vasu on the first day. Now it was like having a middle-aged man-eater in your office and home, with the same uncertainties, possibilities, and potentialities.

This man-eater softened, snivelled and purred, and tried to be agreeable only in the presence of an official. He brought in a khaki-clad, cadaverous man one day, a forestry officer, seated him and introduced me, 'This is my best friend on earth, Mr Nataraj; he and I are more like brothers than printer and customer or landlord and tenant.'

'Actually, I am not a landlord and don't want to be one,' I said, remembering how much more at peace I used to be when my attic was tenanted by junk. Woe to the day I had conceived the idea of cleaning it up.

How did Sen and the poet change their behaviour with regard to Vasu's presence in the press? What could have caused this? What do you think the expression 'did not save him' suggests about Sen's relationship with Vasu? Choose a few adjectives to describe Vasu's treatment of Sen.

What name has Nataraj given Vasu? Does Vasu know about this? Do you think it is appropriate? Does Vasu treat all the people in the room the same way? What adjectives does Nataraj use to describe Vasu, when Vasu is dealing with an official? What does this suggest about Vasu?

How does Nataraj come to terms with Vasu's presence in the

attic? What is the tone at the end of this extract? What conflicts do you expect to arise between Vasu and the other men?

Now read the following extract, narrated by Nataraj. Do you sympathise with Nataraj? Why?

I had been brought up in a house where we were taught never to kill. When we swatted flies, we had to do it without the knowledge of our elders. I remember particularly one of my grand-uncles, who used the little room on the *pyol* and who gave me a coin every morning to buy sugar for the ants, and kept an eye on me to see that I delivered the sugar to the ants in various corners of our house. He used to declare, with approval from all the others, 'You must never scare away the crows and sparrows that come to share our food; they have as much right as we to the corn that grows in the fields.' And he watched with rapture squirrels, mice, and birds busily depleting the granary in our house. Our domestic granary was not built in the style of these days with cement, but with a bamboo matting stiffened with mud and rolled into cylinders, into whose wide mouth they poured in the harvest, which arrived loaded in bullock carts. That was in the days before my uncles quarrelled and decided to separate.

I was appalled at the thought that I was harbouring this destroyer, but I hadn't the courage to go up to him and say, 'Take yourself and your museum out of here!' He might do anything – bellow at me, or laugh scorn-fully, or rattle my bones. I felt dwarfed and tongue-tied before him. Moreover it was difficult now to meet him; he was always going out and returning late at night; sometimes he was away for three days at a stretch. He returned home late because he did not want his booty to be observed. When he was at home he worked upstairs with the broth and moulds; one heard the hammering, sawing, and all the other sounds belonging to his business, and sometimes during the day he hauled down packing cases and drove off to the railway station. I noted it all from my seat in the press and said to myself, 'From this humble town of Malgudi stuffed carcasses radiate to the four corners of the earth.'

Who is the 'destroyer'? Why does Nataraj not throw the man out? Which words indicate this?

Why do you think the reader is told about Nataraj's treatment of insects and animals in the first paragraph?

Compare the first sentence in this extract with the last sentence. How have things changed in his property? What are the speaker's feelings about the change? Which words suggest this?

What is the speaker's tone when he talks about the past? Is there a change in tone when he describes the present? What do you think could happen next to Nataraj?

Now read the next extract, and list the people mentioned in it.

'Oh, iron-willed men! Very good. I agree with you. Don't tolerate any disturbance.'

'That elephant belongs to no one but the Goddess on the hill road. If anyone tries to harm it . . . ,' began Muthu and Vasu cut in, 'Why don't you mind your tea-shop and keep off the flies, and leave these issues to others? Don't try to speak for any elephant.'

'We know what you have been trying to do, and we aren't going to stand any nonsense,' the veterinary doctor said. 'I have examined Kumar and know him inside out. He is in perfect health, more sober than any human being here.'

'So what?' asked Vasu.

'If anyone wishes to drive him crazy, he'll not succeed, that's what I wish to say.'

'Doctor, you may have an American degree, but you know nothing about animals. Do they have elephants in America? Try to get into a government department, count your thirty days and draw your sinecure's allowance. Why do you bother about these matters? Poet, say something in your monosyllables. Why are you silent? Don't be smug and let others fight your cause. Sell me a copy of your poem as soon as it is read. That's all? Now be off, all of you.'

The journalist warned him, 'We are not bothered about you. We'll leave you alone. You leave our procession alone. This is a sacred function. People are out there to be with their God . . . '

'If God is everywhere, why follow Him only in a procession?'

The journalist ignored this remark and said, 'Hundreds of men and women and children with the chariot . . . '

'What's this special point about women and children? You are all prac-tising chivalry, are you? If men are to be caught in a stampede, why not women and children also? What's the point in saving women and children alone? What will they do after their men are stamped out?'

Who is Kumar? Is he also the 'him' in paragraph 5 ('If anyone wishes to drive him crazy . . . ')?

How does Vasu out-argue each of the men in the extract? Do you think Vasu is serious or teasing the men with his opinion about the stampede?

What do you think of Vasu? Does the writer indicate in any way whether he approves or disapproves of Vasu?

Now read the final extract. Who do you think is the 'I' in this extract?

'He drew another chair beside his, and commanded the woman to sit down with a fan in hand and keep the mosquitoes off him. He hated mosquitoes, from what the woman tells me. He cursed the police for their intrusion, which had made him break his cot-frame to show off his strength and now compelled him to stretch himself in an easy chair instead of sleeping in his cot protected by a mosquito-net. Armed with the fan, the woman kept away the mosquitoes. He dozed off. After a little time she dozed off too, having had a fatiguing day, as you know, and the fanning must have ceased; during this pause the mosquitoes returned in a battalion for a fresh attack. Rangi was awakened by the man yelling, "Damn these mosquitoes!" She saw him flourish his arms like a madman, fighting them off as they buzzed about his ears to suck his blood. Next minute she heard a sharp noise like a thunder-clap. The man had evidently trapped a couple of mosquitoes which had settled on his forehead by bringing the flat of his palm with all his might on top of them. The woman switched on the light and saw two mosquitoes plastered on his brow. It was also the end of Vasu,' concluded Sastri, and added 'That fist was meant to batter thick panels of teak and iron . . . '

'He had one virtue, he never hit anyone with his hand, whatever the provocation,' I said, remembering his voice.

'Because,' said Sastri puckishly, 'he had to conserve all that might for his own destruction. Every demon appears in the world with a special boon of indestructibility. Yet the universe has survived all the *rukshasas* that were ever born. Every demon carries within him, unknown to himself, a tiny seed of self-destruction, and goes up in thin air at the most unexpected moment. Otherwise what is to happen to humanity?'

(R.K. Narayan *The Man-Eater of Malgudi*)

List the verbs used to describe Vasu's situation in relation to the woman, mosquitoes, and the police. What does this reveal about Vasu?

Why did Vasu have to sleep on a chair? How did this bring about his death?

What is the sound of Vasu hitting his forehead compared to? Is it an effective comparison? Can you think of some other comparisons?

Read the last paragraph again. Does this story fit into the mould of a fable? Why? Do you think this was a fitting end for Vasu?

What is the thing that is remembered about Vasu, now that he is dead?

Now we are going to read a point of entry, and several 'stepping stones', which will take us through a whole novel: Chinua Achebe's *Things Fall Apart*. From the title, what do you think the novel might be about?

As you read the point of entry, underline the different fears that are mentioned.

Okonkwo ruled his household with a heavy hand. His wives, especially the youngest, lived in perpetual fear of his fiery temper, and so did his little children. Perhaps down in his heart Okonkwo was not a cruel man. But his whole life was dominated by fear, the fear of failure and of weakness. It was deeper and more intimate than the fear of evil and capricious gods and of magic, the fear of the forest, and the forces of nature, malevolent, red in tooth and claw. Okonkwo's fear was greater than these. It was not external but lay deep within himself. It was the fear of himself, lest he should be found to resemble his father. Even as a little boy he had resented his father's failure and weakness, and even now he still remembered how he had suffered when a playmate had told him that his father was *agbala*. That was how Okonkwo first came to know that *agbala* was not only another name for a woman, it could also mean a man who had taken no title. And so Okonkwo was ruled by one passion – to hate everything that his father Unoka had loved. One of those things was gentleness and another was idleness.

During the planting season Okonkwo worked daily on his farms from cock-crow until the chickens went to roost. He was a very strong man and rarely felt fatigue. But his wives and young children were not as strong, and so they suffered. But they dared not complain openly. Okonkwo's first son, Nwoye, was then twelve years old but was already causing his father great anxiety for his incipient laziness. At any rate, that was how it looked to his father, and he sought to correct him by constant nagging and beating. And so Nwoye was developing into a sad-faced youth.

Okonkwo's prosperity was visible in his household. He had a large compound enclosed by a thick wall of red earth. His own hut, or *obi*, stood immediately behind the only gate in the red walls. Each of his three wives had her own hut, which together formed a half-moon behind the *obi*. The barn was built against one end of the red walls, and long stacks of yam stood out prosperously in it. At the opposite end of the compound was a shed for the goats, and each wife built a small attachment to her hut for the hens. Near the barn was a small house, the 'medicine house' or shrine where Okonkwo kept the wooden symbols of his personal god and of his ancestral spirits. He worshipped them with sacrifices of kola nut, food and palm-wine, and offered prayers to them on behalf of himself, his three wives and eight children.

What was Okonkwo's greatest fear? Pick out the two words used to describe the fear.

Why did Okonkwo not want to be like his father? What word was used to name his father? What did it mean? Do you think Okonkwo was too harsh towards his father?

What do you think of the way Okonkwo treated his family? He is described as ruling his household 'with a heavy hand'. What does this mean? Who do you think chose the adjective? Pick out the evidence from the passage which shows this.

What were the things that indicated Okonkwo's prosperity? What was Okonkwo's attitude towards his prosperity?

What do you think of Okonkwo? What do you think might happen between Okonkwo and Nwoye, his son?

Now read the next extract. Do you think these people believed in life after death? If yes, in what form will it be?

But before this quiet and final rite, the tumult increased tenfold. Drums beat violently and men leaped up and down in frenzy. Guns were fired on all sides and sparks flew out as matchets clanged together in warriors' salutes. The air was full of dust and the smell of gunpowder. It was then that the one-handed spirit came, carrying a basket full of water. People made way for him on all sides and the noise subsided. Even the smell of gunpowder was swallowed in the sickly smell that now filled the air. He danced a few steps to the funeral drums and then went to see the corpse.

'Ezeuda!' he called in his guttural voice. 'If you had been poor in your last life I would have asked you to be rich when you come again. But you were rich. If you had been a coward, I would have asked you to bring courage. But you were a fearless warrior. If you had died young, I would have asked you to get life. But you lived long. So I shall ask you to come again the way you came before. If your death was the death of nature, go in peace. But if a man caused it, do not allow him a moment's rest.' He danced a few more steps and went away.

The drums and the dancing began again and reached fever-heat. Darkness was around the corner, and the burial was near. Guns fired the last salute and the cannon rent the sky. And then from the centre of the delirious fury came a cry of agony and shouts of horror. It was as if a spell had been cast. All was silent. In the centre of the crowd a boy lay in a pool of blood. It was the dead man's sixteen-year-old son, who with his brothers and half-brothers had been dancing the traditional farewell to their father. Okonkwo's gun had exploded and a piece of iron had pierced the boy's heart.

The confusion that followed was without parallel in the tradition of Umuofia. Violent deaths were frequent, but nothing like this had ever happened.

The only course open to Okonkwo was to flee from the clan. It was a crime against the earth goddess to kill a clansman, and a man who committed it must flee from the land. The crime was of two kinds, male and female. Okonkwo had committed the female, because it had been inadvertent. He could return to the clan after seven years.

Compare your answers around the class.

What are the adjectives used to describe the dead man? Are they positive or negative, in your opinion? List the adjectives used to show the high intensity of the sounds. What effect did they have on the people?

What effect did the killing of the boy have on (a) the funeral, (b) Okonkwo? What is the word used to describe the killing of the boy? Can you think of other words which mean the same thing?

Do you think the penalty was too harsh on Okonkwo? What do you think will happen to Okonkwo?

Now read on. Underline the changes that Okonkwo notices in his clan on his return.

Mr Brown's mission grew from strength to strength, and because of its link with the new administration it earned a new social prestige. But Mr Brown himself was breaking down in health. At first he ignored the warning signs. But in the end he had to leave his flock, sad and broken.

It was in the first rainy season after Okonkwo's return to Umuofia that Mr Brown left for home. As soon as he had learnt of Okonkwo's return five months earlier, the missionary had immediately paid him a visit. He had just sent Okonkwo's son, Nwoye, who was now called Isaac, to the new training college for teachers in Umuru. And he had hoped that Okonkwo would be happy to hear of it. But Okonkwo had driven him away with the threat that if he came into his compound again, he would be carried out of it.

Okonkwo's return to his native land was not as memorable as he had wished. It was true his two beautiful daughters aroused great interest among suitors and marriage negotiations were soon in progress, but, beyond that, Umuofia did not appear to have taken any special notice of the warrior's return. The clan had undergone such profound change during his exile that it was barely recognizable. The new religion and government and the trading stores were very much in the people's eyes and minds. There were still many who saw these new institutions as evil, but even they talked and thought about little else, and certainly not about Okonkwo's return.

And it was the wrong year too. If Okonkwo had immediately initiated his two sons into the *ozo* society as he had planned he would have caused a stir. But the initiation rite was performed once in three years in Umuofia, and he had to wait for nearly two years for the next round of ceremonies.

Okonkwo was deeply grieved. And it was not just a personal grief. He mourned for the clan, which he saw breaking up and falling apart, and he mourned for the warlike men of Umuofia, who had so unaccountably become soft like women.

Now list the changes you have underlined. Which of the changes did Okonkwo think positive and which negative? Why?

How is Mr Brown's mission contrasted with Okonkwo and his clan? Which expressions indicate this?

How did the changes in the clan affect the people's response to Okonkwo's return? Does Okonkwo seem a changed man after his return to Umuofia, in your opinion?

What is Okonkwo's attitude towards the men in his clan? Does he feel part of the clan? Do you sympathise with Okonkwo? What do you think could happen next?

Now read the next extract. Do you think Okonkwo should have killed the man?

At this point there was a sudden stir in the crowd and every eye was turned in one direction. There was a sharp bend in the road that led from the market-place to the white man's court, and to the stream beyond it. And so no one had seen the approach of the five court messengers until they had come round the bend, a few paces from the edge of the crowd. Okonkwo was sitting at the edge.

He sprang to his feet as soon as he saw who it was. He confronted the head messenger, trembling with hate, unable to utter a word. The man was fearless and stood his ground, his four men lined up behind him.

In that brief moment the world seemed to stand still, waiting. There was utter silence. The men of Umuofia were merged into the mute backcloth of trees and giant creepers, waiting.

> The spell was broken by the head messenger. 'Let me pass!' he ordered.
> 'What do you want here?'
> 'The white man whose power you know too well has ordered this meeting to stop.'
> In a flash Okonkwo drew his matchet. The messenger crouched to avoid the blow. It was useless. Okonkwo's matchet descended twice and the man's head lay beside his uniformed body.
> The waiting backcloth jumped into tumultuous life and the meeting was stopped. Okonkwo stood looking at the dead man. He knew that Umuofia would not go to war. He knew because they had let the other messengers escape. They had broken into tumult instead of action. He discerned fright in that tumult. He heard voices asking: 'Why did he do it?'
> He wiped his matchet on the sand and went away.

What do you think the words 'At this point' could refer to?

What was Okonkwo's immediate reaction on the arrival of the messengers? How much time has passed after the messengers' arrival before the head messenger speaks? Does it seem a long time? How does the writer achieve this effect?

Trace Okonkwo's actions and reactions from 'sitting at the edge' till he went away. Trace what the men of Umuofia do at the same time. What is Okonkwo's reaction to the tumult?

How quickly did Okonkwo react to the messenger's words? Which word indicates this?

How is this killing different from the killing in the earlier extract? How do you think his clan will react to Okonkwo's killing of the messenger? What do you think will happen next to Okonkwo and his clan?

Now read the final extract. Do you think this is a fitting end for Okonkwo?

> When the District Commissioner arrived at Okonkwo's compound at the head of an armed band of soldiers and court messengers he found a small crowd of men sitting wearily in the *obi*. He commanded them to come outside, and they obeyed without a murmur.
> 'Which among you is called Okonkwo?' he asked through his interpreter.
> 'He is not here,' replied Obierika.
> 'Where is he?'
> 'He is not here!'
> The Commissioner became angry and red in the face. He warned the men

that unless they produced Okonkwo forthwith he would lock them all up. The men murmured among themselves, and Obierika spoke again.

'We can take you where he is, and perhaps your men will help us.'

The Commissioner did not understand what Obierika meant when he said, 'Perhaps your men will help us.' One of the most infuriating habits of these people was their love of superfluous words, he thought.

Obierika with five or six others led the way. The Commissioner and his men followed, their firearms held at the ready. He had warned Obierika that if he and his men played any monkey tricks they would be shot. And so they went.

There was a small bush behind Okonkwo's compound. The only opening into this bush from the compound was a little round hole in the red-earth wall through which fowls went in and out in their endless search for food. The hole would not let a man through. It was to this bush that Obierika led the Commissioner and his men. They skirted round the compound, keeping close to the wall. The only sound they made was with their feet as they crushed dry leaves.

Then they came to the tree from which Okonkwo's body was dangling, and they stopped dead.

(Chinua Achebe *Things Fall Apart*)

What does the District Commissioner refer to as the 'love of superfluous words'? What do you think it means?

What do Okonkwo's friends want the soldiers to do? Why do you think they did not do it themselves?

Do you think Okonkwo was wrong to commit suicide? Is suicide acceptable in some circumstances, do you think? (You may want to look again at Hamlet's soliloquy, 'To be or not to be', on page 172–3.)

Look at your answer to the question on what you think the novel *Things Fall Apart* might be about. Was your prediction close to what you have read in these extracts? Based on your reading of all the extracts, write down what you think are the things that have fallen apart in Umuofia.

EXAMINATION STRATEGIES

When you come to the exams, it is natural to think that you don't know enough. This is the wrong attitude. You MUST trust yourself, and trust what you do know, rather than worry about what you don't know.

Examinations are not designed to see if you have read and remembered the texts on the programme, but to evaluate your progress as a reader of literature. And a good reader of literature is one who has NOT memorised lots of notes and useless information, mixed with a selection of critical opinions: that is an old-fashioned and out-of-date attitude.

If you have read through a good number of the texts in this book, you will have acquired a familiarity with some of the *processes* of reading, and with many of the techniques for examining how texts work, how they say what they want, and how you have reacted to them. And you will have a wide reading frame of reference, so that you can compare texts, across time, across themes, and across genres and cultural boundaries.

The objective criteria listed in 'To the student', and some of the approaches we have repeatedly used, will give you enough material to answer *any* questions examiners could ask.

As we have continually found, there are very often no completely right or wrong answers. So what matters is *what* you have learned, *how* you apply what you have learned, and *how* you express what you have learned. Let's have a look at what this means in practical terms:

You have learned how to read, how to examine adjectives and point of view, choice of words, how a story is built, how characters are seen, how the very beginning and the very end of the text reveal the movement within the text, how each of the four genres is different but need the same reading strategies in many ways. You can refer from any period, any text, from the particular to the universal. Above all, you have learned to interpret, evaluate, express your opinions in your own words; you have found lots of lines and quotations which you can use in any of your answers.

BUT . . . you cannot just regurgitate all the things you have learned, in an answer to a question. You must APPLY what you have learned to the specific question. That means NOT saying everything, but saying only the things which are directly relevant to the question – any more will be irrelevant and distracting (and that is one of the things that can make even the best students get lower marks than they should).

The expression is vital: you have seen in your reading how important graphology is – no examiner likes to mark scripts that are difficult to read and badly laid out. Paragraphs, well-organised sentences, and lots of easy-to-read words are what *you* prefer to read. Well, so do the examiners! Layout and presentation are, in their way, just as important as getting the grammar and sentence structure right.

It is a good idea to refer two or three times during your answer directly to the question: that will keep you on the right track, and help you to avoid irrelevant excesses. It also helps to keep your attention focused on answering the question instead of showing off unnecessarily.

So, what can you do to prepare properly?

Reread the texts and the authors you are working on. Go over the answers you gave, the written work you did, reassessing the opinions you discussed and seeing if they have changed in any way (opinions are flexible!). Learn a few useful quotations: a well-applied quotation is often worth three paragraphs of explanation. Do some research on the historical period – but relate it clearly to the texts. Base your research on what you want to know, and what will be useful to know.

You might want to use some critical opinions about the text or the writer. But remember – these are not necessarily 100 per cent right; your opinions are valid too. You may use critics to back up your views, or to contrast with your views. As long as you base your views clearly and explicitly on the text, you can't go wrong. (If you go into abstract flights of fancy, you will almost certainly lose marks. Any subjective affirmation has to be backed up with objective reference. The movement in your essays between the beginning and the end can usefully be from subjective to objective.)

Think up lots of questions you might be asked. Good questions and bad questions. Think of ways of answering even the questions you think are awful; that way, you will be ready for them if they do come up. For example, a question like 'What is the main idea in these poems?' is dreadful – but examiners may still use it. The difference between good and bad questions is simple but vital: one offers you the chance to give your views; the other seems to imply that there is a correct answer. Probably the best answer is one that stresses phrases like 'in my opinion', but the important thing is to base the answer on what the text actually says and does, not on what you think the examiner wants to hear.

Compare your own answers and opinions around the class. This is not so that everyone gives the same answer. Quite the opposite! Examiners will bring down the marks of all the candidates whose answers seem to be the same, or too similar. They want to see intelligent, well-reasoned, individual answers. They do not want to see received opinions out of study guides (and they recognise them anyway); they do not want every answer to be the same. And, of course, you should not recycle the same material in more than one answer.

Examiners, like you, have read the texts, and have some ideas about them. Even if they do not agree completely with a student's views, they are willing to give good marks if an answer is well argued, well presented, and well referenced. But it MUST answer the question asked; not just be an all-encompassing treatise on the generalities of the subject. You must be specific. Psychologically *you* have the advantage, not the examiners, because you know how *you* have read and reacted to the texts.

Don't try to memorise useless, forgettable things. Remember the memorable things, and organise them according to the demands of the question. Don't try to write the same as everyone else, and don't be too different, unless you can back up your answer from the text.

Trust the text. Trust the techniques and the experience you have acquired in working on the texts in this book. Try to communicate the positive learning and enjoyment that you have got out of the course. Be confident – go to the exam in order to show what you know, and to show how you can adapt your learning to whatever questions they throw at you.

You should not see it as a contest between you and the examiners – they want you to like the texts, and want to share your enjoyment, and to verify your learning.

Section 1

p.4

The original version of the text by William Carlos Williams is as follows:

This Is Just to Say

I have eaten
the plums
that were in
the icebox

and which
you were probably
saving
for breakfast

Forgive me
they were delicious
so sweet
and so cold

p.6

The title of the poem by Hilary Tham is *Offerings*. The missing words are (stanza 1) 'sunrise', (stanza 2) 'midday', (stanza 3) 'sunset', (stanza 4, line 1) 'midnight', and (stanza 4, last line) 'I crushed them in my despair.'

p.10

The missing word in the poem by Fadzillah Amin is 'ronggeng'. The poem's title is *Dance*.

Section 2

p.13

Ambrose Bierce *The Disinterested Arbiter*.

> Two Dogs, who had been fighting for a bone, without advantage to either, referred their dispute to a Sheep. The Sheep patiently heard their arguments, then flung the bone into a pond.
> 'Why did you do that?' asked the Dogs.
> 'Because,' replied the Sheep, 'I am a vegetarian.'

p.14

Ernest Hemingway *In Our Times*.

> They shot the six cabinet ministers at half past six in the morning against the wall of a hospital. It rained hard. One of the ministers was sick with typhoid. Two soldiers carried him downstairs and out into the rain. They tried to hold him up against the wall but he sat down in a puddle of water. There were wet dead leaves on the paving of the courtyard. The other five stood very quietly against the wall. Finally the officer told the soldiers it was no good trying to make him stand up. When they fired the first volley he was sitting down in the water with his head on his knees. There were pools of water in the courtyard. All the shutters of the hospital were nailed shut.

The order of the sentences is 9/10/5/6/4/7/11/8/2/3/1.

p.22–3

The title of the story by Grace Paley is *Mother*.

p.23

Catherine Lim *The Journey.*

Richard liked to tell his friends, 'To me, to be able to sit for half an hour, just dreaming away, is a rare luxury,' and he was having this rare luxury now, while waiting to be called into the consulting room. Richard leant back and sighed with pleasure. The satisfaction which a man feels when at the age of thirty two, he has become the managing director of a large and established firm, commanding a salary that has enabled him to buy a large detached bungalow in one of the most prestigious housing estates in the country, two cars, one for himself and one for his children to be driven to school in by a chauffeur, a diamond ring for his wife that would cost a whole year's salary of some of his wife's working friends – this satisfaction cannot be merely called pleasure. It is pure bliss, and Richard felt it stir the depths of his soul. He was not one to be complacent about his good fortune; he was profoundly grateful for it and in this warm glow of gratitude, he thought of his mother, aunt and grand-mother who had pooled whatever money they had to send him to school and, later, to college. Now he was repaying them ten-fold; he sent back a generous sum of money to them every month, and he told them in his letters, and on the few occasions when he saw them, 'Leave that sleepy little village. Come to the city. Come and stay with me. You'll have all the comforts you've ever wanted. You'll have servants to cook for you. You can go shopping in the many shopping centres here. Get out of this backwater. Good Lord, it's such an *ulu* place that one will die of boredom and misery there. My dear Grandma, Mother and Aunt, won't you come? There are three extra bed-rooms in my house – and all air-conditioned too!'

They said no, politely. Grandmother said the air-conditioner was not good for her old bones. The last time she had come down for a holiday, she and Aunt suffered so much; Mother could bear things a little better. The three women had left in a hurry, and Mabel had sighed with relief. 'It was such a trial with those three women in the house,' she had confided to some of her friends at the office. 'My mother-in-law slipped on the Italian marble floor in the bathroom and nearly injured herself. My grandmother-in-law has the obnoxious habit of chewing betel nut all the time and she once spat out the red juice in my patio. Would you believe it? I found a blob of that horrid stuff near my white cane chair. Oh, the horror of living with these people from the *ulu* places! Fortunately, it is not a permanent thing. My hubby asked them to come and stay with us more than once, but they weren't keen, because they're frightened of the air-conditioning. So we've done our part.'

Women, sighed Richard, they were all like that, inclined to be too fussy and house-proud. Was Mabel house-proud! Richard's heart glowed in fond recollection of his wife's fine taste and artistry, evident everywhere in their beautiful bungalow, from the dark brown timbered ceiling, right down to the very table napkins. The best, or nothing, Mabel said. She scoured the best shops, she bought the best things. When the boss and his wife came to dinner – the little coos of delight and admiration uttered by that charming, unassuming couple as they were shown round the house which they praised lavishly. Mrs Harris was particularly taken up by the Chinese antique table which Mabel had put in the corner of the hall. Mabel played down its price – 'Oh, it cost a few hundred dollars,' she had said casually when asked, but it had cost four thousand dollars; he had written a cheque for that amount when the delivery man came.

And now Richard's head became busy with mental arithmetic – Four thousand dollars – Why, when he was a boy, living in that little village in that wooden house with a well near it and a thatched-roof latrine a few feet away – that sum would have represented two years' earnings to his mother, grand-mother and aunt! His mother and aunt earned, if he remembered correctly, about a hundred dollars a month from their washing of clothes, his grand-mother about fifty dollars from the sale of her cakes and puddings which the coffee-shop people came to collect every morning. Richard did some quick calculations: it would take the three of them more than two years to earn the sum which Mabel spent on this one antique, which, as Mabel was always pointing out, did not make her feel as guilty as the *other* antiques. Put it down to my absurdity, she had laughed. But Richard thought fondly of the absurdity that had netted a clear ten thousand dollars; for Mabel had bought a quantity of antiques – pots, chests, chairs, tables – from a dealer in an obscure shop in a dark lane and sold all of them two weeks later for a cool profit of ten thousand. That ten thousand had been immediately converted into some shares which had soon afterwards risen in value. It's Mabel's golden touch, Richard told his friends in an exuberance of spirits.

In celebration of the success, Mabel and he had gone shopping for things to decorate the house with, and for the children. Annabelle's piano (which was already three years old) was replaced by a brand new one, and Mark had a go-kart which pleased the boy no end.

His children – how fortunate, how absolutely lucky they were. They had all the toys and clothes which he and his sisters never had. 'Toys, did you say?' Richard would pretend to explode in articulate incredulousness. 'Toys? Never! You know what, we didn't even have proper food. I remember it was plain rice and some thin vegetable soup every day, or some cheap fish, that was all. No pork, no chicken, no eggs, except during the Chinese New Year.

Nothing, except the cheapest food; at one time, we had plain rice and "tau-foo" for days.'

The girl Annabelle wanted to know what 'tau-foo' was; Mark, abandoning the Lego set he was playing with, made ready to demand some 'tau-foo'.

Richard remembered the old wooden house well. He was born in it; he grew up in it. It was the very essence of filth and degradation. The floor was beaten dirt; it was only years later that his mother had the cement laid. The furniture was old and rickety and bug-infested; the one mattress in the house was stuffed with coconut fibre, and was also bug-infested, and he remembered how he and his sisters had spent hours digging up the bugs hidden deep in the folds of the mattress, and killing them in a little saucer of kerosene. He never remembered himself and his sisters having proper towels, proper toilet soap, proper toilet paper. His aunt cut up old newspapers into little squares for the purpose. The latrine was one thing which, in his recollections, never failed to make him want to retch. It consisted of a raised wooden hut, four feet by two feet; the wooden floor had a round hole over which a person squatted directly over a waiting receptacle, an old rusty bucket. Once – he must have been eight or nine at the time – he had fallen through the hole, and his mother had taken a long time to clean him up, drawing up one bucket of water after another from the well. He had recounted this incident once to Mabel and had immediately regretted it, for she had felt quite ill and had forbidden him to talk of such things again. He remembered how he once fell ill – was that surprising, with the conditions as they were! – and how his mother, grandmother and aunt practically doused him in those horrible-looking, horrible-tasting herbal medicines that everyone in the village resorted to in times of illness. He remembered how, with his head bursting with fever, he tossed about on the hard coconut fibre-stuffed mattress, which was torn in some places so that the bristly fibre poked out and hurt his skin. There was no window in the room he was in; his mother had placed a chamber-pot near his bed for him to ease his bowels or vomit into, and he remembered the whole place stank and choked him. His aunt did a peculiar thing to cool his burning forehead; she cut up a potato into little thin pieces and spread them on his forehead, saying that that would take away the heat. Afterwards she showed him the blackened pieces, explaining that the blackness came from the fever which had transferred itself to the pieces of potato.

The superstitiousness of the three women was unimaginable; he wondered whether if his father were alive, conditions would have been more bearable? His grandmother was always prescribing strange cures for little sick children whose mothers came to her for help. Once a little girl was chased by a dog, and fell ill the next day. The girl's mother came tearfully to Grandmother, and Grandmother got the girl's father to pluck out a bit of fur from the dog, and put it behind the girl's ear! He remembered that the parents carried the terrified child to their house, as she had resisted all their attempts to have the fur put behind her ear. But Grandmother took the child into her arms and touched and spoke to her so soothingly that at last she quietened down. Fur behind the ear of a frightened child! Mabel had been most amused, but she had cautioned him not to tell the children; they might develop superstitious or morbid notions.

He wondered how, with such an environment, he had managed to be where he was now. How culturally deprived had been his environment, how starved of the requisites of mental and emotional growth. Thank God Annabelle and Mark would never know such deprivation. He never had a toy; he remembered that the only toy he had had was a plastic bear with a broken nose which his mother had asked from someone for him, and he had treasured this toy and kept it hidden from his sisters.

One of his sisters had died. It was tetanus. She had stepped on a rusty nail, and his mother had applied some medicine, but three days later, she was dead. He remembered how grief-stricken his mother, grandmother and aunt were. The ignorance of those days! The women were convinced that an evil spirit had entered his sister's body, and caused her death. Evil spirits, evil spirits – they were said to cause every illness and misfortune. How many deaths had been caused as a result of this belief – Richard felt grateful for the regular medical check-ups that he and his family were able to have. The nurse now appeared to summon him into the consulting room and he thought, Good. I shall be well in time for my golf. Shall pick up Mabel from the hairdresser's, and then drive on to a nice, relaxing game.

He cancelled the game. He took off his 'Arrow' shirt and the Pierre Cardin tie that Mabel had given him for his last birthday, and sat down numbly on his bed. The children were clamouring, 'Daddy! Daddy! Come and see our drawings!' but Mabel sent them out to play with the neighbour's children, and then quietly joined him in the room.

'What shall we do now?' he asked her in abject self-pity, and she burst into tears which became uncontrollable sobs. She sobbed miserably for a long time, and he continued to sit very still and gaze at the floral pattern of the brown-and-gold carpet on their bedroom floor. Mabel then sat upright and said that the doctor could be wrong – many doctors had been proved wrong in cases like this. But Richard told her the doctor in his case was positive; he gave him one year at most.

'I blame him,' said Mabel bitterly. 'You have been going to him regularly for the past four years, and how is it possible that he didn't detect it earlier? It seems impossibly irresponsible to me. And the fees he charges.' She rang him up. She tried to keep her voice down, but it rose to a high pitch and finally Richard persuaded her to calm down.

'Richard,' she sobbed again, 'what's going to become of me and the children? Why didn't you give up smoking when I told you to?'

His mother, grandmother and aunt were told eventually, although Mabel had objected, saying, 'We'll keep this to ourselves as far as possible. I don't want people hurrying over and pretending to feel sorry for us. The children must be protected from all this.'

The three elderly women asked if they could come, and when Richard wrote back, 'Please do. I want to see all of you again,' they came. They avoided the sight of Mabel, and she, on her part, fretted. They brought along a certain herbal mixture which they said was good for him, but Mabel here put her foot down and said, 'No. Richard's under the best medical treatment here. The doctors will not tolerate any traditional *ulu* cure.'

Grandmother told her two daughters, privately, that she would have liked to spit in Mabel's face but had refrained from doing so, as it would have upset Richard. He was not in a condition to be upset. The three women stayed out of her way entirely; they ate separately, and Mabel took the children away to her sister's as frequently as she could. She appealed to her husband with tears in her eyes. 'Darling, I'm not trying to be nasty to your folks, but it hurts me badly when I see them foisting their nonsense upon you, and you in this condition too. I want you to have none but the best; you deserve it, darling. Let me take care of you.'

He had said wearily, 'Mabel, leave them alone.' He wanted to add, 'They bring some comfort to me,' but had remained silent after that.

They went home after some time, Grandmother embittered and angry, the two others silent and sad, and he felt a pang, but he let them go, and Mabel was less fretful.

He suffered. There was no pain as yet – but he suffered. He looked at his magnificent house (which a few days before a crew of men and women from the Television Department had arrived to film for a documentary which was to be called 'Lovely Homes'. Mabel had invited them over a month before, before they had learnt of the sad development). He looked at this lovely home of his, and he suffered keenly. Everything about him gave him pain, for he had worked so hard to get all these, and now they were dust and ashes in his mouth. He was still going to his office; he thought he might as well continue working, as sitting at home would be unbearable. Mabel had been consulting one specialist after another. One evening she came home with an excited look on her face and announced that she had found a specialist – the best cancer specialist in the world, based in New York. His chances of recovery under this specialist would be so very much increased. The expense would of course be enormous – but what was money? She was prepared to sell all the shares, her jewellery.

Richard said, 'I'm a doomed man. I'm not going to make any journey to New York.'

Mabel was sad. 'It's no use,' she told her sister. 'I can't make him go to that specialist I told you about. I wonder what I can do to make him agree to make that journey?'

Richard dozed off a great deal. He thought of his boyhood in the small *ulu* village. He thought of the time when he was ill and lay on the prickly coconut fibre-stuffed mattress with the chamber-pot nearby. He remembered how he had felt very ill and had wanted to vomit, but the stuff couldn't come out. He had agonised for a few minutes, making great retching noises in his throat, and he remembered his mother and aunt coming in. His mother's hands were still wet from her washing, and she wiped them quickly on her dress and came to him. She held him close and soothed his chest by rubbing it with slow gentle downward movements with her fingers. His aunt stood by, talking in low tones and then exclaiming happily when at last the vomit came out, and he lay back on the pillow, soothed. He remembered that his grandmother made him a brew, a black, bitter drink which she said was most effective when drunk in moonlight. He was sleeping when she gently picked him up from his bed and carried him outside, where the moonlight was streaming upon the house in a wonderful glow of warmth and peace, and she made sure his face was touched by the moonlight as he drank the brew. His grandmother tried to distract him from the bitterness by telling him a story about a moon goddess. He remembered it was a silly story, but it had the effect of calming him down and allowing him to finish the brew.

In one of his dreams, Mabel was there as his grandmother carried him into the moonlight to drink his medicine. She tried to snatch away the bowl of brew from her hands, shouting, 'What nonsense! What nonsense!' Grandmother resisted, and in the ensuing struggle, the drink spilt all over him and stained him black. Mabel's face was hidden from him; in the darkness she continued screaming at them, and it was then that he woke up.

He told Mabel that he was going to make the journey for his recovery. He would go by train, and his mother, grandmother and aunt would meet him at the terminus and take him home. He was going home – When Mabel understood, she shrieked in agony. How can you be going back to that rotten little *ulu* village? Who will take care of you? What medical facilities could possibly exist there? How could she go to see him, with the business to see to and the children to take care of and the household affairs to manage? Mabel collapsed in tears, hurt beyond expression, struck to the depths of her soul. How could he think of such a thing? Was he sure that – Didn't he want to –

But he said, 'I'm making the journey. I'm going home.'

Section 3

p.28

Edward Bond *Bingo*.

JONSON: What are you writing?
SHAKESPEARE: Nothing.

[*They drink.*]

JONSON: Not writing?
SHAKESPEARE: No.
JONSON: Why not?
SHAKESPEARE: Nothing to say.
JONSON: Doesn't stop others. Written out?
SHAKESPEARE: Yes.

[*They drink.*]

JONSON: Now, what are you writing?
SHAKESPEARE: Nothing.

Section 7

p.109–11

Dance Like a Man by Mahesh Dattani was first performed in 1989.
In the Name of Love by Ramli Ibrahim was first performed in 1991.

Section 9

p.135

The title of the second poem by Wilfred Owen is *Futility*.

p.137

James Berry *Fantasy of an African Boy*.

> Such a peculiar lot
> we are, we people
> without money, in daylong
> yearlong sunlight, knowing
> money is somewhere, somewhere.

Everybody says it's a big
bigger brain bother now,
money. Such millions and millions
of us don't manage at all
without it, like war going on.

And we can't eat it. Yet
without it our heads alone
stay big, as lots and lots do,
coming from nowhere joyful,
going nowhere happy.

We can't drink it up. Yet
without it we shrivel when small
and stop forever
where we stopped,
as lots and lots do.

We can't read money for books.
Yet without it we don't
read, don't write numbers,
don't open gates in other countries,
as lots and lots never do.

We can't use money to bandage
sores, can't pound it
to powder for sick eyes
and sick bellies. Yet without
it, flesh melts from our bones.

The order of the stanzas is d/e/c/f/b/a.

Section 11

p.172

Oscar Wilde *The Importance of Being Earnest*

GWENDOLEN: Mr Worthing, I have something very particular to ask you. Much
depends on your reply.

CECILY: Gwendolen, your common sense is invaluable. Mr Moncrieff, kindly answer me the following question. Why did you pretend to be my guardian's brother?

ALGERNON: In order that I might have an opportunity of meeting you.

CECILY [to GWENDOLEN]: That certainly seems a satisfactory explanation, does it not?

GWENDOLEN: Yes, dear, if you can believe him.

CECILY: I don't. But that does not affect the wonderful beauty of his answer.

GWENDOLEN: True. In matters of grave importance, style, not sincerity, is the vital thing. Mr Worthing, what explanation can you offer to me for pretending to have a brother? Was it in order that you might have an opportunity of coming up to town to see me as often as possible?

JACK: Can you doubt it, Miss Fairfax?

GWENDOLEN: I have the greatest doubts upon the subject. But I intend to crush them. This is not the moment for German scepticism. [Moving to CECILY.] Their explanations appear to be quite satisfactory, especially Mr Worthing's. That seems to me to have the stamp of truth upon it.

CECILY: I am more than content with what Mr Moncrieff said. His voice alone inspires one with absolute credulity.

GWENDOLEN: Then you think we should forgive them?

CECILY: Yes. I mean no.

GWENDOLEN: True! I had forgotten. There are principles at stake that one cannot surrender. Which of us should tell them? The task is not a pleasant one.

CECILY: Could we not both speak at the same time?

GWENDOLEN: An excellent idea! I always speak at the same time as other people. Will you take the time from me?

CECILY: Certainly.

[GWENDOLEN beats time with uplifted finger.]

GWENDOLEN and CECILY [speaking together]: Your Christian names are still an insuperable barrier. That is all!

JACK and ALGERNON [speaking together]: Our Christian names! Is that all? But we are going to be christened this afternoon.

GWENDOLEN [to JACK]: For my sake you are prepared to do this terrible thing?

JACK: I am.

CECILY [to ALGERNON]: To please me you are ready to face this fearful ordeal?

ALGERNON: I am!

GWENDOLEN: How absurd to talk of the equality of the sexes! Where questions of self-sacrifice are concerned, men are infinitely beyond us.

JACK: We are. [Clasps hands with ALGERNON.]

CECILY: They have moments of physical courage of which we women know
absolutely nothing.
GWENDOLEN [*to* JACK]: Darling!
ALGERNON [*to* CECILY]: Darling!

[*They fall into each other's arms.*]

INDEX OF AUTHORS